INTRUDERS

Also by Budd Hopkins

Missing Time

INTRUDERS

The Incredible Visitations at Copley Woods

BUDD HOPKINS

Random House · New York

Library of Congress Cataloging-in-Publication Data

Hopkins, Budd, 1931–
    Intruders: the incredible visitations at
Copley Woods.

    1. Unidentified flying objects—Sightings and
encounters—United States. I. Title.
TL789.3.H64   1987   001.9'42'0973   86-29806
ISBN 0-394-56076-0

Manufactured in the United States of America

9 8 7 6 5 4 3 2

First Edition

This book is dedicated to the memory of
J. Allen Hynek

Acknowledgments

It is ironic to realize that this book would not exist but for the painfully complex experiences of Kathie Davis, her family, and all the others—Susan Williams, Sandy Thomas, Pam, Andrea, Ed Duvall, Dan Seldin, Joyce Lloyd, Lucille Forman, Margaret Bruning and the rest—whose accounts appear in these pages. Their names may have been changed to protect their privacy, but they know who they are and I wish to extend to each of them my profound gratitude for their cooperation and my respect for their bravery in allowing these difficult stories to be told. There are many others whose similarly harrowing accounts are not included here, men and women who have gradually become my treasured friends and to whom I also wish to extend my gratitude.

The help I have received from medical and scientific consultants has been essential to this work, and I particularly want to acknowledge the contributions of Dr. John Burger, Dr. Paul Cooper, Dr. Don Klein, Dr. Robert Naiman, Dr. Christina Sekaer, psychologists Aphrodite Clamar and Elizabeth Slater, and for their work on soil sample analysis, Cullen Hackler and Paul Lander. I wish to express my thanks to Joseph Santangelo, Travis Whitehurst and Lew Willis, researchers whose efforts have enabled me to pursue certain avenues of investigation in these cases. Two colleagues in particular—David Jacobs and Joseph Nyman—have been invaluable friends, confidants, critics and careful readers of this manuscript; I am very much in their debt. They have supplied me with major amounts of advice, information and caution—though not necessarily in that order—and have thereby helped to make this a stronger book. Finally, I would like to thank April, my wife, and Grace, my daughter, for tolerating the theft of family time that this project has represented. I could say that it will never happen again, but I know I would not be believed. Despite this, I want them to know how much their forbearance and understanding has contributed to the creation of my book and how essential their spoken and unspoken support has been to my life.

Contents

Illustrations appear in a section following page 146.

A Note to the Reader

Whether you are a physicist, a housewife, a UFO researcher or a dabbler in the occult, this book will almost certainly strain your credulity to the breaking point. One of the many things we don't like to admit about the human mind is its basic inability to accept or even to vividly imagine an "unrealistic" or deeply unpalatable truth. Though we can entertain almost any wild idea "in theory," a profoundly unsettling concept can be almost impossible to believe—to really believe—despite the weight of evidence and the pressure of logic. One historic example of our inability to comprehend and believe a chilling truth is delineated in Walter Laqueur's book *The Terrible Secret,* a work dealing with the Holocaust.[1] Laqueur's research established that by the end of 1943, when a sizable portion of the world's population had read or been told of Hitler's systematic liquidation of the Jewish people, this ongoing horror was simply not believed. The Nazis were evil, we seemed to be saying, and truly barbaric, but *that*— the systematic murder of children and old people and men and women —that just couldn't be true. Obviously, in this context even eyewitness accounts were irrelevant. Laqueur describes a meeting between Jan Karski, a Polish eyewitness to the slaughter, and Judge Felix Frankfurter, a man whose brilliance and intellectual resiliency cannot be doubted. Karski told Frankfurter of what he had seen and heard, but Frankfurter replied that "he did not believe him. When Karski protested, Frankfurter explained that he did not imply that Karski had in any way not told the truth, he simply meant that he could not believe him—there was a difference."[2]

When we shift to the subject of this book a certain analogy comes to mind. (Obviously I do not mean to compare the unspeakable horrors of the Holocaust with the events reported here. An analogy exists only in the methods we use to avoid such deeply disturbing testimony.) Surely a majority of the world's scientists believe in the probability of extraterrestrial life existing somewhere in our inconceivably vast universe, and that some of these life forms are possibly more advanced than our own. Many scientists in fact maintain an active interest in SETI—the search for extraterrestrial intelligence. And yet almost none of these scientists have taken the time to look into the UFO phenomenon as it inarguably exists: a phenomenon consisting of tens of thousands of reports of apparent craft sightings, landings, photo and radar evidence and accounts of the temporary abduction and examination of human beings. Obviously the UFO phenomenon as I have described it may offer immediate evidence of extraterrestrial intelligence, right here and right now. But the scientific community has not investigated these reports and then rejected them; for the most part scientists have only the vaguest idea of the weight and the specifics of the evidence.

There is an all-too-human reason for this lack of curiosity. The idea of an extraterrestrial intelligence existing "out there" somewhere, but not as yet possessing a technology that allows travel between solar systems, is an easy, logical and comforting concept to hold. We on earth remain, according to this model, detached and unaffected, passively listening for distant, intelligent signals sent to us across the "unbridgeable vastness" of space. The possibility that extraterrestrial intelligence may already be visiting our planet, as the UFO evidence implies, and treating the human species as laboratory specimens for some elusive and perhaps unfathomable purpose —that is a truly disturbing idea. We all know, of course, a basic scientific truth: It can't happen here. Justice Frankfurter's remark is apt; despite the eyewitness descriptions and all the other categories of evidence, "I just cannot believe it."

Shortly after my book *Missing Time* was published I appeared on a radio interview program to discuss the UFO phenomenon. The talk show host proclaimed himself a skeptic. "I'm very, very skeptical of this whole UFO business," he announced proudly. "Travel from one solar system to another is simply not possible. You can't get here from there, wherever there is. And even if there are extraterrestrials flying around, they'd never do what these UFO occupants are supposed to be doing." After listening to these and other items from his long, complicated list of what is and what is not possible, I told him that of the two of us I was by far the more skeptical. "I'm so skeptical," I said, "that I find it beyond me to deny the possibility of anything."

And so my request to you, the reader. Do not prejudge. Realize that if any aspect of the UFO phenomenon as reported is true, then any of the rest of the reported phenomena may be true too. Try not to put anthropomorphic limits on what may be an entirely alien intelligence and technology. The true skeptic cannot, at the beginning, accept the impossibility of anything.

INTRUDERS

1
The September Letter

At first, as you drive by, the flat stone walls of the house seem neutral and prosaic. Nothing more, really, than masonry curtains to shelter and conceal the family life within. The tall maple trees of the surrounding Copley Woods provide a second barrier against unwanted attention. It is easy to pass the Davis home without noticing anything at all unusual, but when you are told what has been happening within and around these gray stone walls the very soil they stand on begins to feel unnaturally charged.

The neighborhood itself is normally peaceful enough, and pleasantly typical of middle-western, middle-class suburbia. The houses have enough distance between them to allow natural privacy and isolation, and the area is just far enough away from downtown Indianapolis to suggest an almost rural environment. The Davis family owns three acres of land in the Copley Woods and lives quite comfortably there with an impressive array of automobiles, kitchen appliances, television sets, and a backyard swimming pool. Robert Davis is a good provider. In keeping with the Davises' desire for anonymity I shall characterize his occupation only as highly skilled, technical, and obviously well compensated.[1] Besides Robert, four others live in the Davis house: his wife Mary; their daughter Kathie, a divorcee; and her two children, Robbie and Tommy. In September of 1983 I received a letter from Kathie Davis, a letter which triggered a two-and-a-half-year investigation into certain extraordinary events in and around the Copley Woods.

Though I am by profession a painter-sculptor who lives and works in New York City, I have gradually become more and more deeply involved in examining reports of UFOs—Unidentified Flying Objects. In 1981 I wrote a book on the subject, *Missing Time,* a documented study of seven UFO abduction accounts I had investigated, along with UFO researcher Ted Bloecher and psychologist Dr. Aphrodite Clamar.[2] The end of my book, which Kathie Davis read in the summer of 1983, provided a link to the Davis family and the Copley Woods affair. As an afterword I had asked anyone who felt that he or she might have had an experience similar to those dealt with in *Missing Time* to write me at my publisher's address. Among the hundreds of letters that arrived in response, from places as divergent as Australia and Norway, Lebanon and Canada, was Kathie's intriguing account. Subsequently she told me that she had written an earlier note and then had torn it up, assuming that I would probably not be interested. Her second letter, however, the one she actually mailed, triggered an investigation the extent of which she clearly could not have foreseen. It has involved the skills of chemists, radiologists, medical practitioners, psychologists and other specialists. I have made four trips to Indianapolis to interview various principals, and Kathie has come to New York three times. In-depth psychological tests and interviews have been employed, as has "lie detection" in the form of voice stress analysis administered by a professional in the field. Ultimately, the Copley Woods affair has yielded more new information—unsettling information, it must be said—about the nature and purpose of the UFO phenomenon than any case yet investigated. This is a very large claim to make but I believe the evidence fully justifies it.

No aspect of this phenomenon is as controversial—or as dramatic—as a so-called "abduction report" of the type I shall deal with in this book. Over the years hundreds of otherwise credible people have described being somehow immobilized in their cars or homes or wherever and then taken by UFO occupants into landed UFOs for what appears to be a kind of physical examination conducted while the abductee is stretched out upon a table. What seems to be externally imposed amnesia usually prevents the abductee from recalling the full scenario of his or her experience, which generally lasts an hour or two. (Hypnosis has been the most useful method investigators have employed to aid the victim's recollection.) Now we would willingly dismiss any one of these accounts, taken alone, as nothing more than an intrinsically unbelievable aberration. But as we shall see the overall patterns in these cases are so remarkably consistent, often down to tiny details, and people reporting these experiences are often so inherently credible, that the phenomenon simply cannot be dismissed. However one wishes to theorize about these accounts —that they represent some strange new mass psychological delusion or that they represent descriptions of real, physical experiences—something important is going on, something which demands open-minded, scientific investigation.

The first widely publicized UFO abduction, the Betty and Barney Hill case, occurred in 1961 in the White Mountains of New Hampshire.[3] Driving late at night, the Hills saw a moving light which gradually approached their car, and eventually they pulled off the main road for a closer look. The object hovered low enough, finally, for them to see that it was a structured craft of unusual shape. Barney Hill, using binoculars, was able to make out the ship's occupants looking back at him through a horizontal row of windows. A moment or two later their conscious recollections of this event ended and the next thing they knew they were driving along the original route and slowly becoming aware that they had somehow "lost" two hours since they had first noticed the light. In the days and weeks that followed, Barney Hill began to suffer from extreme anxiety, insomnia and nightmares. Eventually he developed an ulcer, and as his condition worsened, he sought medical and psychiatric help. His psychiatrist, Dr. Benjamin Simon, felt that he was suffering from some kind of unremembered trauma, and therefore began a series of hypnotic regressions to uncover and ventilate the problem. It was in this context that Barney Hill recalled what had happened during the missing two hours: The UFO had landed that night, and he had been paralyzed and then taken on board along with his wife. Separately they had been subjected to some sort of physical examination. Dr. Simon had regularly given Barney the posthypnotic suggestion that he would not consciously remember the material recovered during hypnosis once the trance ended. This device provided a control. When Betty Hill was later regressed, she knew nothing of her husband's recollections, so her congruent descriptions of the craft, its interior and its occupants were extremely important. This encounter, when it became public knowledge in 1966, was immediately ridiculed and derided because of its content, though neither the veracity nor the mental stability of the Hills has ever been convincingly challenged. Today it can be seen as a watershed event in the investigation of the UFO phenomenon.[4]

The modern era of UFO *sightings*—accounts of strange, silent, dislike craft seen in the sky—had begun years before, during World War II, when these objects were thought by Allied pilots to be enemy secret weapons.[5] This theory went out the window when captured German pilots reported seeing the same things, and assumed them to be an American secret device. After the war UFOs were seen over the Scandinavian countries, and the Air Force then assumed that they were experimental *Soviet* rockets. Yet none seemed to crash, no debris was found, and so eventually that explanation was also abandoned. Not until the later nineteen-forties did the extraterrestrial theory begin to gain a foothold, though it was still difficult to believe that these things might actually be piloted —that there might in fact be some intelligent something inside at the controls.

The Betty and Barney Hill case gave us the first inkling of what was to become a flood of similar abduction reports, straining our credulity even further. I had had a daylight UFO sighting in 1964—an event that generated my interest in the subject—and yet when I read the details of the Hills' encounter I could not accept the idea that such a thing as an abduction by UFO occupants was possible.[6] Using Justice Frankfurter's distinction, it was not that I thought the Hills were lying, it was that I just could not believe them. My own subsequent investigations of similar UFO sightings, however, slowly and inexorably led me to accept the possibility that abduction encounters might literally be occurring as described. As the evidence mounted and case report followed case report, I became convinced of the importance of this aspect of the UFO phenomenon, and by 1977 concentrated my efforts in this area of research.[7] The result, in 1981, was the publication of my book on the subject and, eventually, Kathie Davis's recognition while she read it of certain patterns and details that applied to herself and her family.

One of the central ideas in *Missing Time* was my guess that many people—perhaps thousands—may have had UFO abduction experiences and yet *consciously* remember almost nothing to indicate they had suffered these traumatic encounters. The pattern of evidence we had uncovered suggests that a kind of "enforced" amnesia can efficiently erase from conscious memory all but the very slightest recollections of such experiences. In one of the seven similar cases we investigated, "Steven Kilburn" described nothing more than a deep-seated fear of a certain stretch of highway and his "feeling" that something had happened to him there that possibly involved a UFO. Unlike Betty and Barney Hill he did not recall sighting a UFO, he was not aware of any missing time, or even of seeing anything unusual. But after investigating his case with the help of Ted Bloecher, two psychologists and a polygraph operator, I came to the conclusion that his sketchy, though emotionally loaded, initial recollections did in fact conceal a full-blown UFO abduction experience. Under hypnosis Steve relived a traumatic encounter very similar in its details to the Hill case.[8]

A second extremely important pattern emerged from these early investigations, a pattern which the Copley Woods affair amply illustrates. It appears that most UFO abductees have had more than one such experience, their first abduction generally occurring in childhood around the age of six or seven. Often they are picked up and examined several times after that, though these later encounters are rarely reported past the age of forty or so. An analogy which immediately springs to mind is the human study of endangered animals, in which zoologists tranquilize and tag or implant transmitters in sample animals to trace their subsequent wanderings. I presented evidence in my book indicating a similar interest by UFO "occupants" in certain human beings who are apparently treated like experimental subjects requiring reexamination at intervals across the years. And as we shall see, there is evidence that these human subjects have also been somehow "tagged."

A third point dealt with the issue of the still-visible scars which apparently resulted from the UFO occupants' systematic, quasi-medical examinations of three people when they were first abducted as children. In the illustration section I reproduced three photographs of these small, straight scars as they currently appear, respectively, on the back of the calf, above the knee, and on the hip of the three different abductees. (By profession they are a corporation lawyer, a microbiologist and a news media employee). As in the Hill case, hypnosis was used to break the memory blocks and to elicit descriptions of the "surgical" procedures which caused the cuts, as well as detailed recollections of the occupants' physical appearance and of the interiors of the UFOs themselves. Though we do not have any indication of the purpose of these incisions, their physical character suggests a cell-sampling operation of some kind. Over the past five years I have encountered twenty-seven more abductees who bear similarly acquired scars, though a number of these marks are of a different type. Instead of a short, straight cut, seven are circular, shallow depressions— scoop marks, one might say—about one quarter to one half inch in diameter. The photographs I reproduced in *Missing Time* gave Kathie Davis yet another reason to write to me. She, her mother, her closest

friend and her next-door neighbor all bear nearly identical scars on their
lower legs, all apparently resulting from earlier UFO abduction experiences.

Though Kathie mailed her letter in August, it was not forwarded to me
by the publisher until September. She told me later that while she was
reading the book she had begun to realize that she herself had had many
of the same partial memories, UFO abduction dreams and disturbing
mental flashbacks as the individuals I described. The effect of it all had
been extremely unsettling, though in her initial communication she decided not to refer to her own deepening anxiety.[9] Because of a personal
reticence that I soon recognized as one of Kathie's basic qualities, she
preferred to tell me about other things first.

When I opened her letter some fifteen color photographs spilled out.
I recognized immediately a familiar image from UFO "landing trace"
investigations—a circular area of ground in which all the grass appears to
be dead, as if it has been subject to heat or to some other form of radiation.
Ted Phillips, an investigator who is particularly interested in this kind of
report, has catalogued over twelve hundred cases in which UFOs apparently have physically affected their surroundings.[10] Many of the photographs in his files, such as those taken of the site shortly after a UFO was
observed on or just above the ground near Delphos, Kansas, closely resem-
ble Kathie's enclosures. (See illustrations.) But even more important, later
analysis of the affected soil in both cases showed that the degree of
calcification, of soil dehydration, was very similar—and equally difficult to
account for.

Kathie began her letter by explaining that there were two things she
wanted to inform me about—the event documented in the photographs
and a "missing time" incident that occurred years before involving her
older sister. She wrote first about the more recent incident.

> . . . Around the first week of July, 1983, at about 8:00–9:00 P.M.,
> I was preparing to go out and sew a little at a neighbor's home, and
> while I was standing at the kitchen window I noticed a light in the
> pool house and the door was open. I remember shutting it earlier,
> so I knew it shouldn't be open, let alone have the light on, so I
> mentioned it to Mom. She looked and wondered what was up, but
> neither one of us were at all alarmed. When I got ready to leave I
> decided to drive round the turn-around to make sure no one was out
> there, as Mom would be alone with the kids (my sons Rob, 4, and

Tommy, 3). When I did, the light was off and the door shut, and the garage door was open (which is always kept shut). When I got to Dee Anne's house (one street over) I called Mom and told her what I saw and asked if she'd like me to come home and check it out, and she sounded rather nervous (not at all like my Mom). She said she'd seen a big light by the pool house, and it moved up to the bird feeder and grew to about two feet in diameter. But she didn't see any beam. It was just like a spot light on the bird feeder, lighting it up, but nothing else around it . . . When I got there it was gone, and I looked all around the property (with my Dad's .22. I'm chicken)! I did finally find my dog Penny hiding under a car out back. Usually she carries on something fierce when anyone she doesn't know is on our property. It's not like her to hide and have to be coaxed out from anywhere, especially by me. She's usually all over me. I didn't see anything, so I went back to sew and later that night Dee and I and her daughter came back about midnight and went swimming. Right after that night our yard was burned, by what we don't know. Nothing will grow there now, no matter how much water we give it, and wild animals won't go on it. At first, even Penny would walk halfway around the yard to avoid walking on it. She'd sniff it and run the other way. Birds will no longer go near the bird feeder either, and we have always had tons of birds every day, especially red birds. Well, that's the story of our back yard mystery. It's still here for anyone who wants to see it, more or less unchanged.

When taken together, several things Kathie mentioned in her account of the strange backyard lights and the dead area on the lawn suggested to me the possibility that a UFO landing had taken place, despite the fact that neither she nor her mother remembered having seen anything that could be called a craft. The unusual behavior of her dog is typical of many UFO sighting reports in which dogs, horses and even cattle seem to be dramatically affected by low-level or landed UFO's. This phenomenon, it has been theorized, may be a reaction to disturbing sound frequencies outside the range of human hearing. Often the animal continues for a time to be wary of the site where the disturbance took place.[11] The small moving lights that Kathie's mother described have also been mentioned many times before in conjunction with low-level UFO sightings.[12]

But the photographs, of course, presented the most graphic evidence in support of Kathie's claim of a drastic, nearly overnight change in the

Davises' lawn. The main area was a circle, eight feet in diameter, in which all the grass had turned brown and was now crumbling away. Extending out from this circle was a forty-nine-foot-long swath which ran perfectly straight and was nearly three feet in width. Here, too, the grass was dead and disintegrating. This long track ended in a nearly perfect arc, and seemed absolutely artificial. Two smaller "jogs" appeared to emerge from the main circle, and one of these contained a deep crack which looked, superficially, as if it had been caused by intense heat. The photographs were clear and effectively showed the mysterious damage, but Kathie had still another story to tell. Her letter continued:

Now about Laura. My sister Laura is thirty-five years old. She's always been very level-headed and not much imagination. Always the realist. Anyway, in the summer, about 1965, she left one evening about 4:30 P.M. to take my mother to Bingo. On the way home from dropping her off, as she was passing the church on 10th Street, she suddenly was compelled to pull into the church parking lot around back. She noticed there weren't any cars around and thought it quite strange for a Sunday afternoon in that busy area. When she parked she looked up and saw something she'd never believed before then. It was silver, and I believe she said the lights were red, green and white, flashing somewhat (flickering might be a better word). It was hovering soundlessly . . . over the lot about telephone pole high, right over her car. All she remembers now is she reached over to turn down her radio to see if it made noise, and then the next thing she remembers is it's dark out and she looks up and this thing is gone and she's driving down the street. When she went to get Mom that night they drove around looking for it but never saw anything else.

In this brief account of her sister's 1965 experience, Kathie includes three intriguing details that turn up frequently in abduction accounts. First, there is the suggestion of external control over the abductee. One simply finds oneself compelled, as Kathie put it, to drive down a particular road, enter a parking lot, leave one's house, or whatever, for no apparent reason. The decision is remembered as odd—even irrational—and frequently a witness will say something like "I didn't even know there was a road there, but I found myself turning off the main route to drive down it. I stopped next to this field, and there was a UFO hovering above the trees." No one knows how this psychic control is enforced, but it is a basic component in many UFO abduction reports. The potential abductee is apparently "set up" in a place that permits the UFO and its occupants to operate efficiently, safely and covertly. So far, all the UFO abduction cases I have investigated have had this kind of tactical plausibility, a fact that weighs in on the side of their physical reality.

The second and more crucial indication of a possible UFO abduction was the fact that Laura "lost" a period of time. First it was about five o'clock in the afternoon, and the next thing she knew it was several hours later, since darkness had fallen. One common characteristic of an abduction experience is the merging in memory of its onset and its conclusion, a joining so seamless as to leave the abductee with no *feeling* that he or she has actually lost any time, despite what clocks and simple vision may establish beyond any doubt. This partial and apparently externally imposed amnesia can be extremely effective. Laura remembered sitting in her car and looking up at the UFO, but her very next recollection after that was of driving down a street with the UFO no longer in sight.[13] It is significant that she reported these odd recollections to her mother that very evening—in 1965—at least a year before the public at large was aware of the symptoms—or even the existence—of such bizarre events.[14]

The third indication of a possible abduction was, of course, the presence of the telephone-pole-high lighted UFO itself, as centerpiece to her recollection. But there was more. In *Missing Time* I had described the use of hypnosis in recovering forgotten details in such cases, and I had recounted some of the vagaries of both the method and its results as it had been employed by the various psychiatrists and psychologists who aided our investigations. Kathie's letter continued, bringing up an event that, in this context, was particularly interesting:

About ten years or so later [circa 1975] Laura went to get hypnotized to lose weight, and while her girlfriend who went with her did great, she experienced some quite terrifying experiences. The first night she came home [after the hypnosis], shortly after she went to bed she woke up and she couldn't talk or hear. [She also suffered temporary distortion in her vision.] Her husband took her to the emergency room and they gave her tranquilizers and sent her home. This went on . . . gradually getting better. She noticed that she was doing the exact opposite of what the hypnotist had suggested. He told her that potato chips and candy were fat slices, I guess so it would gross out her subconscious and she wouldn't want to eat them.

But instead, everytime she ate them she felt markedly better. And when she called the hypnotist to ask him what the heck was happening to her and could he fix it, the moment she heard his voice she became violent and wanted to kill him. You have to know Laura. She's very much *not* like this at all, very common sense, down to earth, easy going. He suggested she had some sort of "block" and that it would probably be best if she didn't see him anymore, to go to someone else . . . The effects gradually wore off, but she was left with one strong thought: that by the year 2000 the world would be totally different than we know it, but it would be only for the young and strong.

Having finished her account of the mysterious backyard lights, the marks on the ground, and her recollection of her sister's UFO experience, Kathie added a final cryptic paragraph:

My mother and I have had a couple of unusual experiences, mine mostly in the form of vivid dreams, and Mother and I both have the same scar on our right legs. She said she got hers when she was a girl playing outside. I don't remember when I got mine, but it seems like I had it all my life. They are in the same place and look exactly alike. A nurse once told me it looked like a scar left by a bone marrow test or a pin inserted in my shin bone from a break. At first I only had one scar but now I have two, on the same leg, about 3½" apart . . . I got this one when I was about 13, but I can't for the life of me remember how. I used to play in the woods by the pond a lot, and I may have got it there, but I don't remember how.

Kathie closed her letter with an address and a phone number. Though I could not anticipate it at the time, her account of two suggestive incidents has expanded into the most complex UFO case I have yet encountered. Usually, when I received letters in response to *Missing Time*, they were read and then stacked in a cardboard box to be answered later when time permitted, a batch at a time. If the tone of the letter sounded urgent and the narrative followed the pattern of symptoms I recognized as suggestive of a buried abduction experience, I often phoned the writer directly. The "Kathie Case" fit this special category. I called her for the first time on September 15, 1983. A number of phone conversations ensued, leading up to arrangements for Kathie to visit New York in the middle of October for an intensified investigation of her experience and a series of hypnotic regressions.

During these phone calls I talked with Kathie, her mother, her father and her sister Laura. All four speak with a familiar middle-American accent—I was born in Wheeling, West Virginia, so I know it well—and an earthy, candid directness that conveys the habit of honesty. One of my first conversations was with Kathie's father, Robert. I asked him his recollections of the circle and patch of dead grass which appeared on the lawn behind his house.

Well, I've been working about ten years on this damn yard out there, and the backyard was the best part of the whole place. I don't know what did it. It's not fungus. I don't know what the devil it is, but something or someone or whatever has wiped out a hunk of my damn ground. The circle and that line away from it is still just like it was, and it's been there about three months. It hasn't changed at all. The grass just grows up to it and quits.

Robert, Mary and Kathie all agree that it took perhaps three days for the grass to die completely and then to crumble away to brown powder. The marks were unmistakably clear by the Fourth of July, when Mary remembered pointing them out to her grandson. Shrubbery near the bird feeder, where Mary had first seen the small ball of light, began to die also, and as we shall see, there were other odd organic changes in the Davises' backyard.

I also asked Kathie's father his opinion of both of his daughters' basic truthfulness. Robert and Mary have raised four children—three girls and a boy—and I have met them all. As I began to know them better, I felt that they all were honest and innocent of the need to embellish or invent exotic incidents. Robert was more emphatic: "If they ever made anything up I'd whack their butts for them, so they never did."

In fact, after talking to the other family members I realized that Kathie had a tendency even to understate the strangeness of events in the Davis clan. She was less prone to sound the alarm than to try to explain things away, and she only wrote to me when she had photographs to back up her and her mother's accounts of the peculiar backyard lights and ground traces. At the end of that letter she had referred, almost reluctantly, to some vivid dreams she had had, and in one of our earliest phone conversations I asked her about them. The most recent and for her the most unforgettable occurred in the summer of 1978, when she was nineteen years old, newly married, and living with her husband in a small attic apartment in a suburb of Indianapolis.

The dream was extraordinarily frightening and realistic, Kathie recalled, an experience as vivid now as it had been then. It began in the middle of the night with Kathie sitting up, awake, facing two strange, gray-faced creatures who stood alongside her bed. One of them was holding a small black box with a glistening red light on its top. The "man" who held the box moved closer and handed it to Kathie, and as he moved the other figure moved too, in absolute unison. In an account she wrote later she described it this way: "When they handed me the box I remember thinking, 'Oh, please don't come any closer!' Just as I wrote that I felt the terror, and it all felt *too* real. The feeling, the dream! For just a flash I thought this could be real, I don't know. *The terror is real.*"

She described the figures as having large heads and skin that was "dingy white, almost gray." Their eyes were "pitch black in color, liquid-like, shimmering in the dim light." She mentioned that she could not remember seeing hands when the box was passed to her, and that the figures were so close to the bed that she could not see their lower legs or feet.

I don't remember if there was a mouth and nose, or ears. I just remember the eyes best, and the general shape. They were between four and five feet tall, I guess, and slight of build. He called me by name and seemed to talk to me like I was a child. I don't know why I feel this but it didn't bother me.

He said "Kathie" and handed me the box. I said, "Can I have it?" He said, "No. Hold it. Look at it." I did. Then he took it from me gently after a minute. I said, "What is it? What's it for?" He said, "Look at me." Then I thought, "Do I have to?" but I did. He said, "When the time is right you will see it again, you will remember and you'll know how to use it." I said, "O.K."

I was scared, petrified, but as soon as I heard my name, and when I looked at his face, his eyes, I could calm down enough to communicate. I felt more physically relaxed, almost sleepy again, and quieter mentally. I just kept thinking, "Just don't come any closer and don't touch me and I'll be O.K. God, please don't touch me! Don't move closer to me, please!" They never touched me and they moved slowly, cautiously. I never saw them leave, I just woke up.

Kathie said that this "dream" seemed utterly real—she was in her own bedroom, and everything appeared exactly as it normally was, except for the presence of her strange visitors. Her husband was asleep beside her through the entire ordeal, yet she made no effort to alert him. About three A.M. she awoke slowly, as if from an anesthetic, as she put it, and roused her husband to tell him of her bizarre recollection. The following day she told her mother as well as her sister Laura. I have since interviewed both women as well as Kathie's ex-husband on this point, and all three recall Kathie's having told them at that time—1978—of her frightening "dream." All the details she has described predate the publication of *Missing Time*. (She also did not see the film *Close Encounters of the Third Kind* until her father took the whole family to see it a year later, at Christmastime.) I am satisfied that in 1978 she had almost no knowledge of the typical "bedroom visitation," nor of this commonly reported UFO occupant-type. Her images and memories cannot be ascribed either to "contamination" by reading the UFO literature or by viewing its Hollywood version as created by Steven Spielberg's special effects department.

In the past seven years I have investigated literally scores of accounts similar to Kathie's dream recollection, and I am always on the alert for certain symptoms that suggest the dream was not a dream at all, but instead was a real event—a partially recalled UFO abduction experience. Though many UFO abductions are remembered normally and apparently in their entirety, the way one might recall a mugging or a frightening accident, some degree of amnesia accompanies the majority of these experiences. We simply do not know whether amnesia in these situations is a natural, internally fueled defense against unsettling memories; whether it is an externally imposed phenomenon by which UFO occupants conceal their operations and, as it were, help the abductee to live as normal a life as possible after such an experience; or some combination of these two factors. But if, as I suspected, Kathie's dream was a real event, her conscious recollections were undoubtedly only part of a longer, more complex buried experience. The first thing she remembered was not awakening, but rather being already awake and sitting up in bed. She had only a hazy sense of how the dream ended, so, like a number of UFO abduction accounts, her story had a middle but no real beginning or end. I made a mental note that when she came to New York this would be the first incident which we would explore through hypnosis, the method we relied upon to pierce the veil of amnesia.

In the time between my receipt of Kathie's original letter and the day of her arrival in New York in mid-October, I was on the phone with at least one member of the Davis family almost every other night. UFO research may be frustrating from some points of view but I'm sure it has the full support of the telephone company. Indianapolis, even in the off-hours, is a costly connection, and few of our calls were short. Each of the Davis family members' recollections seemed to spark still more accounts of other apparently unconnected and as yet unreported incidents. It was as if each person had for years harbored an odd memory or two, and until I began asking questions along lines that I knew from past experience could be fruitful no one assumed that these memories were possibly significant—or, for that matter, part of a larger pattern within the UFO phenomenon.

When, for example, I began asking the Davis family members about their dreams, especially any frightening, recurrent dreams, another previously hidden pattern emerged rather dramatically. Kathie had written to me a second time, enclosing photographs of the similar mysterious scars on her and her mother's lower legs, and in this letter she complied with my request by describing another dimly remembered "dream" from her childhood:

> Me and Mom are hiding in a closet because there's a big thing in the sky, and Mom is real scared. Then suddenly she's pulled from the closet and I'm terrified that *I'll never see her again*. I don't understand why we're supposed to be scared of the thing in the sky. We lived on Michigan Street then. We were in my closet. That's it. That's all I can remember, and it's very unclear.

In a later, completely separate interview with Kathie's mother, I asked Mary if she had ever had any recurrent, disturbing dreams that remained vividly in mind over the years. She said that there was one puzzling dream that she had had frequently as a young woman, which was both terrifying and extremely realistic and which involved her eldest daughter. In this dream she had hidden in the closet of Laura's room because "two people" were in the house who "wanted to take my child." This closet—which she dreamed of exactly as it was in reality—had a trapdoor in its ceiling which led to an attic crawl space. In her panic she opened it and pushed Laura up into the attic to hide her from the nameless threat outside. The dream always ended there, and Mary would then wake up terrified. The similarity between Kathie's and her mother's dreams is remarkable except for one odd but central detail—Kathie places herself in the dream, while Mary remembers that it was Laura she was hiding in the attic. This apparent contradiction, which still has not been resolved, can be explained various ways. First, there is the possibility of "contamination," that as a small child Kathie heard her mother's vivid account and applied it to herself rather than to her sister Laura, thereafter remembering the dream as if it were her own. It is also possible that Mary misremembered her own dream. But there is a third, more disturbing possibility. When I interviewed the Davis family in Indianapolis and inquired about any odd fears or phobias any of them might recall, Laura told me that she has always had an intense fear of just such attic spaces as she remembers from their old Michigan Street home. Her own terror about it is such that she insisted her husband nail shut the ceiling trapdoors leading to attic crawl spaces in both the houses they have lived in since their marriage. Despite this deep-seated and unusual fear, Laura claims to remember nothing of a childhood attic experience, while Kathie recalls the "dream" of hiding with her mother in this same closet. And so, considering the recollections of all three, a third possibility suggests itself: Could there have been two separate invasions of the house years apart, with Mary reacting the same way both times by hiding her littlest child in the closet?

Not until our third phone conversation did I ask Kathie if she had, herself, ever seen anything she took to be an actual UFO, an unidentified *flying* object as opposed to the odd light in the pool shed or the two strange figures in her "dream." She answered somewhat hesitantly that she and two other girls—teenagers—had several times seen odd moving lights late at night when they were driving around, in Kathie's phrase, "out in the boonies." I asked for details. "My friend Dorothy and I sometimes cruised around spying on Dorothy's boyfriend. We always seemed to have a good time but we don't remember what we did. But one time I remember we saw this weird light. It was flashing like a strobe. I said, 'Hey, look at that light up there,' and then somebody said, 'It's a UFO,' and we all started giggling. And then it got closer. And it started flashing. We all got a creepy feeling. I was more fascinated than I was scared. I remember that we stopped the car to look at it." Kathie's memories at this point became vague, so I made a note to inquire further into this incident, too. I asked her to visit her friend Dorothy and find out what she remembered about that night, and the next day Kathie called me. "I was really surprised," she said. "When I got Dorothy on the phone,

I told her you wanted to know what she remembered about the time we saw the flashing light and stopped the car. She said, 'Do you mean the light in the sky or the light on the ground that we got out to look at?' Now, the strange thing is I don't remember seeing any light on the ground. I barely remember getting out of the car. I don't remember anything else about it at all, except that Roberta was hiding on the floor in the backseat, scared to death and wanting to go home. The whole thing was peculiar. I remember that I spent the night at Dorothy's, and that we had barely gotten in bed when her parents' alarm clock went off and it was time for them to get up for work. I know it was almost dawn when we came in, but I can't for the life of me remember what we did all that time. Dorothy doesn't know what we did either, but she remembers how late it was." And then Kathie, recognizing the irony of the situation, chuckled and said, "I remember one of us saying, 'Time really flies when you're having fun!' " As the reader will learn, Kathie's conscious recollections of that night concealed an extremely harrowing UFO abduction experience, an event of crucial importance for our understanding of the UFO phenomenon.

One of the requests I made of Kathie and her family was that they carefully go over the ground behind their house near the burned area and look for any marks or disturbances that they may not have noticed before. I also asked for samples of the soil inside the damaged circle and control samples from the undisturbed ground immediately adjacent to it. By going back to her appointment book Kathie had been able to fix the date of the backyard events—the lights, the armed search, her mother's account of the illuminated bird feeder, etc.—as having been June 30, 1983. So my request for soil samples, following the receipt of her first letter, came two and a half months after the event. I knew, therefore, that any evidential weight the samples might once have had was now probably compromised.[15] But Kathie's search at the burned circle yielded an important new find: About two feet out from the eight-foot-diameter circle, equidistant from the center and from each other, were four small holes, finger-thick and about three inches deep. These small holes, which could easily have been made by some sort of fixed, symmetrical landing gear, have their precedents in other similar UFO cases, as we shall see.

During a September phone conversation one of the most disturbing series of events in the ongoing Copley Woods affair came to my attention through Mary Davis. I was speaking to Kathie one evening when she said, almost reluctantly I thought, that her mother asked her to tell me about the strange phone calls. It seems that in 1980, when Kathie was pregnant with her second son, Tommy, she received a phone call that was indecipherable. Above a background noise that roared like a factory in full swing she heard a voice moaning and muttering but using no syllables she could understand. She assumed at first that it was a friend playing a practical joke on her, so she broke in and asked humorously what was going on. The voice continued without even a pause to acknowledge the question. She asked again, and after several requests and no apparent response of any sort she hung up. This occurred on a Wednesday afternoon. The following Wednesday, at about the same time—3:00 P.M.—she received another nearly identical call. And the next Wednesday and the one after that. No words were ever audible, and there were no apparent sexual overtones. The gender of the voice itself was indecipherable.

The phone calls continued for months, coming every Wednesday afternoon at around the same time. Sometimes Kathie listened for many minutes, fascinated by the weird sounds, and sometimes she hung up quickly. At one point early in this saga she decided she should probably report these incidents to the telephone company and the police, but since the voice, whatever it was, seemed harmless enough she decided not to try any legal remedies. She did, however, decide to have her phone changed to an unpublished listing. On a Monday afternoon the telephone company called to inform her that the change had taken effect, and to give her her new unlisted number. A few minutes later the mysterious caller phoned again, sounding angry, according to Kathie, but clearly establishing the fact that acquiring an unlisted number meant nothing at all; she was as accessible as ever. It was the only time she received one of these calls on any day but Wednesday.

One of the reasons Kathie's mother asked her to tell me about these calls was that Mary herself had answered the phone one Wednesday when Kathie was out. Mary said the voice had been very strange to listen to. She gave me her impression of the guttural sounds, the moans, and the background roaring and clicking noises. Both Kathie and her mother felt that the voice seemed sometimes to be angry, sometimes sad, and sometimes emotionally neutral. On one or two occasions Kathie sensed that the sounds were actually threatening, but there was never any sense of interplay, of conversation. Whatever the voice was, it proceeded in a monologue, making no allowance for any response.

Luckily, on another Wednesday afternoon during that period, Kathie's friend Dorothy came to visit. She answered the phone at Kathie's request

so Dorothy, too, heard the moaning, the guttural noises and all the rest.
There are now three witnesses to this strange phenomenon, and their
descriptions are remarkably congruent. The calls continued throughout
the nine months of Kathie's pregnancy, but within a week after Tommy's
birth on September 26, 1980, they ceased abruptly.

What is one to make of this business? Is it connected to the UFO
phenomenon in some way? There are, in fact, precedents in the literature
that document this kind of unusual event in other UFO situations.[16] One
peripheral fact may be involved here, and it is disturbing to consider.
When Kathie came to New York in the middle of October 1983, I had
many questions for her. Since I routinely try to inform myself about the
mental and physical health of each UFO witness, some of my questions
had to do with Kathie's medical background. She has had a long struggle
with several chronic, possibly psychosomatic illnesses—colitis, irregular
heartbeat, acute anxiety, insomnia and so forth. In group therapy her
psychologist thought that there was some as yet undiscovered cause for
her problems, such as a buried trauma, a particular unremembered event.
As she answered my questions about her medical history, I asked about
the health of her two boys. They were fine, she said, and then paused.
"Tommy, my youngest, has a speech problem. He's three years old but
he doesn't talk yet. He just makes this sort of moaning sound. I've had
him thoroughly tested. They've done brain stem and brain wave analysis,
and so on, and he's normal. He's very bright. He just doesn't talk yet."
Later, when Kathie was alone with a woman colleague of mine, she told
her, with barely concealed emotion, that the situation worried her a great
deal. She said that Tommy sounds very much like the mysterious caller
who repeatedly phoned her during her pregnancy.[17]

One of the earliest conversations I had with the Davis family concerned
the 1965 "missing time" UFO episode reported by Kathie's sister. I spoke
to Laura at length about this sighting which, the reader will remember,
occurred in a church parking lot, and with one chronological difference
her account closely corroborated the version Kathie had outlined in her
letter.[18] Laura had taken her mother to a bingo party on a Sunday
afternoon in the early fall. The game began at 5:00 P.M., so she assumes
it was very close to that time when she drove by the church on her way
home. (The church was about ten miles from the place she had deposited
her mother sometime before the bingo began.) She does not know why
she felt compelled to pull into the entrance and then drive around behind
into the church parking lot, but this is what she did. She simply stopped
the car, and at this point her daytime memories end. In the next instant

it was dark out, and above her she could see a large, hovering UFO with multicolored lights flickering around its bottom edge. Laura could hear it "humming or whirring, making a sound like a top would make—an airlike sound." She lowered her window and leaned forward to turn down the radio, hoping to hear the UFO more clearly, but suddenly it began to accelerate and in a few seconds was out of sight. As she drove home she realized that something was radically wrong. A portion of this puzzling sequence of events was missing, an unsettling mystery that, over the years, bothered her whenever she thought about it.

One fascinating and suggestive new piece of information did surface during the interview. Laura told me that when Kathie was questioning her, Kathie had asked if she had been at all frightened while she was looking at the UFO. "I told her I wasn't frightened at all, ever. I just felt amazed by this huge thing in the sky, only a hundred feet or so above me. Kathie said, 'You were never, even for a second, afraid?' and I said, 'No, never. Not when I first saw it, not when I heard its humming sound and watched the lights on it, and not even . . .' " Laura said that here she stopped herself; she had been about to say, " 'Not even when I got back in the car.' And I thought, Oh, was I ever out of the car, because I don't remember being out of the car." It was a sudden half-memory, a glimmer, perhaps, but one that hinted at the forgotten part of the experience. Perhaps, during the missing time period, she *had* been out of the car. It was an idea that opened a Pandora's box of possibilities.

Later, I asked Laura if she had read my book *Missing Time*, which deals with just such time-lapse situations, and she said that Kathie had lent it to her, but she had only read parts of it. "It made me very uneasy to read your book, and I couldn't finish it." She told me that she had seen *Close Encounters of the Third Kind*—a UFO film which does not deal directly with abductions—and said that it hadn't bothered her at all. "But when I saw the movie about the couple in New Hampshire [*The UFO Incident*, the film account of the Betty and Barney Hill abduction[19]] it scared me to death. I had to turn the TV off. When I got in bed I couldn't sleep. My eyes were wide open. I tried to sleep, and finally I thrashed around so my husband would wake up, but he never did. I hardly slept that night." I have investigated enough similar cases to recognize in Laura's account and subsequent behavior many of the signs of a traumatic—and buried —UFO abduction experience. Everything I was learning about the Copley Woods affair underlined my desire to go to Indianapolis and see for myself.

Seven years before, I had investigated the first of scores of UFO reports that turned out to involve an abduction, and which established a by now familiar pattern. In that first case a young man, Steven Kilburn, was immobilized after his automobile was pulled off the road as if by some powerful external force.[20] He was then approached by five short, grayish, large-headed humanoid figures. Like Kathie and so many other abductees, Kilburn's attention was drawn almost hypnotically to his captors' eyes, which he described as "really shiny . . . black. I don't see any pupils or anything . . . and they're big . . . they're black and endless. Like they're liquid or something . . . I keep looking at these eyes looking at me. God. I feel like I'm under a microscope."[21] It is worth noting that in Kathie's 1978 "dream" she also describes the small, gray-skinned figure's eyes as "pitch black in color, liquid-like, shimmering in the dim light . . . When I looked at his face, his eyes, I could calm down enough to communicate." Kilburn was taken inside the UFO and placed upon a table where he underwent an intermittently painful physical examination which included the taking of a sperm sample. Later he was returned to his car and the memory of this traumatic encounter was somehow temporarily blocked.

Since the Kilburn case I have worked directly with over one hundred people who apparently have had the same kind of UFO abduction experience. These individuals, it should be pointed out, come from every educational, social and economic level of our society. I have investigated the cases of three different abductees who hold Ph.D. degrees. Other abductees I've worked with include a psychotherapist, a police officer, a lawyer for the United States Government, a farmer, an army officer, a business executive, a well-known writer, an artist, a registered nurse, and so on— a nice cross section of the community. Now after investigating this sort of abduction account, the researcher ultimately has to take one of three basic positions. First, he can decide that the witness is a liar, a deliberate hoaxer. Second, he can conclude that the witness is somehow deluded, that the experience did not physically take place but instead was some kind of psychological aberration. The third and only other option is that the witness's account is an honest attempt to remember an actual event.

As to the first option, I am convinced that none of the apparent abductees I have worked with is deliberately trying to perpetrate a hoax. Publicity cannot be considered a motive. Only two of them have ever given me permission to use their real names in any report I published. None have ever asked for any reward, financial or otherwise, for their accounts. None, in my opinion, had any visible motive to invent such a bizarre story, and in the few cases when polygraph tests were used, the witnesses passed them.

The second possible explanation of these abduction accounts—the psychological explanation—is by far the more plausible, and it is here that I have made the greatest effort to find an alternative to their literal truth. In 1981 Dr. Aphrodite Clamar, Ted Bloecher and I received financial support from the Fund for UFO Research to undertake a study of this central issue.[22] We hired a highly recommended, highly qualified psychologist, Dr. Elizabeth Slater of New York, to administer a full battery of psychological tests to nine people whose abduction experiences we had previously investigated, and whose veracity seemed beyond doubt. Dr. Slater was told absolutely nothing about the UFO connection. She knew only that we had a research project that required the "blind" testing of our nine subjects, that we were interested in any psychological patterns that might emerge among them, and that we were interested, naturally, in any psychopathology that might be present.

In June of 1983 Dr. Slater completed her tests, which included the Minnesota Multiphasic Personality Inventory, the Rorschach, the Wechsler Adult Intelligence Scale, the Thematic Apperception Test and a projective drawing test. She found no major mental disorders amongst the nine; none was paranoid, schizophrenic or otherwise emotionally crippled. There was, however, something of a pattern. Though all nine were above average in intelligence, they all shared certain "deficits," to use the psychological jargon. In Dr. Slater's words, each of the nine evinced "a degree of identity disturbance, some deficits in the interpersonal sphere and generally mild paranoia phenomena."[23] I asked Dr. Slater to translate some of these phrases into laymen's language for me. In general terms, though several of the nine subjects were extremely successful in life—in career, social and economic position and so on—all suffered a lack of self-esteem. None seemed fully at ease physically, "at home in their bodies, and comfortable with their sexuality," in Dr. Slater's words, and all suffered from a degree of distrust and wariness, though none could be called paranoid. "They're just more vigilant, more hesitant to trust, than the average person," she said.

After Dr. Slater handed us her report, we told her about the UFO connection, and I explained a little about UFO abduction accounts. She was, as one might imagine, flabbergasted to find out that this was the experience her nine subjects shared. In answer to our final request she applied herself to the task of writing an afterword to her report, a reevaluation of the test results in the light of this new information. She read my book *Missing Time*, hypothesized about the psychological effects one might expect from such an experience, and then wrote a summation. Her conclusions are extremely important for any attempt at a "psychological theory" of UFO abduction accounts, so I will quote from them in some detail:

> The first and most critical question is whether our subjects' reported experiences could be accounted for strictly upon the basis of psychopathology, i.e. mental disorder. The answer is a firm no. In broad terms, if the reported abductions were confabulated fantasy productions, based on what we know about psychological disorders, they could only have come from pathological liars, paranoid schizophrenics and severely disturbed and extraordinarily rare hysteroid characters subject to fugue states and/or multiple personality shifts . . . It is important to note that not one of the subjects, based on the test data, falls into any of these categories . . . In other words, there is no apparent psychological explanation for their reports.
>
>   . . . From another, more speculative point of view, one can consider how UFO abduction as reported in Mr. Hopkins' *Missing Time* might affect the victim . . . Certainly such an unexpected, random and literally otherwordly experience . . . during which the individual has absolutely no control over the outcome, constitutes a trauma of major proportions. Hypothetically, its psychological impact might be analogous to what one sees in crime victims or victims of natural disasters, as it would constitute an event during which the individual is overwhelmed by external circumstances in an extreme manner . . . [and somehow] stripped of any mental capacity to resist physically.
>
>   . . . Psychological traits which arose consistently in the subjects first included a surprising degree of inner turmoil as well as a great degree of wariness and distrust. Logically, such emotional upheaval and accompanying caution about the world might certainly follow in the wake of an experience as described above.
>
>   Furthermore, if one considers the skepticism and disrepute that is typically encountered with reports of UFO sightings, then not only are we characterizing UFO abduction as inherently traumatic, but we must add that it would likely carry social stigmatization as well . . . Assuming for the sake of argument that abduction has

actually occurred and that presumably its occurrence would be very
rare, it then becomes something that cannot be readily shared with
others as a means of obtaining emotional support. Consequently,
one would likely find a deep sense of shame, secretiveness and social
alienation among the victims, who would have undergone a profound experience that could not be comprehended or accepted by
others. The closest analogy might be the interpersonal alienation of
the rape victim, who has been violated most brutally but somehow
becomes tainted by virtue of the crime against her.

As Dr. Slater pointed out in her addendum, the results of the nine
psychological test batteries obviously cannot prove that our subjects were
actually abducted. The project does, however, establish two major points:
that a trained psychologist testing nine individuals "blindly" found absolutely no psychological explanation for their abduction accounts, and also
that each exhibited the kind of "psychic scarring" such a trauma would
be likely to inflict.

In my effort to explore any possible psychological explanation for UFO
abduction accounts, I have dealt with a number of other psychologists and
psychiatrists who have been most helpful and generous with their time,
though the subject is still so controversial that several are not anxious to
be publicly identified with the undertaking. Three psychiatrists and two
psychologists have conducted hypnotic regression sessions over the years
with a number of possible UFO abductees. Two other psychiatrists have
interviewed our subjects and, in one instance, led a kind of group therapy
session with a gathering of six abductees. None of these psychological
professionals have presented to me, even tentatively, a psychological theory that might explain these bizarre accounts. And even if such a theory
did exist, there would still remain the problem of explaining the physical
evidence—the scars, marks, temporary disappearances, etc. It is perhaps
also significant that none have ever encountered in their clinical practice
any clearly psychotic patients who described this kind of UFO abduction
experience. It is obviously not a commonly held delusion. God, the devil
and the CIA are still popular, it seems, but UFO abductions are not a big
item with the genuine lunatic fringe.

And so we find ourselves left with the third and so far the only un-
damaged explanation for UFO abduction accounts. It is at once the most
incredible and yet the simplest theory of all: These clearly frightened,

demonstrably honest people are simply telling the truth about what happened to them.

When I completed *Missing Time* I thought that more abduction
accounts would continue to come to light, but I was not prepared for the
truly vast numbers that apparently exist. And instead of becoming somewhat more vague in its contours, the abduction phenomenon now seems
more precise, more focused, more *real* than I could ever have imagined.
I had resolved not to write another book unless I learned some new and
important truth about the phenomenon. In the intervening five years that
condition has been met, clearly and dramatically. The impetus for this
present study is my growing awareness of what seems to be a long-term,
specific, experimental purpose behind what I had thought were the
UFOs' somewhat random, information-gathering forays.

At this point I must warn the reader once again: The assertions I am
about to make are "unbelievable," "inconceivable"—yet I am certain that
existing evidence supports their truth. Almost everyone who has ever
reported a UFO abduction experience has described the behavior of the
abductors as peculiarly neutral and objective, displaying neither malice
nor human warmth. The general image used by the abductees is that of
a laboratory environment, in which they are the tranquilized specimen.
Many reports describe the taking of samples, which sometimes have
included sperm and ova. In thirteen cases that I have investigated, family
members from different generations of the same family seem to have been
systematically abducted, at varying times and locations, leading one to
infer that these abductions represent a genetically focused study of particular bloodlines. In the Copley Woods affair, Mary Davis was apparently
abducted as a child and again as a young mother. Her daughters Kathie
and Laura—but not, it seems, her other two children—were abducted
later, at different times and places. At least two of Mary's *grandchildren*
have reported disturbing encounters with similarly described humanoid
figures. Both mother and daughter bear virtually identical scars on their
lower legs from apparent childhood abductions, and there is evidence that
both Kathie and her son Tommy have had implants inserted near their
brains, one through the nasal cavity and the other through the ear. Such
apparent implants—an outrageous and paranoia-inducing idea if there
ever was one—have been recalled, both with and without the aid of
hypnosis, in eleven abduction cases I have investigated.[24] The object most
often described is a tiny ball, only two or three millimeters in diameter,
that is put in place by means of a long needle. (One remembers the

analogy with human zoologists who methodically install tiny transmitters in sample animals to facilitate later tracking.)

The pattern of UFO interest in generations of particular families is clear. In a Canadian case, a father was abducted as a young man and decades later his son experienced a series of such encounters. In an Erie, Pennsylvania, family, both mother and daughter have apparently undergone the same abduction experiences over the years, while in Connecticut, Vermont and Florida cases mothers and sons were separately picked up and "examined" by UFO occupants. But most disturbing is the apparent motive behind this concentration by the UFO phenomenon upon various family bloodlines. In this book I will present new and compelling evidence that an ongoing genetic study is taking place—and that the human species itself is the subject of a breeding experiment. I am fully aware that this idea is so outrageous that one's natural response upon reading it is to echo Justice Frankfurter's remark about the Holocaust and simply announce that one cannot believe it, period, regardless of the evidence. But I ask that you hear me out. If what I report in these pages is true, as I believe it is, our view of the cosmos and our place within it will be forever changed. With the stakes that high the evidence must be attended to.

2
The Missing Hour

It was not until October—nearly a month after I received her initial letter —that I actually met Kathie Davis face to face. It was an odd, sweet and emotional occasion that will be told in a later chapter, but I would like to describe her here, nevertheless. Though she is of medium height, she is a large, broad-shouldered, big-boned woman, and despite the various illnesses she has suffered, her body is a strong one. Her kind, intelligent face is surrounded by short, curly, dark blond hair. After I had been with her a while I noticed that her hazel eyes vary slightly in hue, one from the other, a feature which helps explain why her glance is so subtly arresting. Kathie is a careful observer, but her attitude towards the strange events she has experienced is tinged with irony and a sense of resignation.

During the three-year period of our investigation I saw Kathie undergo rather pronounced changes. When we met, she was an unemployed and recently divorced woman with two small children, living at home with her parents. As the investigation progressed and she began to understand more about the cause of her deep-seated anxiety, she began to gain self-confidence. Eventually she went back to school and trained for a new career; she now has her own apartment and is self-supporting. Her old anxiety is still there, but its effects are no longer crippling.

Though Kathie's education was obviously less than Ivy League, her

intelligence and range of information are self-evident. Her conversationsal
style can be salty and only casually grammatical, but one discovers that
she is highly sophisticated in surprising ways. (I have always thought that
the autodidact, as it were, knows all about it but doesn't know how to
pronounce it, while the college graduate often has that situation reversed.
Kathie is a good example of my theory.) She has considerable talent as a
visual artist, as several illustrations in this book demonstrate, but I discovered that she has another quality which I respect whenever I sense its
presence: a particular kind of insight into others, an ability to read and
understand people, not in a mystical way, but with simple, practical,
intuitive awareness. The German word is apt; Kathie is a true *Menschen-
kenner*, a "knower of men." If I were to go to a party and meet new people
or visit old acquaintances, I would include her on a very short list of those
friends whose opinions I would solicit immediately after leaving. What
did you think of him? How do you read her? Is he possibly more intelligent
than he seems? Her gifts in this area are rarer than one supposes, and very
much to be cherished.

Kathie's initial September letter had presented only a general outline
of the events leading up to the appearance of the strange lights and
desiccated soil in the Davises' backyard. When I first read it I had no
reason to think that this apparent UFO incident could possibly have
involved an abduction, and so our investigation focused on other issues.
But after two visits to Indianapolis and many wide-ranging interviews with
Kathie, her family and neighbors, I gradually came to realize that the
sequence of remembered events just did not cohere. No matter how we
looked at it, there was at least an hour missing from Kathie's recollection
of that night. What finally emerged after extensive investigation is, on the
basis of its compelling physical evidence alone, one of the most important
UFO abduction cases on record.[1]

It began very casually on a summer day like any other. June 30, 1983,
was hot and muggy in the Indianapolis environs. The temperature
reached 85 degrees, though the skies were somewhat overcast. Shortly
before dinnertime Kathie set off to attend her regular Thursday evening
therapy group, a program she had joined to help her cope with years of
insomnia and paralyzing anxiety. She returned home at the usual time,
around 7:15 P.M., ate her supper, and then put her boys, Robbie and
Tommy, to bed. After dinner she called her friend Dee Anne to arrange
an evening of sewing at Dee Anne's house. (The two women shared a
modest business venture together, making clothes to order for friends.)

The first peculiar observation was made a little before nine o'clock, as Kathie was telling her mother her plans for the evening. She glanced out the kitchen window and noticed a light shining from the little pumphouse near their swimming pool. Though I was aware of some of these details from her original letter, subsequent personal interviews provided a great deal of new information. I learned, for example, that there was something odd about the color of the illumination in the poolhouse.

The door was open and there was a funny-colored light glowing from inside . . . a white light, more like a fluorescent light than the usual yellowish bulb we had there. I asked my Mom to look at it. I told her that I had just been out there and I remember the door was closed. Mom said not to worry about it, it was nothing, and just passed it off, but I had a really strange feeling when I first saw it. It was kind of eerie.

A few minutes later, when Kathie left to visit Dee Anne, things had changed. Now the pumphouse was dark and the door was closed, but the garage door—which had been shut—was open. The trip to her friend's house is only a five-minute drive, so when Kathie arrived, about 9:15, she called her mother immediately and told her about the garage door, asking if she wanted her to come home and search the property for a possible intruder. Kathie knew that her father would not be back from work for at least two hours, and that in the meantime her mother would be alone with Kathie's two little children. Nevertheless, Mary declined her daughter's offer, saying that everything seemed all right at home and she shouldn't bother. A moment later, however, as Mary stood at the kitchen sink, she noticed a strange round ball of light surrounding the bird feeder in the backyard. This small feeder, sitting atop a four-foot pole, is located about twelve feet from the kitchen window. Mary described what she saw this way:

It was a pale white light. It wasn't real bright. I could see the bird feeder through it, and I thought, "Gee, where is that light coming from?" I leaned out to see if a car was coming, and then I thought, you know, that's impossible, no car could shine its lights over behind the house. And there wasn't any beam. It was just there. It was round and about as big as a basketball, but I could see the bird feeder through it. Then it just sort of faded out, all at once.

And so, only a few moments after she had talked to Kathie, she called her back and said that perhaps after all she should come home and look around.[2] Kathie, sensing a slight uneasiness in her mother's usually reassuring tone of voice, left immediately. The time sequence now becomes particularly important. Most crucial are the hour Kathie arrived back home and the approximate time she left to return to Dee Anne's. Fortunately we can estimate both with near certainty.

Dee Anne's eleven-year-old daughter Tammy had been out shopping with her grandmother that night. The store closed at 9:00 P.M., and Tammy remembers that they arrived back at her mother's sometime before 9:30 and that Kathie had already left. Both Kathie and her mother recall that Kathie arrived at home around 9:30. She went straight to the closet and took out her father's rifle to provide herself a little spiritual edge over any possible intruders. Her mother reminded her that the rifle was unloaded, but Kathie replied that that was all right, she'd take it anyway. Mary chuckled and said, "What are you going to do with it—beat 'em to death?" Undaunted but nervous, Kathie went outside to search for prowlers. She and Mary both recall that she seemed to be gone no more than ten minutes. When she returned to the kitchen she told her mother that everything appeared to be normal, and that she was now going back to Dee Anne's, not to sew, but to get Dee Anne to come back with her for a "moonlight swim" since it was such a hot night. If she had been outside only for the ten minutes she remembered, she should have arrived at Dee Anne's sometime between 9:45 and 10:00. In fact she arrived about *11:00* P.M., and probably a little after. There is a period of at least an hour of missing time.

Both Tammy and Dee Anne recall that Kathie came very late, suggesting they all go for a swim. It seemed like a good idea so they quickly put on bathing suits. Kathie borrowed one of Dee Anne's, but Tammy for some reason decided to change when they got to the pool.[3] They remained at Dee Anne's no more than fifteen or twenty minutes before returning to the Davises', where they discovered that Kathie's father had just come home from work. Robert Davis worked a late shift and never arrived home before 11:30, and that night, everyone remembers, was no exception. Kathie, Dee Anne and Tammy arrived, then, sometime after 11:30, having spent, by all accounts, no more than twenty-five minutes changing clothes at Dee Anne's and driving over for their swim. Kathie had somehow lost the hour between ten and eleven o'clock. But more strange things were about to occur.

As they headed towards the pool, Tammy, barefoot, decided to walk on the grass to the left of her mother and Kathie, both of whom kept to the gravel path. At some point in the yard she "stepped on a place where there wasn't any grass, and it felt warm, like warm cement," as she told me later. (See illustrations.) "My foot felt tingly and kind of numb." Having brought her bathing suit with her, Tammy went into the little pumphouse to change. As she did so, she began to feel nauseated and dizzy. When she came out and joined the others in the pool "something did not feel right." Dee Anne said that from the moment she arrived in the backyard she felt uneasy, "like somebody's watching us." It was a very distinct feeling, though when she mentioned it, Kathie tried to downplay it. "I'm out here all the time, swimming by myself," Kathie said. "It doesn't bother me." But she described other problems that arose.

So we were swimming around and I dunked my hair back and got it wet, though I didn't get my face under the water. And Dee Anne looked at me and I looked at her and all of a sudden we're both freezing, though it's about eighty degrees out. It was a really warm night. She asked Tammy if she was cold and she said she was, so we decided to get out. We'd only been in a few minutes, too, but I was having trouble with my eyes. Everything was starting to look real hazy. I was the first to dry off because I couldn't see very good, and the longer I sat there the more I couldn't see. Everything was sort of white and I hadn't gotten my eyes under the water, you know, for the chlorine to do that. Everything was white with halos around the lights. It was weird, and I kept rubbing my eyes and they started burning. I went to the eye doctor two days after that and he said I had something like conjunctivitis in both eyes. I had a lot of trouble with them. There was even some pus. It was nasty.

The three swimmers had yet another problem. They began, nearly simultaneously, to feel quite nauseated. (In Tammy's case it was a deepening of the condition that had begun when she first entered the poolhouse.) Though it may appear an odd reaction to this kind of illness, they all three decided that what they needed was to eat something. They put shirts and shorts or jeans over their damp bathing suits, borrowed some money from Kathie's father, and headed for a local fast food restaurant that they knew would be open late. When they arrived, their nausea had become worse, so instead of ordering any food they simply turned around and headed

home. All of them considered it peculiar that it had happened so quickly and so similarly to all three, and that Kathie's eye problem had also surfaced so suddenly. Tammy and her mother had both had their heads under water, but neither suffered any difficulties with their vision. As Kathie said, "It was just weird. I remember being so cold. We were shivering, and Tammy's lips were blue. It was so foggy and we were freezing and it was the middle of summer. And then we all began to feel really sick."

Joyce and Bernie Lloyd—as I shall call them—are the closest neighbors to the north of the Davises. On this same evening, June 30, Bernie left after dinner on an errand with his son.[4] Joyce was dusting and tidying in the dining room, and glancing occasionally at the TV set in the living room. There was a sudden flash outside in the direction of the Davises' backyard, behind the trees that separate the two houses, and then a low, vibrating sound. Joyce felt her house begin to shake. The chandelier in the dining room moved slightly, and as the noise increased, the television picture turned completely red and all the lights in the house dimmed and flickered. Then everything returned to normal—the sound ended as mysteriously as it had begun. Joyce sat back in her chair stunned, confused, thinking immediately that there had been a small earthquake. Her next thought was that she should call the Davises' and see if they were all right. Perhaps their house had been struck by lightning. Maybe that was the flash she had seen through the trees. But she told me much later that when she thought about calling them, it was as if she simply couldn't do it. Something was preventing her from such a simple, normal act. The time, she noticed, was 10:45 P.M.

Bernie came home shortly afterwards. He is a very skeptical man when the subject of UFOs is mentioned, and by the time I interviewed him, months had passed since the incident in the Davises' backyard. He knew, of course, what we suspected, and he had seen the burned circle and swath in the Davises' grass. In this context I asked him what was going on in his house when he came in that night. He admitted immediately that his wife had been very upset. I phrased my next question this way: "On a scale of one to ten—one is your wife telling you she ran into a friend at the supermarket, and ten is her calling you in panic to say that she's barricaded herself in the bedroom and three men are trying to get at her—on that scale of emotion, how would you describe her that night when you walked in?" "She was a good, solid eight," he replied. "She was definitely scared."

He added that when he came up on the porch she was already at the door, telling him of the strange flash over near the Davises', and the noise and the vibration, and her fear that there had been an earthquake. He tried to think of an explanation, and suggested that perhaps a car had hit a utility pole, and that that was what had caused the lights to flicker and the house to shake. Bernie also told me that when he came home that night, a little after 11:00 P.M., all the digital clocks in the house were flashing and had to be reset. Something had definitely affected their power supply, at least momentarily.

When one adds the Lloyds' account to the others, the meshing of time and incident becomes very significant. Now any theory as to what happened that night must explain a number of anomalous incidents, from the physical effects in the Davises' yard and the electrical and other disturbances at the Lloyd's, to Kathie's inexplicable missing hour and the odd lights she and her mother saw earlier. The UFO abduction phenomenon, as I have pointed out, has very specific, recurring features. In order to test the possibility that Kathie had been abducted that night, I tried to see if the evidence so far supported these known patterns. UFO abductions are most commonly reported to last between one and two hours.[5] Therefore, if Kathie was taken shortly after she went outside with her rifle about 9:30 or 9:40 P.M., the abduction could easily have ended about an hour later, at 10:45, and by that reckoning the flash and sounds and strange electrical effects Joyce Lloyd reported at that time could have coincided with the UFO's departure.

Another pattern in many UFO abductions demonstrates their selective nature. If particular individuals within a group are the targets, and they are, for example, riding in an automobile with others who are not desired, these others are often "switched off," put in a state of suspended animation, until the targeted individuals are returned. In the David Oldham case, an abduction I discussed in *Missing Time,* Oldham was riding in the backseat of a two-door car.[6] When the car was stopped and the abduction began, his two friends in the front were somehow switched off. Oldham pushed the seat—and his companions—forward and got out only with great difficulty. He walked on, compelled as it were, towards a huge light, and later, after the abduction was over, struggled back into the rear seat past his "suspended" friends. By the time their animation returned David's memories of his UFO experience had vanished, and were not restored until he was hypnotically regressed years later. When Kathie and her mother heard Joyce Lloyd's bizarre account they were both surprised by the fact that they heard or saw nothing unusual that night except the odd lights they had described earlier. But if Kathie had been abducted and her mother "switched off," then it might follow that neither would have been consciously aware of the flash and sounds which Joyce described as having emanated from their backyard.

The marks in that backyard were, of course, a crucial clue to the mystery. The grass in the circle and straight swath began to wither and die immediately after June 30, and by July 4 the pattern was dramatically visible. But the odd physical effects of the event were soon to multiply. The hedge in the immediate area of the bird feeder also began to wither, and ultimately Robert Davis had to cut the plants back almost to the roots to force new growth. The degree of damage to portions of the hedge was in direct proportion to their proximity to the bird feeder. In the spring the Davis family had planted a few tomato plants in the general vicinity of what became the burned circle. The fruit these plants eventually produced were abnormally large and so mealy as to be inedible.

Kathie's eye problems and nausea were not the only symptoms of her experience that night. She began to suffer some degree of hair loss, and felt generally unwell for days afterward. She was also troubled by a low-level pain in her right ear and slightly impaired hearing over the next few weeks. One can hypothesize that whatever affected the Davises' yard was the source of a powerful and destructive form of energy, a force strong enough to heat the ground so that it was still warm to the touch forty-five minutes later when little Tammy walked across the "baked" area in her bare feet. The nausea and dizziness the three swimmers felt suggests the presence of some residual radiationlike effect, as does Kathie's later hair loss.[7] The bizarre electrical effects that occurred in the Lloyd house give another dimension to the power of these emissions, an elusive mix, perhaps, of microwave and other forms of radiation.

Shortly after I received Kathie's original September letter, I asked her to send me samples of the soil within the burned circle as well as control samples from unaffected areas a few feet away. A few days later I received them, neatly packed in plastic Ziploc bags. Kathie explained that the samples from within the burned area had not been easy to dig up. The ground inside the circle was so hard that she had to jump up and down on a spade to break into the compressed earth. The first thing I noticed was that the color of this sample was a light grayish brown, in contrast to the rich brown-black of the soil from unaffected areas nearby. The texture is hard and dry, having more the appearance of gravel than of soft, pliable loam. The soil samples were taken in the middle of September, unfortunately more than ten weeks after the incident, so several different possible testing avenues had been already somewhat compromised. (See illustrations.) Crystallographic and spectrographic analysis showed no apparent differences between the two samples. However, it was necessary to heat the unaffected sample in an oven at 800 degrees Fahrenheit for six hours to achieve the same color as that of the affected soil, though without duplicating its solidified appearance. Clearly, the amount of energy emitted by *something* in the Davises' backyard that night was enormous, though we have no idea of its nature.[8]

The later history of the "baked" circle and the straight swath is equally interesting. Because there was no grass at either spot, when the first winter snow came it covered the bare ground evenly and made the pattern of the marks even clearer. And when the temperature rose above freezing and the snow began to melt, it melted first over the affected areas, again rendering the marks clearly visible. (See illustrations.) I photographed the area in late May of 1985, nearly two years after the original event, and the mass of the circle was still almost devoid of vegetation, despite Robert Davis's attempts to plant new grass seed. I also noticed a general absence of insect life—anthills, burrows, etc.—though the grass has begun to creep in from the perimeter of the circle, shrinking its circumference somewhat. One can speculate that if a UFO landed at this spot, then the long, bare path connected to the circle may indicate the direction of its takeoff since it leads away from a tangle of overhanging tree branches and wires and towards the open sky. Here, the vegetation has grown in much more densely, though this pattern, too, is still clearly visible two years later. If a UFO landed and rested on the circular area for perhaps an hour, and then took off across the straight swath, one can hypothesize that the straight swath would then have received a lower dosage of whatever radiation was present.

One final point should be made about the "baked" areas on the Davises' property. When Kathie first sent me the photographs of her backyard after the June 30, 1983, incident, I asked her father about any underground pipes that might run through the area. The photograph of the forty-nine-foot-long straight swath raised the possibility of some kind of leaking, or recently laid, pipeline, though clearly the ground had not been recently dug up; its dead grass was of one continuous growth with the living grass next to it. Still, it was an issue that had to be explored. Robert Davis explained that ten years previously he had installed beneath the backyard a septic system consisting of a geometric pattern of drainage "fingers" extending out at right angles from a central line. These pipes were the only ones beneath the backyard. But the forty-nine-foot swath of dead soil that had appeared so suddenly and mysteriously ran *at an angle* to his system, crossing his drainage pipes at only three points and thus eliminating any possible connection between the two lines. And as I know from my property on Cape Cod, septic systems *encourage* the growth of vegetation rather than inhibiting it, which invalidated any "sewerpipe theory" at the outset. In the words of Erma Bombeck, "The grass is always greener over the septic tank."

In October of 1983, Kathie came to New York, and we met for the first time. Our initial investigation focused on her "dream" experience of 1979, and a later, similar encounter. Because Kathie's conscious recall of both incidents was clearly incomplete, we decided to employ hypnosis to aid her memory and to overcome any blocks that might be present. Dr. Aphrodite Clamar conducted the first two hypnotic sessions, and I took over for two more. (These initial explorations will be covered in later chapters.) Kathie proved to be a fine hypnotic subject, but it was not until my first trip to Indianapolis in January of 1984 that I suggested we try to regress her back to the night of June 30, 1983, when the peculiar physical damage occurred on the Davis property. She had never been eager to talk about that event, and so was even less inclined to think about exploring it hypnotically.

On my last night in Indianapolis we drove to her friend Dee Anne's house, where I conducted an interview on the events of that evening. Dee Anne's account supported my growing suspicion that there was a period of time missing from Kathie's conscious recollections. We chatted about the strangeness of the entire sequence of events, and then Kathie suddenly said to me, "Why don't we do the hypnosis now? If we have to do it about that night, let's get it over with. And Dee Anne can see how nice hypnosis can be, how relaxing." (Kathie has always been reluctant to undergo hypnosis in her own house, an interesting condition in itself.)

And so we began in the usual way. (For more about the process of hypnosis, see Appendix B.) Kathie made herself comfortable on the couch, and I started the calming induction process, part of which involves picturing a placid, beautiful ocean beach. She had been through this procedure on eight previous occasions, but in a moment she began to tremble. "I want to wake up," she said, her voice quietly urgent. "Wake me up. Now." I quickly counted backwards from five to one, having given her the customary instructions, and at "one" her eyes opened and she sat up. It was obvious that she was extremely frightened. She told us that when she began to glide into a relaxed, familiar trance state she suddenly saw herself standing at the window looking out at the light in the poolhouse.

> I just couldn't go on. My head would start to hurt and I would think I can't go any further or I'm going to die. I just . . . my body . . . my body felt like it was going to die. I don't even know what I was afraid of. I just felt like my body was going to die if I remembered any more, so I had to wake up.

I felt Kathie's hands and they were very cold. Her breathing was still agitated, but she was slowly regaining her composure. I said that her asking to be brought out of the trance demonstrated the control the subject has during the hypnotic process, and that that should be a reassuring fact. I wanted to calm her any way I could, but it was not easy. She had had a real shock:

> I never felt that kind of scared when I was with Dr. Clamar, or when we did it before. But this voice, this voice in my head kept telling me if I remember any more I'm going to die. "Feel your body. Feel it. You're going to die if you remember any more. Feel your head, it's going to burst, your chest is going to cave in and you're going to die if you remember any more." Something in my mind kept telling me this and I started feeling real cold all over like I was dead. I just wanted to wake up. It was bad . . . I just started to see myself standing in front of the window looking at that funny light . . .

I pointed out that we hadn't even completed the induction process when she began to react with great fear. I had not yet mentioned the night of June 30 or any other detail designed to lead her back to that experience.

> But I knew what we were headed back to. We'd just been talking about it with Dee Anne. It's been on my mind all day. But I've been chicken about trying to go back to it. I didn't want to. Man, I really thought I was going to die.

I asked her if the voice was her own, telling herself that she was going to die, or if the voice seemed external—another voice telling her this.

It wasn't me. I'm telling myself relax and enjoy this feeling and you're going to feel great when you wake up. And I'm listening to what you're saying, and I'm relaxing, and this other thought kept fighting its way in. But every time I'd tell myself just relax, take a deep breath, and don't think about standing in front of the window. Just think about a beach and relax. I'd try to picture a beach and I'd see it, and then it would fade out. I'd be standing back in front of the window and I'd hear, "You're going to die if you remember any more." It was just like a voice bursting through. I'm scared.

I tried as best I could to reassure her, to calm her fears, to explain that there seems to be no malice, no retribution present in this kind of UFO experience, despite the apparent threats. Nevertheless, there was obviously no choice but to put the June 30, 1983, incident on the back burner, to be looked into at a later time. The full narrative of what happened to Kathie that night was not to emerge until my second visit to Indianapolis in November 1984. But in the meantime she had several vivid and important memory "flashbacks." Hypnosis often seems to open the gates of normal recollection; frequently after a regression session the subject goes on to recall more and more pieces of the puzzle in separate, disconnected dreams and sudden flashes of memory. Shortly after her first abortive attempt at hypnotic recall, Kathie made a dramatic and spontaneous breakthrough: She recalled standing in the doorway of the garage and looking out into the yard at an egg-shaped craft, supported on four jointed legs. She also recalled a ball of light less than two feet in diameter seeming to move up and down her body, painfully irradiating her with light as she stood paralyzed and unable to respond. It was a particularly disturbing memory, and an extremely vivid one. The quick sketch she made of the UFO, showing the part of it that was visible as she stood in the doorway, closely resembles the egg-shaped craft in a little-known South African abduction case, of which I was at the time unaware.[9] (See illustrations.) More importantly, the UFO, as she recalled it, was located exactly above the burned circle in her yard.

When I returned to Indianapolis I was eager to explore this June 30 incident, and on the eleventh of November the hypnotic session finally took place. I spent an extra amount of time inducing the trance, calming Kathie, reassuring her that it would be all right, now, to remember. We began with her mother's phone call to her at Dee Anne's and her drive back home. She described coming into the house and deciding to take her father's rifle with her.

KD: I just felt real strange. Something wasn't right and I want something to protect me. The hair on my arms was standing up on end and I felt all tingly everywhere. *(She stirs uneasily)*

BH: What's happening, Kathie?

KD: I don't know. I just don't feel right. I went down the sidewalk and down the steps and across the yard. I got to the poolhouse and I reached out to open the latch and it was real rusty and hard to open. It was stuck, but I got it open. I was afraid to open the door. I thought about my dog. I wondered where she was. I pulled the door open and stuck my gun in and hollered, "You've got three seconds to give it up," or something like that. I gave them three seconds and then reached in and turned on the light, and nobody was there. Everything looked fine, and I was relieved. *(Kathie now describes walking to the back of the property, towards a large shed, where she finds her dog Penny. At this point in her narrative she shifts to the present tense, indicating a deepening of the trance state)* She won't come with me. She's just going off. I still feel real creepy . . . like some-body's watching me from the woods . . . but he won't fool with me when he sees this gun. So glad I have it. I guess I'll go to the garage and look around. *(Kathie stirs and jumps slightly)* Are you touching me? Somebody's touching my arm . . .

BH: I didn't touch you, Kathie. How does it feel?

KD: It feels just like somebody's touching me lightly, although it's stopped now. *(Kathie describes heading towards the garage to look around. The garage is attached to the house, and the rear "pedestrian" door opens into the backyard.)* Something was touching my arm, and it felt like they were running their fingers on me. It didn't hurt. It was creepy, and it wouldn't stop. *(She resumes her narrative)* I turn on the garage light and stick the gun in and holler the same thing—I have a gun and you've got three seconds—and then I go in and it's quiet and everything looks fine . . . I walk over and look behind a cabinet and I look behind a stack of mattresses and everything's O.K. . . . Now I'm starting to feel real strange. My head really hurts and now I'm starting to feel real tingly and hot. I've got to get out of the garage . . . *(She tenses and stirs uneasily)*

BH: What's happening, Kathie?

KD: I can't see. Everything's all white . . . very irritated.

BH: It's O.K., Kathie. You're all right. Tell us what you're seeing and feeling.

KD: *(Very agitated)* My head hurts so much . . . I can't move . . . feels like a . . . I can't see anything . . . even when I shut my eyes it's all white . . . I feel like I'm stinging, like there's little things crawling all over my skin. I can't, I can't do anything about it . . .

BH: Where are you, Kathie? Are you by the garage?

KD: I don't know. I can't see . . . Now something's pinching my arm . . . the muscle . . . the same arm that was touched . . . *(Sighs deeply)* I feel fine now. My ear hurts and my arm feels like somebody's holding me. But I feel fine . . .

BH: Somebody's holding your arm? Do you feel fingers?

KD: No, just the . . . around my arm . . . I don't know. But my ear hurts . . .

BH: Are you still holding your gun?

KD: No. I'm not holding anything. I'm just standing . . . and there's something holding my arm and it feels like somebody's poking my ear with a pencil or something. It feels like I've got an ear infection, and my ear hurts real bad. I want to keep moving my arm out to touch my ear but someone's holding my arm, and I can't walk, and I still can't see because everything's all white, and my eyes are shut. I don't think I want to see.

BH: *(Calms her)* Kathie, what did you see just before this happened?

KD: I saw the doorway. I guess I'm still in the garage standing in the doorway, looking out. I saw a round ball of white light looking right at me . . . It's about the size of . . . a little bigger than a basketball.

BH: At your head height?

KD: Yes. Close. I'm right past the concrete. *(The concrete slab behind the garage is about five feet from the burned circle where the UFO apparently rests.)* I'm not scared. I feel better.

BH: Can you move in any way, now?

KD: No. I'm just standing here looking at the light and it's looking at me. I guess it must have turned off 'cause I can see. Now it's going down towards the ground real slow, and now it's going back up again, and it stops where it was before. I don't know what to do. It isn't hurting me except for my ear. It's just sitting there, and I want to know what it is.

BH: Can you see anything else around there, in the yard?

KD: *(After a pause)* There's a lot of dark things in the yard . . . I can't really see what they are . . . they're just there. I think there's six. Six dark things. They're not very big, but I can't see what they are. I don't think I want to get any closer . . . They're kind of shaped like big bullets. I think they're just an outline. They're not moving. *(Kathie describes them as being about her height, smooth and featureless. Everything is still, and then she sighs deeply, nervously.)*

BH: What happened, Kathie?

KD: The things are starting to move. They're getting in a line . . . They're coming towards me, but not directly at me. *(Long pause)* Now they're gone, except one.

BH: How close were you from the line?

KD: Too! *(She sighs, in obvious fear)* I hear my name . . . It said *(whispering)* "Kathie!" Something touched me! It reached and touched me, but I didn't think it was close enough to touch me. On my neck. It made me cringe . . . *(Long pause)* I'm tired. The bullet thing is gone. There's just the light, now. *(Suddenly agitated)* I can't see! I feel like it's going all through my body . . .

Once more I calmed her, and after a moment it became clear that the episode had ended and Kathie was no longer remembering what had happened near the landed craft. Her next remark was in a normal voice, as she resumed her previous conscious recollection: "I think instead of sewing I'll go swimming . . ." I asked where her gun is now. "It's on the floor . . . in the garage. I guess I dropped it. I turned around to shut off the light and I saw it there on the floor, near the doorway." I asked her how she feels at this point. "Funny. Sick to the stomach. And my ear hurts. I can hardly hear out of it."

I asked where her mother was when she went into the house. "She's standing in the doorway looking out the screen door. She looks all pale and sleepy. I told her everything was all right. But I guess it wasn't all right, and I guess she already knew that if she was standing in the doorway . . . but I don't know, I don't know, I don't know. I just don't want to think. I don't want to sew, I don't want to think. My head hurts . . ." I calmed her and then brought her out of the trance.

Watching Kathie relive that night had been grueling for me, so I knew how profoundly upsetting it must have been for her. The general tenor of the experience had been physical—the disturbing touches at her arm, the painful intrusion in her ear, the blinding light that moved up and down her body, apparently causing the tingling and the heat. There were more specifically physical recollections than visual ones, though Kathie told me afterwards that she had seen, dimly, the egg-shaped UFO to her left as she stood in the garage doorway. "I knew it was there, but I didn't want to look at it. I was more worried about the dark things, and whenever I could see anything I tried to keep my eye on them."

Her account differed in several important ways from the standard abduction report. First, she did not describe the usual short, gray-skinned UFO-occupant type, though her recollections did suggest a humanoid "presence" holding her arm and inserting the pencil-like object in her ear. "The touch," she said, "was gentle, like a person would touch you." The odd, bullet-shaped things that formed a line and approached her rather indirectly seem more robotlike, in her description, than humanoid. She told me later that they moved as if they sensed her fear and were acting, somehow, to avoid frightening her more deeply—but that, of course, is an admittedly subjective reading of the situation. Much of the time Kathie could not see because of the extreme light that flooded her. She said that it was as if she, herself, were lit up internally, glowing with as much intensity as the white balls of light. She described the initial shock and pain as being like a bolt of lightning hitting the center of her chest and then flowing all through her body.[10] She does not specifically recall being *inside* the craft, stretched out on an examining table, though her recollections do not rule out this possibility.

These peculiar globes of light, somewhat larger than basketballs, seemed to be all over the Davis acreage that night. Kathie recalled that they appeared to be attached to the UFO's outer structure, but were able to move independently away, as if they could become separate "exploring" devices. (See illustrations.) One can theorize, then, that the UFO landed, dark and unlit, beneath the trees on the Davis property *before* Kathie left to drive to her friend's house. What she saw, glowing from inside the pool shed, was one of these globes of white light, and later her mother saw a second globe illuminating the bird feeder. When Kathie returned and went outside to look for intruders, she herself became the object of the white light's attention. The UFO literature is full of case reports in which white lights are described as moving back and forth above the abductees' bodies, presumably scanning or examining them—to use a handy anthropomorphic image.[11] But unfortunately, as with most of the large questions about the UFO phenomenon, we simply don't know what these lights are, or why they do what they do. In this particular instance, however, it may be significant that the maximum blinding irradiation came at the outset of Kathie's experience and then again at its very end.

More immediately interesting to me was Kathie's account of the insertion of a pencil-like object into her ear, and her subsequent discomfort and hearing deficiency. Of the fifty-eight people I've worked with who have recalled nearly complete abduction experiences, eleven have reported the insertion of what seem to be tiny implants into their bodies. (There are indications that this operation may have occurred in more than this particular 19 percent.[12]) Six have recalled a thin probe of some sort with a tiny ball on the end having been inserted in a nostril, and they feel pain when the probe apparently breaks through at the top of the nasal cavity. Two reported the same type of probe entering the region of the eyesocket, and three recall the probe's going in through, or behind, the ear. (Kathie is herein listed twice, since she also remembers a nasal implant.) Specific hypothetical reasons for these probable implants—as well as the medical evidence for their existence—will be gone into later; it is necessary now only to point out that in every case the destination of the probe lies in the region of the brain.

As I have said before, UFO abduction accounts must be taken seriously because of the repetitive pattern of details described in widely separate cases. In November of 1984 I knew of only one "ear implant" case—Kathie's—but three months later I had become involved with a second. In February of 1985 I was contacted through a radio call-in program I was appearing on in the Miami, Florida, area by a woman I shall call Sandy Thomas. Sandy would not speak on the air; she simply left her phone number with the station and asked to be called back. She had been too upset, she told me later, to try to talk during the broadcast. She wanted to report a dream she had had recently—on December 28, 1983, to be exact—which she felt had been almost too real to have been literally a dream. The essence of her recollection was that she had been awakened in the night, paralyzed, and then taken from her house by three shadowy, large-headed figures. She was transported to some sort of circular room, placed on a table, and a thin tube of some sort had then been inserted in her left ear. There is much more detail to her story, but she remembered being taken back to her home and placed in her bed, where she awoke in great fear, feeling quite ill. "I must have perspired a lot, too," she said to me later, "because my hair and neck were all wet. Even the pillow was wet." She immediately roused her husband and told him in detail what she remembered of the experience. She said that though she was feeling physically ill, she was still so frightened that she insisted he stand guard while she went to the bathroom. As I questioned her further about her recollections it became clear to me that she had not called the radio station merely to report a nightmare; though she did not say so, it was obvious that she felt this was something more than a typical bad dream. A number of things she and her husband told me during several phone calls led me to believe that there might well be other similar experiences in her family, and so, since I was going to be in their vicinity for a few days, I decided to interview them in person.

The Thomases live in a sunny, modest bungalow near Saint Augustine with their ten-year-old son and a number of pets. Sandy was at first quite nervous about trying hypnosis as an aid to recollection, but ultimately she decided that it was better to explore her situation than to continue in fear and doubt, not knowing if she had been dreaming or if she really had been taken from her bedroom that night. I assured her that there was no way I could clarify the issue for her, but that by reliving her experience through hypnosis she would more easily be able to answer the question for herself. Her recollections in the trance state followed the "dream" very closely, but with a great deal more vividness and detail. I will present here just the section of the transcript dealing with the apparent ear implant. Sandy has been taken into a large round room, and is lying on a flat table. Her fear has lessened at this point—it had been intense at the beginning of her account—and she states that one of the "men" tells her she is going to go to sleep for a while.

ST: I'm feeling angry.

BH: Why?

ST: Because I'm here, and I didn't want to be.

BH: They said that you were going to go to sleep for a little bit, is that right?

ST: Yes, and I'm glad. I would rather be asleep. *(Pause, sighs)* He's going to put some water in my ear.

BH: What's the water in?

ST: It's not a needle . . . it's like a tube . . . *(Long pause)* I just want to go to sleep real fast.

BH: How do you feel?

ST: Awful. Just limp and awful, and this tube is sticking in my ear . . . My neck's turned.

BH: Is this tube a thick tube or a thin tube . . . let's start with the idea of a pencil's thickness. Is it bigger than that or littler or what?

ST: Smaller. And now it's out.

BH: How'd it get out?

ST: The tall man took it out, and my hair's wet. *(Long pause)* Now there's a small, tiny one—like a light. There's a light.

BH: Do you mean a small, tiny tube?

ST: Yes. Very small, with a tiny light on it. It lights on the end. And it's in my ear. And they make me move my jaw. *(Pause. Speaks brightly, quickly)* That's it.

BH: That's it . . . did they say "That's it"?

ST: That's what they said, "That's it! That's not so bad." *(Long pause)* Now they want to see if I can walk. *(Pause)* They're so stupid. They make the table go down to maybe the height of a chair, and I'm supposed to get off and . . . just walk. But I'm cold again, and scared . . . My hair's wet against my neck and it feels awful . . .

BH: Does your ear hurt, Sandy? *(A leading question on my part, which makes the wording of her answer all the more interesting)*

ST: I have an itching . . . between my ear and my throat.

BH: Is it on the skin or inside the skin, or where is it?

ST: I guess it's inside. It feels like sometimes when you get a tickle and you can't reach it.

Many more things surfaced during this long hypnotic session, and when I brought Sandy out of the trance state she was extremely upset. She cried on her husband's shoulder, and a few minutes later I tried to comfort her, too, but it was clear to me that she did not want to admit to herself that these recollections were something more than a mere bad dream. There was evidence to support the physical reality of her account. *Something* had wet her hair and neck, a condition her husband had also observed that night. The Thomases and I knew that perspiration that heavy and that localized—she had been dry everywhere except that one place—was an unacceptable explanation. Sandy told me, and her husband concurred, that she complained for several days afterwards of an unsettling "itch" in her left ear, and that when he looked into it it appeared to be red and irritated. But there was one last emotional moment before I left. Sandy and I sat at her kitchen table while she worked on a sketch of the gray-skinned, large-eyed figures she recalled from her "dream." (See illustrations.) When she was finished, I did something I immediately regretted. From the material I had brought with me, I handed Sandy a page

of drawings of very similar UFO occupants made by witnesses in other ,
UFO abduction cases. She glanced at these sketches for what seemed to
be only a split second; then she burst into tears, jumped up and rushed
out of the room. It was as if she were a rape victim who had just been
shown mug shots of her tormentors.

The main resemblance between Sandy's and Kathie's abduction accounts is, of course, the similarly described ear penetration, but there are
other parallels, too. Each reported feeling nauseated after the experience,
and each endured several days of discomfort in the area near the affected
ear. As the reader will learn, there are still other, more profound resem-
blances. Both women have young sons who also seem to have suffered
UFO abductions, and like Kathie, Sandy had apparently been abducted
at least twice before her December 1984 experience. Most disturbing of
all, there is evidence that Sandy and Kathie have been similarly "utilized"
in some sort of genetic experiment, a subject we will explore in later
chapters.

Because of the relatively large tracts of land in the Copley Woods and
an ingrown habit of respecting one another's privacy, the Davises are not
on intimate terms with their neighbors. Therefore, when I visited Kathie
and her family I made it a point to ask anyone close by if they had seen
or heard anything unusual on that June night in 1983. The people living
to the south of the Davises were away on vacation at the time, so they
had nothing to report. But a very interesting incident occurred to the
neighbor who lives directly across the street, to the west of their home.
The problem with her account is that the witness is unsure of its date;
despite its fascinating details we cannot with any certainty connect it to
Kathie Davis's June 30 abduction.

Sometime in the summer of 1983 this neighbor, "Martha Elkins," was
awakened by a loud roaring sound that made her house vibrate and so
terrified her that she felt sure a jet plane was about to crash into her home.
(This ongoing description, the reader will recall, is very much like that
reported by the Lloyds, the neighbors who live to the north of the
Davises.) Martha leaped out of bed and ran to the window. A nearby
nightlight flickered and her digital clock began to flash, indicating an
interruption in its power supply. Though she could see nothing, Martha
assumed that a crash was imminent. Oddly, the roaring and the vibration
continued, seeming to remain in more or less the same place rather than
passing quickly overhead. After a few moments the source of the sound
apparently changed direction, moving slowly away on a more northerly
course, and shortly thereafter it was gone.

Martha said that the three digital clocks on the same side of the house as her bedroom were flashing and had to be reset, though the digital clocks in her kitchen, living room and guest room—the opposite side of the house—were unaffected. The home of her closest neighbors was near that unaffected side, and when Martha asked them the next day what they had seen or heard, they had absolutely nothing to report. They had not awakened and had had no temporary power outage in any part of their house. I interviewed them later and all three family members confirmed this apparent absence of effect, a situation Martha finds almost impossible to believe. She said to me that she had never felt so close to death. The roaring was so intense and the vibration so frightening as her lights flickered and flashed that she finds it inconceivable that the entire neighborhood wasn't awake and terrified. Joyce Lloyd, who can date her similar account to the night of June 30, and who thought the surrounding area was undergoing an earthquake, was also amazed that no one else seemed to have reported these effects. One is led to speculate, based on the apparently narrow zone of electrical interference, that the sounds and vibrations were also strictly localized. How that idea can be squared with our present knowledge of physics is only one more UFO mystery.

The June 30, 1983, Kathie Davis case must be seen as one of the most important abduction accounts in the UFO literature for a very compelling reason: The physical evidence in this case, such as the "landing trace" marks on the Davis property, is so very extensive, more so than in any UFO abduction report I know. Not only Kathie, the principal figure in this encounter, but her friend Dee Anne and Dee Anne's daughter Tammy all suffered similar physical aftereffects, presumably because they were near the landing site only minutes after the UFO's departure.[13] Kathie's account of undergoing an "ear operation" during her abduction —a procedure previously unknown to me—received support a few months later when Sandy Thomas, in Florida, described virtually the same experience, and the same physical aftereffects. The electrical interference, the vibration and sounds described by the Lloyds and their neighbor—if, in fact, the two events occurred the same night—provide even more data for analysis. The June 30 landing is surely the most "visible" event so far in the ongoing Copley Woods saga. It is not, however, the most significant or portentous, as the reader will soon learn.

3
Kathie in New York

It seems, now, a very long time since that day in September 1983 when I received Kathie's original letter about the events in her backyard and the information about her sister's missing time experience. In the months that followed, the case took on an ever-expanding, nearly epic quality, and now directly involves over twenty people, four of whom, under hypnosis, have recalled UFO abduction encounters. Another two hypnotic subjects have remembered what I take to be pieces of an abduction scenario, but remain for one reason or another partially blocked in their recall. Seven have described with considerable detail low-level sightings of apparent UFOs in the area. And there is evidence ranging from very strong to merely circumstantial that seven others may also be harboring "forgotten" UFO abductions.

This bizarre saga is so complex that only parts of it can be retold in these pages. So, in an attempt to be inclusive I have appended at the end of the book short accounts in outline form of most of these other incidents. The story cannot be told in a strictly linear, chronological way. The order in which I learned of particular incidents is not necessarily the order in which they were investigated. Some of these accounts are marginal and some are intimately connected with Kathie Davis's own experiences. Nine people have undergone regressive hypnosis and I have conducted personal interviews with another nineteen. (Three others were interviewed by telephone.[1]) But despite the complexity of the case and the number of people involved, Kathie Davis is beyond any doubt the central figure in this complex story.

So far I have not described in any detail the way we actually met, an event which occurred in mid-October when Kathie made her first visit to New York. I have referred to the many phone calls we exchanged before that visit, and the new information that various members of the Davis family provided me with almost daily. When Kathie and I finally agreed on a mutually convenient date for her trip I began to prepare in earnest. I scheduled a program of interrogation and hypnotic regression sessions to explore that new information as thoroughly as possible, and I set up a semi-social evening so that I could introduce Kathie to some other investigators in our area. But above all I was looking forward with great curiosity to actually meeting her. Like almost everyone else I have encountered in her situation—people who are beginning to suspect they have undergone consciously *unremembered* UFO experiences—Kathie was becoming very disturbed about what our investigation might disclose. By telephone I tried to ease her anxiety, a condition she assured me she had lived with most of her life. In addition to chronic anxiety Kathie suffers from the kind of insomnia which is synonymous with night fear, fear of the dark, of the particular loneliness and isolation an insomniac feels in a house of sleepers. She told me that she always sleeps better during daylight hours and that often at night she keeps a light and her television set on to ease her nervousness and help her feel less vulnerable.

Over the years I have observed this sort of free-floating, apparently unreasonable dread in many people who have undergone consciously unremembered yet traumatic UFO abduction experiences. It has led me to shift the emphasis in my investigations from simple information gathering to a currently much larger place for therapeutic considerations— helping the abductee deal with fear and uncertainty and an inevitable sense of isolation from those who have not had to suffer through this truly unearthly experience.[2] As with rape victims—and on some level UFO abduction is a species of rape—membership in a support group of fellow victims can be very helpful. I frequently employ a kind of buddy system in such situations, a technique which has given real aid and comfort to people who are beginning to explore, through hypnosis and other means, their buried traumatic encounters. Thus, an abductee who has already been through such an extensive, in-depth investigation can be contacted when needed by an individual beginning his or her personal search. But there is one crucial ground rule: The abductee whose case has already been investigated is not permitted to give any information as to the *content* of his or her abduction experience—descriptions of the UFO, its occupants, technical procedures, sequence of events, etc. The only permissible area of discussion is, however, vast and emotional: how one deals with the knowledge that such literally unbelievable events may have actually happened. How one tries to integrate this kind of unthinkable experience into one's life. How one deals with the fear and uncertainty that this knowledge engenders.

I gave Kathie the New York phone number of "Sue," a woman close to Kathie in age who is intelligent and deeply sensitive to the psychological wounds inevitably suffered by anyone who has undergone this kind of experience. In keeping with the pattern I have come to think of as almost invariable, Sue was first abducted as a small child, in her case at the age of five. She had a series of experiences after that time culminating in a particularly traumatic abduction that occurred when she was sixteen, in a suburban area about thirty miles from New York City. She and a friend, a sixteen-year-old boy who lived in her neighborhood, saw a large orange light descend on a nearby hill. They went to see what it was, and two hours later inexplicably found themselves a quarter of a mile away from the hilltop, feeling odd and having no recollection of what had happened in the intervening time. Sue complained afterwards of a pain at her navel and the feeling that her face had somehow "been sunburned," but the psychological aftereffects were more disturbing. Sue comes from a comfortable, upper-middle-class Jewish background, and her behavior until this time had been exemplary. A deep unease soon began to manifest itself, and within a year or so after this experience she had begun to use drugs as a way to keep her apparently rootless anxiety at bay. Knowing Sue as she is now, an efficient and well-paid businesswoman, involved in a stable and loving relationship with an interesting man, it is difficult to imagine her as the fear-ridden heroin user that she became during the many months she spent in college. Emotional support from her family, years of psychotherapy and her own strong will each undoubtedly played a role in her gradual emergence from these problems. Eventually she felt strong enough and determined enough to explore what may have been a central cause of her anxiety, the traumatic UFO experiences that lay just below the surface of her conscious recollections.[3]

Sue was an ideal and generous confidante for Kathie. After an initial very long phone conversation from her office, Sue provided Kathie with her unlisted home number in case Kathie felt she had to talk at any hour of the day or night. Separately both Sue and I assured Kathie that apparently nothing had ever happened to anyone once an investigation had begun into his or her UFO encounters. We insisted that from now on she would be left alone by "them," by whoever had been carrying out these disturbing abductions in the past. The beginning of serious investigation, I told Kathie, would mark the end of her UFO experiences. I was wrong, very, very wrong.

Kathie made arrangements to leave Indianapolis by bus on Thursday, October 13, and she would arrive in New York the next day. Everything seemed fine. However, about 2:00 A.M. on the morning of October 3, Sue was awakened by a long-distance phone call from a very frightened Kathie. Kathie had been lying in bed reading and idly watching television when she heard her name called, firmly and precisely. It was somehow "in her head" rather than aloud, but it seemed as if two voices were speaking in unison. "Kathie!" She felt a cold, paralyzing fear, and after a moment jumped up and fled from her room. She ran downstairs and immediately called Sue in New York, saying that she knew something terrifying was about to happen to her. Sue sleepily tried to calm her. She suggested she take a tranquilizer or a drink, and to turn up the phonograph and the TV and go back to bed. Sue's advice did not help much, Kathie admitted later. They chatted a while and after ending their conversation, Kathie slipped back into her state of dread.

She took a tranquilizer but cursed the fact that it would take many minutes to have an effect. She was too terrified to go back to bed, so instead she went to her parents' room and wakened her mother—her father was a sound and determined sleeper—telling her only that her heart was pounding and that she felt ill. "Take some aspirin," her mother answered drowsily, "and try to sleep." But as Kathie turned to leave, a small ball of light whizzed down the hall past her. "What was that?" she asked, and her mother answered, "It must be lightning." But the ball of light had clearly been in the hall, only a few feet from Kathie. Outside there was absolutely no sign of a storm.

At this point Kathie was more frightened than ever, and more determined not to return to her room alone. She went into her sons' room, picked up little Tommy, her three-year-old, and carried him into bed with her. Now that she had some company she was not so afraid, so she turned up her television set and began to read. Surprisingly, she found herself becoming drowsy and she soon fell asleep. At some later time she was awakened by her mother who was standing in her doorway. "What do you want?" her mother asked. "Why did you call?" Kathie said that she had been sleeping and had not said anything, but Mary insisted that she heard someone calling her that she thought was Kathie. At this moment the two women noticed a low humming sound coming from somewhere outside the house. Kathie was too frightened, now, even to look out the window. Mary said that maybe there was a truck parked in front with its engine idling, so she went downstairs to investigate. She glanced out the front windows and saw nothing on the road near their house, but, as she told me later, she was too frightened herself to go outside and actually look around—and up, where the sound actually seemed to be located. She went back upstairs and eventually mother and daughter went back to sleep.

In the morning when she awoke, Kathie felt an extreme stiffness in her neck, and her arms and shoulders felt exhausted, as if, she explained, she'd "spent the night lifting weights." When her mother came down to breakfast she also described having a stiff neck and a dull pain in her arms and shoulders. Their complaints were identical. Kathie called me that morning and told me about the events of the night before. I asked if she could see any unusual marks on herself or her mother, but she said she hadn't noticed anything. I inquired about the state of her bedclothes and nightgown. She left the phone to look, and then came back to report that there were a few tiny bloodstains on her sheet, clustered at the top in the place where her neck would have rested. Later she found a few more small drops of dried blood on the bottom sheet, over to one side, but near the region of her lower back. I have since seen these stains. They are small, discrete drops, perhaps one eighth of an inch in diameter. None is smeared or blotted. They are quite precise, as if Kathie had been very still when they marked the bedclothes.

This new development was deeply upsetting to me. I had truly believed that once our investigation started, Kathie's UFO encounters would cease. Though this had apparently been the case in previous investigations, I was aware that my belief rested as much on hope as experience. I *wanted* it to be over. Kathie had suffered enough. Yet something disturbing had obviously happened to her on October 3, something only partially remembered but clearly possessing a physical dimension. Her mother had very likely had the same experience. Sue's attempt to help via the telephone and my earlier assurances had made no difference whatsoever. The UFO phenomenon simply does what it wants, when it wants to.

On Friday, October 14, I took the subway to the Port Authority Bus Terminal to meet Kathie's bus. Her inevitably uncomfortable overnight trip from Indianapolis took about seventeen hours. She had left her children with her mother and was coming to New York for the very first time in her life, at her own expense, to stay in the studio of a stranger —myself—and explore some of the most inherently disturbing experiences one can ever know. She had told me that I would easily recognize her; she was overweight, traveling alone, and would be wearing a certain color coat. The bus pulled in and there she was, smiling a shy, sleepy little smile and obviously wondering if she or I—or both—were hopelessly crazy to be doing what we were doing.

Kathie was tired, thirsty, hungry, and in need of a cigarette and a ladies' room. After we took care of several of these requirements we headed back to my Chelsea studio via her first New York subway train. Kathie was surprised to come through the experience unscathed. Knowing what she had heard about New York subways, she naturally expected we would be mugged or at least shot at. Curious as to the source of her information, I asked if she had ever been to New York before. With a twinkle in her eye she answered no, she hadn't, but she'd seen a lot of Charles Bronson movies. I liked her immediately.

One of the things I discussed with Kathie on our first afternoon together was her medical history. Broaching that subject was tantamount to opening Pandora's box. Since her birth in 1959 poor Kathie had suffered just about every medical anomaly I had ever heard of. Her overweight condition seems to be the result of hormonal imbalance. She began menstruating regularly at the age of seven, the beginning of her pubescence. By the age of ten she had grown to her present height, 5' 3½", and was under treatment for high blood pressure. At the age of fourteen she was operated on for gallstones, and her gallbladder was removed. She has suffered from hepatitis, and almost died during a severe bout with pneumonia which presented all the symptoms of what is now known as Legionnaires' disease. She has had her appendix removed and once spent two weeks in traction because the two *extra* vertebrae in her spine somehow fused. Very early in 1983 she was hospitalized with what seemed to be an asthmatic attack. A lung collapsed and she was treated with an intravenous bronchial dilator; she suffered an apparent allergic reaction to the medication and spent the following two weeks in the hospital. After the traumatic events of the summer of 1983 Kathie began to exhibit symptoms of heart arrhythmia, and on one occasion the irregular heartbeat was so disturbing that paramedics had to be summoned.

The tale of Kathie's health problems is long and depressing, which makes her courage and physical resilience all the more remarkable. In 1983 doctors were certain she had contracted Cushing's disease, since she exhibited all its symptoms, but the test results, luckily, were negative. Hypoglycemia, hyperadrenalism and high blood pressure have all been chronic problems, and allergic reactions to certain medications have compounded her difficulties. Kathie has not been spared her share of what used to be called "female problems." When she had her appendectomy the surgeon also removed some cysts on her ovaries, and though a hysterectomy was contemplated, it was finally not performed. The birth of Kathie's younger son, Tommy, was smooth and uneventful, but her first son, Robbie, very nearly did not survive. He was born two months prematurely, by caesarian section, after Kathie suffered sudden kidney failure. Robbie's heart stopped twice during the delivery, but he survived in the intensive care unit, and now, years later, is flourishing.

Certain of these medical details may be significant in the light of the UFO experiences Kathie and her family have undergone, and I offer them here merely as raw material for speculation. As a young teenager, Kathie noticed a small bump on the front of her shinbone, as if there were a round, movable object just below the skin. There was no pain connected with it, only a kind of low-level discomfort. With her fingers Kathie could move this object around, perhaps a half inch or so from a slight subcutaneous indentation where it normally rested. During one of her medical visits she pointed it out to her doctor and he decided to dissolve the cyst by injecting it with a medication. The object, however, turned out to be impenetrable and the needle broke off. Later, when Kathie went to the hospital for her gallbladder operation, her doctor announced that he would remove it surgically while she was under the anesthetic. When she had regained consciousness and left the recovery room he came into the ward and showed her a small, calcified object. It was quite remarkable, he told her. When he first pressed lightly down with his scalpel, the skin opened and the cyst shot straight up several feet into the air, hitting the metal reflector of the surgical lamp with a ping, and as it dropped back he caught it in his hand. It had startled everyone in the operating room. "You have a smart body," the doctor told her. A small fatty pad had formed between her shinbone and this floating—eventually flying—cyst, protecting the bone in a kind of "natural insulation" process. Kathie never really inquired, and thus does not know, what lay at the heart of this calcified mass.

It is ironic that what should be one of the easiest, most natural things

for a UFO investigator to do is often one of the most difficult: listening
carefully to the witness and taking particular note of what the *witness* feels
is especially significant. We tend to let our knowledge of other cases and
patterns dictate what we "select out" as being particularly significant in
the subject's account. This, I am sorry to say, is what happened during
my first interview with Kathie, in the context of her medical history.
Almost the first thing she told me was an event that had always bothered
her, and that made no sense either to her or to her doctor. Of all the
difficulties she'd endured, this was the most emotionally painful. Possessing normal, healthy appetites, Kathie had been sexually active, though her
knowledge of contraception was almost nil. In fact, she had been very
lucky and had never had an accidental pregnancy. In late 1977 she met
and soon fell in love with her husband-to-be; they made plans to be
married in the spring of 1978. Early in 1978, however, Kathie realized that
she was pregnant.[4] Positive blood and urinalysis tests confirmed the fact.
Kathie was elated, as was her fiancé, and the date for the wedding was
moved up a few months. Things were proceeding happily and her body
was beginning to undergo subtle changes—until one day in March when
Kathie awoke with what seemed to be a normal menstrual flow. Her
mother assured her that such things sometimes happened and that she
shouldn't be too alarmed, but a visit to her doctor confirmed her fears:
She was no longer pregnant. Yet there had been no apparent miscarriage,
no physical traces that would attest to a natural abortion. She just wasn't
pregnant anymore. Her doctor was perplexed, but for Kathie the experience was truly shattering.

Kathie was married in April according to the plan she and her fiancé
had established. She went on to have two sons, Robbie, born in July of
1979, and Tommy, born in September of 1980, but the loss of her first
baby has always been a particularly tragic memory for her. She made all
of this very clear to me on that October afternoon when we talked for
the first time in my studio. Yet at that time I just assumed it was a sad
personal event, totally unrelated to Kathie's ongoing UFO experiences.
Again, I was very, very wrong.

Kathie's very first hypnotic session occurred later that same October
day in the office of Dr. Aphrodite Clamar, with Martin Jackson, an
associate of mine, as an additional observer. (The hypnotic sessions dealing with the backyard landing, recounted in the previous chapter, took
place at a later date). There were two major areas I was eager to explore:
Kathie's 1978 "dream" about the figures in her bedroom, and the more

recent events which triggered her late-night phone call to Sue. We decided to begin with the earlier "dream" experience. Kathie was quite nervous about undergoing hypnosis, so Dr. Clamar used extra care in inducing the trance and making sure that she was comfortable. Kathie said very little. She saw the two small, gray-faced figures standing by her bed, just as they had in her "dream." Her fear was acute and she asked to be put into a deeper trance, but by the end of this first session very few additional images had come to mind. It was clear to all of us that we would have to make a second attempt to explore this experience on another day when Kathie would be less tired and anxious. There had been one interesting physical development, however. More than once during the hypnosis Kathie complained that her throat felt odd and uncomfortable, as if it contained traces of a dripping liquid; she frequently swallowed and cleared her throat. During the next session the reason for her discomfort became vividly clear.

As we drove home, Kathie made a statement that exemplified her basic openness and honesty. "I want to find out what happened," she said. "I know this is going to be scary. It was scary the first time, when I was dreaming it. It might not be anything. It might just be dreams. I don't know. If it is, it would be nice to know it's just dreams. If it's not, at least I'll know what I'll have to learn to live with."

Our second session took place on Sunday afternoon. Again, Dr. Clamar gave a long, careful induction, and again we went back to Kathie's 1978 "dream" about the two small figures in her attic bedroom, but this time the sequence of events broadened dramatically. Kathie recalled awakening next to her sleeping husband, and for some reason getting out of bed. She did not describe seeing the small figures at this time, so I guessed that the moment she was reexperiencing occurred either before or after that confrontation. She described going into the kitchen of their small apartment and standing by the sink, as if waiting for something. After a long pause she felt herself floating comfortably with her eyes closed, seeing nothing. She seemed to be lying down and then she said she was being touched and examined. Next she twisted about in obvious discomfort as she described two thin probes pressing up into her nostrils. It hurt when they seemed to break through in the region of her sinuses. She cleared her throat, swallowing uneasily as she felt something drip at the back of her throat. It tasted bitter and metallic, she told us later, "like blood."

Various other physical recollections followed—pressure at her abdomen and at her neck, for example. Finally she opened her eyes and saw the small, gray-skinned figure standing next to the table on which she lay. (She obviously was no longer in her bedroom.) The "man's" huge black eyes gazed down at her; she felt frightened and then, oddly and almost simultaneously, reassured. There was no communication other than the sense she had that she would not be harmed. Apart from difficulties swallowing and clearing her throat, Kathie appeared to be calm for several minutes. Then she was startled once more as she reexperienced her "dream" of awakening in bed with the two figures standing nearby, holding the shimmering box. It was clear to me now that the morning after this experience, Kathie remembered (as a dream) only the end of her abduction experience rather that its beginning or middle. The gray figure handed her the box, telling her to look at it, and then took it away with the observation—delivered telepathically—that when she saw it again she would understand its purpose. Shortly thereafter she went back to sleep, and having reached that convenient halting place, Dr. Clamar brought her out of the trance. We had more reason than ever before to proceed with the exploration of Kathie's and her mother's recent experience.

This description of thin needles being pressed high up into the nasal cavity is a very familiar one in UFO abduction accounts, and occasionally the abductee has been able to see a very small BB-like ball at the end of the probe. In several reports this tiny—two to three millimeters in diameter—object is no longer present after the probe is withdrawn. And there are some descriptions of a probe being inserted *without* anything on its tip, but when it is withdrawn there is a tiny ball attached.[5] One is naturally led to infer that implants of some sort are being put in place and sometimes removed. An incident that occurred in Truman, Kentucky, in the middle nineteen-forties provides a vivid illustration of this sort of operation.[6] Under hypnosis the subject relived her experience as a five-year-old child. She had been taken by several "little men" into a large, cold, brightly lit craft, and placed on a table. She could not move, and after several intermittently painful physical operations of some kind she became frightened anew:

> SUBJECT: He's . . . he's . . . taking something and putting it in my nose. And I don't want him to. No, it hurts! No, don't, don't, it hurts. No, I can't. No! No! No!
>
> BH: (*Calms her, and then asks what the thing looks like*)
>
> SUBJECT: It's long. It's a long little thing. And he's putting it in my nose, and it hurts, and I don't want it in there. No. Don't let him do that. No, please, no, no, it hurts . . .

BH: What part of your nose does it hurt?
SUBJECT: It hurts in my head. Up in my head, way up in my nose. Far in my nose and I don't want him to do it, 'cause it hurts.

In a September 1981 abduction case involving "Megan Elliott" and her infant daughter "Renee," Megan described this sort of nasal probe being inserted in Renee's nose. This Wood County, Texas, incident was thoroughly investigated by Lew Willis, and his report includes this passage:

HYPNOTIST: Can you see anything on the end of the probe?
MEGAN: Yes . . . Just a little ball.
H: Just how big would you say it is?
M: Oh . . . small.
H: Small, small like a baseball, or a BB, or . . .
M: Smaller than a BB.
H: Smaller than a BB? One final question there. When the probe was extracted, was the BB still there on the end of the probe?
M: (Showing distress) I didn't see it come out.[7]

In *Missing Time* I dealt with three separate instances of apparent nasal cavity implants, and in my investigations since that time I've encountered several more. Yet so far as I know no one has unequivocally established that an implant is currently in place in any abductee. X rays, of course, require that an object be radiopaque in order to be seen, and a two-millimeter object is *very* close to the resolution limit of most CAT scans. I am certain, however, that eventually one of these objects will be located, and then we will have our long-sought-after physical artifact, our "smoking gun." Speculation about the purpose of these possible implants runs to any or all of three unappetizing possibilities: They could function as "locators," in the mode of the small radio transmitters zoologists attach to the ears of hapless, tranquilized elk to trace their wanderings. Or they could be monitors of some sort, relaying the thoughts, emotions or even visual and sensory impressions of the host. Or, and perhaps least palatable, they could have a controlling function as receivers, suggesting the possibility that abductees could, from time to time, be made to act as surrogates for their abductors. I do not wish to dwell on any of these paranoia-inducing theories. Perhaps these BB-like objects have some other, as yet unimagined purpose or purposes. Whenever we consider these large, theoretical questions about the ultimate nature, source and intention of the UFO phenomenon, we must admit that we still have no final answers.

One other odd detail that Kathie recalled is her sense that the two gray figures moved in absolute unison. "When one leaned forward, the other one did, too, in exactly the same way. They moved together, as if they were one." This observation comports with Kathie's having heard her name called, in the October incident, as if by two voices, speaking in unison. David Oldham, describing the small figures he faced during an abduction experience in 1966, was startled when all of them blinked their eyes at the same instant, in perfect unison.[8] In a case I recently investigated, a Minnesota man, driving on a lonely road near the Plate River, was stopped by five tall figures who stood near a large, hovering light. When they began to move towards him, he noticed that they all stepped off simultaneously on the left foot. His first thought was that they must be soldiers on maneuvers, though almost immediately he had reason to drop that idea.[9] I do not know what this clonelike appearance and behavior means, but it is not a constant in abduction reports. More often a witness will recall differences in both the appearance and behavior of various UFO occupants within the same craft. Again, we just do not know how to interpret these seemingly contradictory patterns.

The next item on our investigative agenda was the night in early October when Kathie called Sue at 2:00 A.M. to tell her of having heard her name called, and "knowing" that something terrible was about to happen. In discussing her recollections, she mentioned a segment of that evening's events that she had not previously discussed with me. Just before she went to bed and heard the simultaneously voiced "Kathie!" she had taken a drive to a nearby all-night food store to get something to drink (Kathie consumes large quantities of Diet Pepsi). The first odd detail she remembered was the fact that she had just returned from this food store, a ten-minute drive from her home, with a few items, when she realized she was thirsty and had not bought anything to drink. It was during this *second* trip that she saw a large, brightly lit object in the sky that she assumed was the Goodyear blimp. Something about this second trip to the store remained in her memory as both peculiar and elusive. She came home and went to bed, and then the voices called, there was the humming outside, her fear, and her phone call to Sue.

Unfortunately Dr. Clamar was unavailable for any more hypnotic sessions that week. Dr. Robert Naiman, a psychiatrist who had also done hypnosis for me in UFO abduction cases, had no time to give us, and I was unable to locate another hypnotist with appointments available in the time remaining before Kathie was scheduled to return to Indianapolis. Therefore I decided, with Kathie's immediate approval, to do the hypnosis myself. I set the scene in the usual manner. We began at the point when Kathie returned from her first trip to the store to buy some groceries.

KD: I walk into the house and I'm really freezing . . . Daddy's sitting at the kitchen table. I'm draggin' this stuff and I'm asking him if he wants some of my munchies. He said no. I went up to my room and put my book and my magazine down and my stuff and washed up. I started feeling colder. I'm feeling kinda tingly all over. Kinda, the skin on my arm feels prickly. And . . . the clock *(agitated)* says it's 11:45. And I forgot to get something to drink, 'cause I'm real thirsty . . . Yeah, I go in the kitchen and see if we have any Pepsi. We don't, so I told, I told my dad I was going to get something to drink. I'm feeling prickly or colder than before, and I'm so thirsty . . . And I get in my car . . . and the inside light didn't come on, but then it came on. A second later the key buzzer buzzed. And this is kind of weird, you know, and I'm thinking it's kind of creeping me out. I feel kind of funny, kind of creepy, but . . . and I keep trying to start it, and then I checked my lights and they come on when I start it . . . with the lights on it starts. So I'm hoping I don't get stuck somewhere in this stupid car and I . . . pull out of the driveway. Driving down the street . . . I see something in the sky. I'm right at *X (this location and others deleted)* and I catch a glimpse of this, out of the corner of my eye, and I'm thinking, that's weird. And I go to the [traffic] light and there's no car so I go past the light and I'm going . . . I'm in front of the parking lot at *Y,* and I look up at it again and it's still there. I didn't stop! I slowed down. Now I'm at, I still see it . . . it isn't moving much and I'm at . . . I'm at *Z* . . . I'm looking between two big trees . . . I'm thinking that it must be the Goodyear blimp because Wilma saw the Goodyear blimp this morning real low. I'll bet that's what it is because it looks like it has its message lights on on the bottom, pretty big, too. I stopped the car and looked at it for a minute and it . . . well, I never saw the Goodyear blimp roll like that when it turned. It's awful low. I'm going to watch this thing 'cause it's not going anywhere. It's just . . . going in circles, or rolling or something, and when it kinda rolls it's

. . . rolling over. Instead of turning it rolls to the . . . I don't know, it's really strange. Hmm. Hmm. I'll just keep going. I got to the store. I went to the Seven-Eleven, and now I can't, that ain't . . . I can't see that now. *(Kathie suddenly jumps, lifting an inch or so off the bed, and startling me as much as herself)* GOD DAMN IT!

BH: *(Calming her, assuring her that she's safe)* Everything is all right, Kathie. Just tell us what you're seeing.

KD: Well, hell, I thought I was at the store, but I see the windows, and the lights in the windows at the store, but that guy . . . *(nervously)* was not the clerk. I swear, I thought I was at the store, but then I saw him looking at me. I know him. I'm not scared of him, but I was shocked to see him. I wasn't expecting to see him . . . and he's smiling at me. I mean, he wasn't going to hurt me. I got a twitch in my thumb. Man, he just popped, popped in . . . there he was. He *shocked* me! Don't do that to me, sneaking up behind me and scaring me like that! *(Her voice is frightened, unsteady)* Want me to have a heart attack? And my thumb won't quit twitching. *(Long pause)* I feel quite cold.

There are many details in Kathie's account so far that exactly parallel UFO abduction cases I've investigated in the past. For some reason many abductees describe being physically cold during their experiences. Dr. Clamar employs hypnosis frequently in her regular, non-UFO therapeutic practice, but rarely does anyone report being chilly while in the trance state in her office. Yet so often did this situation occur when the subjects were UFO abductees that she began to keep a blanket handy for use on just such occasions. Two possible explanations for this common reaction suggest themselves. Fear, existing at the threshold of traumatic shock, can cause the subject to feel unusually cold, but there is also some testimony to the fact that the interiors of the UFOs themselves may actually be cold. Hypnosis, as we know, can provide the vividly reenacted illusion of real experience.

At the heart of Kathie's account is the suggestion that her behavior is somehow being externally controlled. She has just visited the store, and yet suddenly she feels the need to return. She describes going upstairs to her room and preparing to settle down to read. But then she starts to feel cold and "tingly all over" and after these odd symptoms she realizes she is thirsty and must go back to the store. Her thirst provides a convenient reason for another trip, though obviously there were other things in the house for her to drink. Odd electrical problems develop as she tries to start her car, all of which seem to deepen her sense of dread, but still nothing deters her from her mission. And then she notices and begins to carefully observe a strange lighted object in the sky.

As the object rolls and maneuvers about, its behavior perhaps literally mesmerizing, she finds herself at what she assumes is the store. It has big windows and lights, but the "clerk" who approaches her, one can assume, has never used a cash register. Her account continues:

BH: Are you in your car, Kathie?

KD: *(Softly)* No, not now. I don't know how I got from my car to where I'm standing. I just gotta . . . I can't stay long. I have to go home.

BH: Now you've talked to him. Does he say anything back to you?

KD: Yeah. *(Pause)* He asked me how I was feeling. I can't remember what he asked. He asked me something, something else. He told me something. I can't remember. *(Very frightened)* I don't want to remember.

BH: *(Calms her, saying that the memories will come back when she's ready to deal with them, etc.)* Can you give us any idea of where you are when this is happening?

KD: I don't know. I'm standing in front of the store but it's not the store. I mean it's big, the big windows, long windows, and all that light coming from the windows, and things in the windows, but he was in there and he came out. I don't remember seeing how he came out. I saw him in there and then I saw him out there and I was standing with him . . . I stopped the car to look at that thing in the sky and then I'm at the store and there's that guy. I don't know . . . *(At this point in her narrative her recollection of the encounter with the small figure and the presumably landed UFO ends and "amnesia" sets in. What follows more or less agrees with her later conscious memories of the trip to the store.)* I went out and bought stuff so I'm going home now. I go home. I looked in the sky all the way home. I even went the other way . . .

Kathie describes the route she takes home as being peculiar, as if she had been a little out of her way from the round trip she would normally have made. When she comes into the house she remarks that her father has gone up to bed.

BH: Do you notice what time it is?

KD: *(Sighs)* It's, well . . . I . . . it can't be that. It don't take no
. . . *(Firmly)* I left at a quarter till twelve and I saw my clock
and it says it's twenty till one, and the Seven-Eleven is maybe
ten minutes away, and I feel a bit creepy again.

BH: Did you get a drink? Are you thirsty?

KD: I think . . . I never got a drink, and I'm not thirsty. *(Appearing
surprised)* Looked at TV for a while. *(Frightened)* I called Sue.

At this point I calmed Kathie and shortly thereafter I brought her out
of the trance. We decided that the second part of the October experience
would be held over for another hypnotic session. Apparently this first part
of the encounter was only a prelude for what would happen later. Kathie
is "lured" out of her house so that she can be approached and told
something—something that frightens her and that she doesn't want to
remember. Something, perhaps, about what would take place later, in the
house, when everyone was asleep? This two-step abduction is, so far as I
know, unique in the UFO literature. It illustrates an unsettling situation
that—unfortunately—I believe to be fairly common: Many UFO abductees seem to be on "shorter leashes" than any of us had ever previously
suspected. They seem to be all too readily available whenever, and for
whatever reasons, they are needed.

Kathie's round trip to the store that night should have taken between
twenty and twenty-five minutes, allowing for her slightly circuitous return
route, but according to her recollections it took nearly an hour. There is
a missing time period of roughly thirty minutes, yet Kathie's recollections
of her encounter with the diminutive gray-faced figure do not account for
that much elapsed time. Clearly more happened during this incident than
she recalled. A few days later she did remember one more exchange.
Moments after the figure first appeared and startled her, she calmed down
enough to think to herself, "It's crazy, here I am about to go to New York
and explore this stuff, and now this happens." The small "man" answered
her thought, as it were, in a very easy way. Kathie's sense of his reply was
something like, "That's nice that you're going to New York. It's nice
you'll see your friends [presumably Sue and me]. It's very nice." As if
nothing made any difference at all—the trip, the upcoming hypnosis, the
investigation, and so forth. There was no sense of a threat, a prohibition,
a warning—only the most casual sense of recognition. It was almost, in
Kathie's view, the way one speaks to a child: "That's nice, that's a very

pretty doll, you're lucky to have a nice doll like that." I didn't say it to Kathie, but this exchange lent me a little peace of mind—something that lately seemed in very short supply.

Our next hypnotic session picked up at the point when Kathie returned from the "store" without having bought any Diet Pepsi after all. She describes watching TV in her bedroom.

BH: Are you enjoying it?

KD: It's all right. I'm not really watching it. I'm just listening to it. My eyes are shut and I'm really tired. *(Sighs)* Oh, no, this is starting to hurt. It's kind of throbbing a little bit.

BH: That pain will melt away slowly . . .

KD: I can still feel it but it doesn't hurt anymore. Something inside of my head feels like it's throbbing, high up, high up under my nose . . . Oh, well, it's probably just my sinuses. If it gets worse I'll just take an aspirin. I can hear something, like a power line. It's got a real high-pitched humming sound, but I don't really hear it, it's like it's in my head, you know. Oh, my arms feel funny. *(Moves nervously)*

BH: What's the matter, Kathie?

KD: I don't know, I feel kind of creepy about the window. I keep looking up at the curtain. It's right by my bed . . . a row of windows. I don't know why I keep looking up there. I got a creepy feeling. It's probably just my imagination . . .

BH: Are you still watching the television?

KD: Unh-huh. I'm listening to it. And tomorrow I'm going to Jimmie's and I'm just thinking about it. I hope he's going to be in a good mood. *(Suddenly startled)* What was that?

BH: What's happening, Kathie? Did you hear a noise?

KD: *(Begins to breathe rapidly, obviously very frightened)*

BH: You're safe here, Kathie. It's over with. You're just remembering something that happened a while ago. You're completely safe. Tell me what you see.

KD: I just heard my name. Oh, boy, it really scared me! I wasn't expecting that.

BH: What did it sound like, Kathie?

KD: Two voices talking at the same time. They just said, "Kathie!" And it was really loud. It wasn't me. Maybe it was Mom. No, it wasn't her. I keep looking out the window. There's nothing there. I'm really getting scared, now. I don't know why I keep thinking something's going to happen . . .

BH: *(Reassures her, calming her)* What's happening now, Kathie?

KD: I got a real bad headache. I'm going to go downstairs and call Sue 'cause I'm scared. I don't want to go downstairs, but I have to call Sue. I don't want to walk by the kitchen window again, and I don't want to walk by the living room window, either. So I'll go downstairs and call Sue and then I won't be so scared. My mom will probably kill me for calling long distance but I'll pay for it myself. I gotta call her. I feel like something's really going to happen.

BH: Do you go down and call her?

KD: Yes. I'm sitting on a chair next to the microwave oven. I'm calling her and I'm really crying and I keep hearing that noise . . . And I thought I saw a light outside in the front room through the curtain . . . I looked and saw the chandelier lights reflecting from the window, but there was another light beside the chandelier light, and I looked again and it was gone. I don't want to go by the window again . . . any window. I don't even want to look at them.

BH: Now, Kathie, let's jump ahead just a little bit. You talked to Sue and told her what you were seeing, and you thanked her and then you hung up. Now you feel better. What are you going to do now? What happens now?

KD: I don't feel that much better—I'm still scared and I still think something's going to happen, even though Sue told me it wouldn't. I still think something's going to happen, so I take a tranquilizer. I know it's going to be an hour before this sucker starts to work. What am I going to do till then? I go back up to my room . . . the lights are still on . . . I never turned them off, and I turn the TV up. I turn on my radio and I get a magazine and I still feel funny, like something's going to happen. And my heart is flipping a little bit, and that just made me more scared. I couldn't stand to be near my bedroom window, so I get up and go in my mom's room. I knock on her door and she says, "What do you want?" I go over to the foot of her bed and say, "My heart's flipping," and she says, "Take your heart medicine and some Pepto-Bismol and go to bed. You'll be O.K." I'm still thinking something's going to happen. So I go out in the hallway, and I'm just standing there for a few minutes deciding what I'm going to do. I don't want to go back to my room and I don't want to go to the bathroom and I don't want to go downstairs. I just want to hide. I believe I turn around

. . . I was going to go to my room, then I change my mind and
decide to go into Robbie and Tommy's room, and just when I
was turning to go into their room I saw a flash of light in the
hallway. And it was like a little ball, and it streaked and flashed
at the same time. It left, like, a tracer almost. It made me jump,
and I stepped back into Mom's door, and I said, "Mom, did you
see that lightning?" And she said, "Yeah." But how could it be
lightning in my hallway? . . . Something's funny . . . it isn't right.
Something's going to happen, I know it. Something bad is going
to happen. So I go into the kids' room and get Tommy. He's
sound asleep. So I pick him up and carry him back to my
bedroom with me. And I feel guilty about waking him up, but
I just can't be in that room again by myself. I'm just so scared.
So I lay Tommy down next to me and he wakes up for a minute,
but he's back sound asleep right away, and I wish I could be.
I cover him up with my cover. I lay down and read some more
Rolling Stone. And this sound's going on and this kid's not
waking up. I got the TV on and I got lights on and I got the
stereo on and I'm reading, and this kid just went right back to
sleep! Oh, I'm going to go to sleep, now. My arms tingle. I'm
going to sleep. My body tingles . . . my whole body tingles
. . . it feels really good. I'm just going to go to sleep. My head
feels like it's floating. It feels real light. My whole body tingles,
especially my upper arms, and my knees tingle real cold. It feels
good. I feel real good. I just feel like I'm floating. My hands feel
like they're on backwards . . . and my thumbs are pointing the
other way. Feels kind of weird, but it feels good . . . just kind
of feels fine. I'm gonna go to sleep. I hear this funny noise
. . . It sounds like somebody's breathing real fast and short. Kind
of puff, puff, only real faint. Only it's not me. I feel some poking,
thumping on my chest, under my left breast. It's kind of like
somebody thumped you. Hmm. I'm asleep, but I can think. I
think I'm asleep . . . I feel fine. It's real tingly. Did you just poke
me under the arm?

BH: No, Kathie, I didn't. Which arm was it?

KD: My right arm.

BH: Do you know what poked you?

KD: I don't know. I can't see. I can't open my eyes. Maybe that's
Tommy I hear breathing, but . . .

BH: Can you hear the stereo?

KD: No.

BH: The television?

KD: No. It's quiet. Now somebody poked me under my left breast. *(Nervously)* This time my right breast and my ribs, by my heart.

BH: *(Calms her)*

KD: I can smell burning matches again . . . It smells like burning matches and it stinks.

BH: Can you open your eyes?

KD: I can't. I can't open my eyes.

BH: Did they poke you through your nightgown?

KD: I don't think I have any clothes on. I don't know. I don't feel any. I feel cold. They're doing something with my chest.

BH: Who's the "they"?

KD: I don't know, I can't see. Whoever's touching me . . . I feel touching . . . I feel cold touches on both sides of my chest, underneath my breasts and alongside of them, and fingers or something cold touching me.

BH: What do they feel like? Do they feel like fingers?

KD: Yeah, sort of, but they're cold.

BH: Are they soft?

KD: Not real soft . . .

BH: Do you still hear that noise?

KD: Just really, really faint . . . kind of . . . I don't know even if it's a noise . . . just a vibration of something . . . It's just low key or whatever . . .

BH: What's happening now, Kathie?

KD: Just feel like my nose is running down my throat, you know, my sinuses are draining . . . I don't remember . . .

BH: You said you don't remember. Don't remember what?

KD: My lawn. I don't remember . . .

BH: We'll come back to that, Kathie. Now let's move back to you lying there and feeling comfortable, and the probing or what-ever it was has stopped. What happens after it stops?

KD: I'm asleep and I feel nice and warm, and like a warm rush through me from my chest to my arms and legs, and I feel fine and I'm just asleep.

BH: Do you feel Tommy there?

KD: No. I feel that pinching on my face again, between my eyes. I don't feel the pain—I just feel the pressure . . . Something's poking me. I'm on my stomach and something's on my neck . . . It feels like a collar on my neck, but I'm still in bed asleep . . . It will go away. *(Moves nervously)*

BH: What's happening, Kathie?

KD: I'm having that dream . . . I must be having that dream about the guys in my room because I'm seeing them again. I just must be having that dream.

BH: Is it the attic bedroom?

KD: I'm not in my attic room. I'm in bed asleep and I see this guy. I see what he looks like. He looks like the same guy I had in my other dream, that's all. This guy smiles at me a lot, not so bad.

BH: Is he there in your bedroom with you?

KD: I don't know . . . He's in my head, I guess he's in my dream . . . I don't know where he is . . . I guess I'm just in bed.

BH: In your dream about him, do you see anything around him, where he is?

KD: Just all blank, all blank, white. Whatever . . . He's smiling. When I first saw him I was scared, but he's smiling and I'm not scared anymore. Why should I be scared of a dream? I feel fine. I feel really relaxed and relieved.

At this point, Kathie's memories of the "examination" and her encounter with the small man seem to come to an end. There is, however, one final surprise.

KD: That can't be right. I must be imagining that.

BH: What's that, Kathie?

KD: I *couldn't* be outside. I wouldn't even go by the windows when I called Sue.

BH: Where are you outside?

KD: In my backyard, I guess.

BH: Let's not try to make sense of this, because dreams are funny and don't make sense. Just tell me what you see. Are you alone outside?

KD: Yeah.

BH: Are you in your nightgown?

KD: Yes.

BH: As you look around, what do you see?

KD: Just my backyard. It's dark out.

BH: Are you standing outside, Kathie?

KD: Yes. I guess I'll go in. I don't know why I'm standing out there. I just go in through the back door and go to bed.

BH: How do you feel, now?

KD: Fine. I'm gonna go to sleep. I must have . . . that part must have

been a dream I was having, or something, 'cause I couldn't have
been outside . . . I'm in bed.

BH: Are the TV and stereo on?

KD: No.

BH: Did you turn them off?

KD: I guess.

BH: Is Tommy still there?

KD: Yeah.

Shortly after this I brought Kathie out of the trance. Though there were
a few minor differences between details she had previously remembered
and those she recalled under hypnosis, the two accounts dovetailed almost
perfectly. It was easy, now, to imagine the entire sequence of events. After
she returned from the store the first time, she begins to feel cold and
"tingly." When she notices the clock she becomes agitated—almost as if
she knows she's late for an appointment—and immediately thereafter
returns to the store. Somehow, she and her car end up not at the Seven-
Eleven parking lot but instead near a brightly lit object she *sees as* the
store.[10] The "clerk," it is now obvious to her, is the small, gray-skinned
figure of previous recollections, and in fact, she told me later that she
"knew" him, that he was familiar to her from her 1979 attic experience.
(Like CIA operatives, abductees also seem to have their regular "han-
dlers.")

Kathie returns home, frightened, apparently unconsciously aware that
there is more to come. Hoping to forestall the inevitable, she phones Sue
in New York, to no avail. Eventually she settles down, and the abduction
begins. As she slips into a possibly prearranged quasi-trance (her description is very similar to that of a normal hypnotic trance), she is somehow
transported out of the house and into the UFO. She is poked and probed,
turned this way and that, in the typical UFO abduction "examination."
Something like a collar is put on her neck, causing her a lingering discomfort, and leaving tiny bloodstains on her pillow. At some point she opens
her eyes and sees the small gray figure once more, but this time against
the blank whiteness that so often characterizes the interior of a UFO. He
smiles at her—with his eyes, as she later informed me; his tiny slit of a
mouth never moves—and she falls back to relaxed sleep. She awakens, of
course, stunned to find herself standing outside, in the backyard, in her
nightgown.

Apart from its unusual two-stage imposition, this abduction seemed typical of the many so-called "bedroom visitation" experiences familiar to UFO investigators.[11] After these two hypnotic sessions in New York I had no reason to suspect the profound significance of that October encounter. Yet months later Kathie was to spontaneously recall a previously un-remembered event that occurred that night inside the UFO. Her later recollections of that occasion are perhaps the most important in the history of UFO research.

4

Robbie, Tommy and the Bogey Man

Kathie stayed with us in Manhattan for six days, but her time was not all taken up with hypnotic regressions and UFO research. She met Sue and her boyfriend, ate Chinese, as we New Yorkers like to say, and did a bit of sightseeing. Charles Bronson movies notwithstanding, she very much enjoyed her visit to the Big Apple. At heart, Kathie is rather conservative. She carefully shepherded her funds, arriving back in Indianapolis with something like forty-three cents left from the money she had allotted for her trip, but with a bag of presents for her two little boys.

In the days and weeks following her return, Kathie and I spoke frequently on the telephone. New—and newly remembered—events in the Copley Woods saga continued to unfold in the slow, inexorable pattern I had learned to expect. But the most troubling event occurred a few days before Thanksgiving and a little over a month after Kathie's visit to New York. She called on the twenty-seventh to give me the disturbing details. She said that she had been nervous all day, feeling "a little creepy, like something was there in the house, and that night I was home alone with the kids. I kept thinking I saw something every now and then, out of the corner of my eye, but then I'd turn and look and there would be nothing there. It was really strange, and kind of spooked me out." Despite her unease, however, the evening passed uneventfully.

I got the kids to bed and then I went to bed shortly thereafter. Well, five in the morning I'm awakened by this bloodcurdling scream, and I nearly had a stroke as I came flying up off the bed, and I ran into my kids' room, and it's my son Robbie . . . Because of the creepy feeling that I was having all that night it really jolted me . . . He was laying on the bed stiff as a board and pale and his eyes were wide as quarters. I thought he was gonna die of fright. I picked him up and I said what's the matter, what's the matter, you must have had a bad dream. He said, first thing he did was he looked me straight in the eye and he said, "Mommy, this ain't no dream." I said, "O.K., come into my room." I brought him in my bedroom and asked him what happened. He said, "Mommy, a man with a big head came in my wall and went in my closet and kept going back and forth, and he wouldn't let me move. And he had lights around his head." And I said, "Honey, it's just a bad dream," you know. And he said, "The man wanted Tommy, Mommy. He wouldn't let me move." I said what did he want Tommy for, and he says I don't know. I kept telling him it's just a dream, calm down. You know, he screamed so loud he woke me up out of a sound sleep between two shut doors, but Tommy didn't even wake up, sleeping in the same room with him. And Tommy's a light sleeper. Usually if you breathe on him he's wide awake. So I thought I had better go in there and get him, too, and bring him in my room with me, just in case.

I left Rob in my room and I went in there and grabbed Tommy, and I turned the light on and I picked him up, and I swear—it was probably by that time my imagination was freaking out—but I could have sworn I saw a flash of light in the closet, out of the corner of my eye, but when I looked there was just, like, nothing, like a shadow, like a kind of fade, you know, like it had been there but it was gone. Like it had left a stain or something, or whatever, but there wasn't anything there. So I picked Tommy up and he never did wake up. I brought him in my room and put him in my bed and he didn't wake up at all, and usually if you just touch him he's wide awake . . . so that was strange, too.

Forgetting for the moment that Kathie's maternal instinct was stronger than her investigative curiosity, I inquired if she had asked Robbie for more of a description of the man with the big head.

No, actually I didn't. I was trying to help him forget it. Budd, it petrified him so bad that he would not go upstairs all day the next day, and he wet in his pants twice 'cause he wouldn't go up and use the bathroom by himself. And it was hell trying to get him to go to bed in that room that night. It's just been the last day or two he slept in his room again, and that was only because I promised to leave the door open.

Subsequent conversations lent more detail to this disturbing account. Robbie mentioned several days later that the man with the big head "had an invisible mouth." When Kathie asked him how he knew that, he replied that the man's mouth was invisible "because whenever he talked to me nothing moved"—a wonderfully apt four-year-old's view of the telepathic communication we usually find in this sort of encounter. Robbie's oft-repeated statement that "the man wouldn't let me move" is, I suspect, his description of physical paralysis, another staple of these reports.

I was curious to find out if Kathie and her family ever talked about UFOs when the children were present, since it was conceivable that Robbie could have been trying to capitalize on the story's attention-getting potential. She assured me that for obvious reasons the adults tried never to mention the subject when either of the boys was in the room. But an incident that occurred a few months later during my first trip to Indianapolis convinced me that Robbie had been deeply frightened that night, and was not in any way trying to connect himself with a "glamorous" adult subject. Kathie, her boyfriend, her children and I had just left her sister's house, and as we drove along I was asking a few questions about one of Kathie's UFO experiences. I spoke without thinking, but Robbie soon made me realize my mistake. "Mommy," he said in a shy little voice, "can we talk about something else? When we talk about this it makes my stomach hurt." I realized that for several days I had been violating the family rule against talking about UFOs in the children's presence—and that poor Robbie was one very frightened little boy.

Just about a week after Robbie's bedroom encounter with the short, large-headed figure, Kathie phoned me with another upsetting piece of news. She had put the boys to bed as usual and the night had passed uneventfully—but in the morning, when she went in to get them up for breakfast, she found Tommy covered with blood. He was sleeping peacefully, yet there was blood on the wall, on the bedclothes, on his face, blood seemingly everywhere. Kathie picked him up and raced off to the hospital emergency room. The doctor examined him and found that he had suffered a massive nosebleed, apparently without waking up. Even more disturbing, the doctor discovered a small hole high up inside Tommy's nostril. He told Kathie that her three-year-old must have punctured himself with a pencil or some similar long, pointed instrument. Kathie insisted that Tommy wouldn't do such a thing, and that if he had he would have cried at the pain and the bleeding. She later looked around his room for a possible implement, pencil or otherwise, and could find nothing. When she told the doctor this, he insisted that since there was a definite wound there, Tommy must have done it with his finger. Kathie pointed out that Tommy has short, pudgy fingers and delicate little nostrils; it seemed physically impossible. The explanation made no sense for another reason as well: Even if he had somehow managed to injure himself that way and begun to bleed profusely, he still would have been too frightened and upset to fall asleep.[1]

My mind immediately registered a different thought. Robbie mentioned that the large-headed man had said he had come "to get Tommy." As he bent over him, Robbie was unable to move and could not see what was going on. Was it possible that one of the tiny BB-like implants had been installed high up in Tommy's nasal cavity, and had, for some reason, "not taken"? Could it have somehow become dislodged a few days later as Tommy slept, causing the middle-of-the night nosebleed? The night the strange figure was in his room Tommy's behavior was unusual: He did not wake up from his brother's terrified screams, nor did he stir when his mother picked him up and moved him into her bedroom. And if the tiny object had somehow slipped out, it could easily have been overlooked by Kathie as she cleaned up the soiled bedclothes.

One of the many letters I received in response to *Missing Time* was from "Margaret Bruning," a resident of central Ohio.[2] She had several disturbing dreamlike experiences to tell me about, but one in particular is relevant to Tommy's situation. She was five years old at the time, and was sleeping peacefully in the bedroom she shared with her younger sister. She awoke as she heard her name called. She was told to go into the kitchen where she saw three men standing outside the back door. "They're wearing uniforms but they're not police," she recalled later under hypnosis. They came into the house as the hook of the hook-and-eye lock magically lifted with no one touching it. The men have "bad eyes," she said, but "they don't have a mouth. No lips . . ." Her next words were tense, as only a frightened little five-year-old child would speak them under the circumstances: "Put . . . me . . . down!" And then, more subdued: "Daddy won't like it."

Margaret is carried outside and towards a large, metallic object which stands partly on her family's land and partly on her neighbor's property. Her tone is one of amazement. "What *is* that?" she says. "If Mrs. Hartman saw it there she'd call the police!" Ultimately she is taken inside the craft and subjected to a "typical" physical examination, and later returned to her bed where she falls peacefully back to sleep. Her initial letter documents her condition the morning after.

> When I awoke in the morning my shorty pajamas had dried blood all over them. I'd had a pip of a nosebleed in my sleep—it had clotted in my braids and a bit had pooled in my ears . . . My mother was awakened by the sound of my vomiting . . . I had swallowed a great amount of blood in my sleep . . . The night following the nightmare I woke mother and our neighbors across the street screaming for help in my sleep.

The UFO phenomenon seems able to exert nearly complete control over the behavior of abductees. In this context, one can understand how a child can undergo a serious nosebleed—even swallowing quantities of blood—without awakening, as was apparently the case with both Margaret and Tommy. My feeling is that Robbie was simply an innocent bystander that November night, and that Tommy was the true object of the strange figure's attention. As the reader will understand from previous accounts, it is highly possible that Robbie's conscious recollections combine the beginning and the end of Tommy's abduction. The figure comes into the room, immobilizing Robbie, and telling him that he's "here to get Tommy." Robbie is then "switched off," put into a state of suspended animation, and Tommy is either taken out of the room for his examination/implantation or the operation is carried out there in the house. If he is taken into a UFO, he is returned a bit later, tucked into bed, and Robbie is "switched back on" into normal consciousness, whereupon he sees the figure bending over Tommy's bed and screams for his mother. Kathie rushes into the boys' room in time to see the last flicker of light, the last trace of the figure's presence, and then things gradually return to normal.

In *Missing Time* I described the case of "Mary," a woman friend of mine and an artist.[3] Though we never unlocked the details of an on-board UFO abduction experience—apparently her amnesiac block was powerful —neither she nor I, for many good reasons, ever doubted that she had had such an encounter. A few years ago when I was visiting her studio she recounted a strange recollection from the middle nineteen-sixties. Mary and her husband were sleeping soundly when they were awakened by screams from both their sons, who were Robbie's and Tommy's ages at the time, four and three. Mary's husband rushed into the boys' room and found them cowering in their beds; a "bogey man" with a big head had come into their room and moved back and forth from the closet to their beds, frightening them nearly to death. Their father naturally put it down to one child's having had a nightmare that somehow managed to infect the other, though both boys said the man was real and had actually been in their room. Twenty years later, when I interviewed the older boy, now a graduate student in college, he could clearly recall the figure. "It was short and had big eyes . . . it also seemed to have an aura or some kind of glow around it. I don't think I could move while it was there. It seemed to speak to my brother, but I don't know what it said. It appeared to come out of the wall behind the dresser, and that's the way I think it left." As he described the experience, he paused and told me that it still upset him to remember it. "You know, Budd, my hands are getting sweaty right now, as I talk about it. It was very frightening." Unfortunately, his brother, who had been ill for several years, died in 1984. His and his parents' are the only available accounts of this strange affair.

The pattern of these generational encounters is clear. Sandy Thomas, the Florida abductee discussed briefly in Chapter 2, has a young son named John. When I visited her early in 1985, I asked her if he had ever mentioned any odd occurrences which she might see as related to the UFO phenomenon. She said that sometime in the fall of 1984 her boy had come into her bedroom in the middle of the night, crying and complaining that a man with a big head and funny eyes had come out of his closet and scared him. Something pinned him down and "bit" him on his back; in fact his back still hurt. Sandy let him get in bed with her and her husband, and after comforting him a while, everyone went back to sleep. A few days later, Sandy asked him to show her where his back had been hurt. He lifted his shirt and pointed to a place above his left hip. During my interview with the Thomas family several months after the incident, Sandy called her son over to where we were sitting so that

I could see for myself what she had found. Raising his shirt, she pointed out a small but distinct circular scar of the same type Kathie and her mother have on their legs. I glanced up at her and could see that there were tears in her eyes as she looked at the mark. Like so many others who have been through these encounters, she does not want to believe they really happened—to her or to her loved ones. Visible, physical evidence only confirmed her worst fears.

There is considerable agreement in these various children's accounts—of which I've presented only a sampling—as to the appearance of the "bogey man," Tommy's recurrent name for him. (See illustrations.) A recent incident demonstrates the point. In February of 1986, two years and three months after Robbie's terror and Tommy's nosebleed, Kathie called me to tell me of a frightening experience the night before. Shortly after she put the boys to bed, Robbie wakened and came into her room. He told her that there was "a red tarantula" moving slowly down his wall, he was afraid and wanted to sleep in her bed. She asked about the tarantula, and he explained that it was "a round red light with things [rays] sticking out like legs," and as it moved it looked like a spider and he was scared. Kathie assumed he had been dreaming, so she pulled the covers over him and he soon was asleep in her room.

A little later, as she was lying on her bed watching late-night television and drinking a Diet Pepsi, she looked up and to her horror saw a small, gray-skinned figure walk past her open door. "I didn't see him out of the corner of my eye either," she told me. "I looked *right at him*. My TV is right by my door. It was the same little guy. He didn't look at me or anything. He just walked by, like I wasn't there. Budd, I thought I was going to have a heart attack. I started to hyperventilate, and I jumped up, and as I started to go out in the hall to my mother's room, there was a bright flash out my window that I could see out of the corner of my eye. Budd, that guy *was there!* He was real little and he didn't seem to be wearing anything, and he looked just like when I've seen him before. But this time there wasn't no amnesia. I didn't forget or anything. I just saw him like you'd see a real person. I got my mother up, and we looked around the house, but there was nothing there. I was so scared I asked my mom to lend me some money so I could spend the night in a motel, but she wouldn't do it. I didn't want to sleep in that house."

I asked Kathie where the little figure seemed to be coming from. "He was coming from my boys' room, right next to mine. Only Tommy was in there, though. I had Robbie asleep in my bed." I suddenly remembered the little red light that had driven Robbie away, leaving Tommy alone in the room. The situation was beginning to seem more orchestrated, perhaps, than coincidental. I told Kathie that when Tommy came home from school she should casually ask if he had had any dreams the night before. She called me about four o'clock. Tommy's speech is still very hard to make out, but Kathie understood that he dreamed "the bogey man" had come into his room. My final request was for Kathie to make a simple, schematic outline drawing of the figure she had seen, and then to make three other, distinctly different figure drawings on the same page. She was to show them to Tommy, and he was to tell her which looked most like the bogey man of his "dream." As one might guess by now, he picked the drawing of the figure Kathie had seen, and later Robbie also selected this figure as the one he remembered from two years before—the man with the invisible mouth who wouldn't let him move.

That week back in November of 1983, when Robbie originally told of the big-headed man in his room and Tommy suffered his drastic nose-bleed, was the occasion of yet one more anomalous event. As the reader will recall, the main reason Kathie telephoned me was to recount the details of Robbie's bedroom experience with the man with the invisible mouth. But that same night she herself had had a peculiar "dream" that she also wanted to tell me about. My attention was immediately drawn to the way she said this recollection first came into her mind. She did not wake up and remember it immediately and vividly, the way most of us recall our dreams—if we recall them at all. When Kathie awoke in the morning, after her ordeal with Robbie and Tommy, she did not even remember having dreamed. Later that afternoon she turned on her television set and lay down to rest, hoping to recoup some of her lost sleep from the night before. It was in this drowsy half-asleep, half-awake state that she remembered—vividly—what she assumed was a dream from the night before. "I remembered that I had this dream, and I kind of dreamed it again, only it was different this time. The same thing happened, but it felt different. I was laying on a table . . ." I interrupted. "On a table?" Kathie paused a moment.

Well, on something. It wasn't a bed. I was laying on a table or something. And I had on my nightgown, and it was, like, pulled up right under my breasts. My eyes were shut, though, and I was real relaxed, and I knew I was on a table . . . I sensed I was laying real flat, and I wasn't on my bed. It was like I was starting to wake up.

And I opened my eyes, and I'm looking down because I'm laying flat
. . . and this guy looks at me, the same guy I've seen before, with
the big eyes. The minute I looked at him he looked at me. And he
has his hand on my abdomen. He says to me, "How are you feeling?"
And I said, "Real tired and kind of crampy," I think that's it, and
he patted me on the stomach, you know, around where the belly
button is, he kind of patted me real gently and said, "That's good."
He was real gentle, real, real pleasant, you know, and he kept looking
at me. And then I felt somebody rubbing me on the temples, real,
real easy, like a massage, and I just shut my eyes and went back to
sleep. And that was it.

I asked Kathie if she was frightened when she saw the man with the large
eyes.

No, I wasn't scared at all. He just asked me how I felt and I said,
"Real, real drowsy, real tired and kind of crampy." I wasn't scared
at all. I felt fine, I guess, I don't know. I was real relaxed . . . I closed
my eyes and went back to sleep. When I got up in the morning,
there was a funny thing. My underwear was on the bed, outside, on
top of the covers. I was sleeping in my nightgown and panties, and
when I woke up my panties were on the bed, up by my hip, right
next to me. I guess I could have taken them off in my sleep, but I've
never done that before. They weren't on the floor, either. They were
right up on the bed, outside the covers.

Kathie said that the next day she felt very "crampy," as if she were
having an unusually difficult menstrual period. She experienced strongly
localized pain in her lower abdomen, in the region of her left ovary. In
fact, she was so uncomfortable, even to the point of having difficulty
walking, that when she called Sue in New York to tell her about Robbie's
encounter, she asked her advice on the matter. Sue suggested that Kathie
check her calendar, and she discovered that this was the day she expected
to ovulate. As I heard these details I could visualize two very different
scenarios. In one, Kathie was simply having an unusually painful ovulation, which often happens, I am told, and managed to work that situation
into a spontaneously generated UFO dream. This possibility was especially likely if her dream took place after she was awakened by Robbie's
cries. In this scenario her physical discomfort led her to sleepily remove
her underwear without remembering that she did so.

The second scenario is more disturbing. In this reading of events, the UFO occupants come into the Davis house and take *both* Kathie and Tommy, while holding Robbie in a "switched off" state until their mission is completed and mother and son are returned to their beds. This encounter—which includes the placing of an implant in little Tommy—has been planned to coincide with the ideal time of the month to remove an ovum from Kathie, an operation which nevertheless causes her some pain and later discomfort. She is kept in a quasi-anesthetized state during this procedure, however, and when she awakens, the watchful, gray-skinned figure reassures her. Seeing she is in satisfactory condition, he once more puts her to sleep and takes her back to her room. Her nightgown is pulled down, her panties are left on top of the covers, and Robbie is allowed to return to normal awareness.

Though it is an extremely uncomfortable issue to face, the fact remains that from the beginning, publicly reported UFO abduction accounts contain details which unmistakably point to an interest by "UFO occupants" in the processes of human reproduction. When Betty and Barney Hill were abducted in 1961 and recounted their stories separately under hypnosis to Dr. Simon, Barney Hill recalled that a sperm sample had been taken from him by his captors. (This important detail was omitted from John Fuller's book on the Hill case, *The Interrupted Journey;* it was probably considered too sensational to include in what was already an "unbelievable" account.) Betty described the painful experience of having had a long needle inserted into her navel, in what her captors said was a pregnancy test.[4] At the time, debunking psychologists, amateur and otherwise, attacked these unpleasant and clearly unerotic recollections as "obvious" sexual fantasies. However, a decade or so later a device similar to the needle Betty described is commonly used in Western medicine. The laparoscope is a long, flexible tube containing fiber optics which are magnified for internal viewing. The instrument is inserted directly into the patient's navel, not for pregnancy tests per se, but for a variety of related reasons—including the removal of ova. So-called test-tube babies are produced by using laparoscopy to locate and remove ova from the female for later fertilization outside the uterus with "the sperm of one's choice." A fertilized egg is eventually "planted" back inside the uterus; if all goes well the embryo develops normally and a healthy, normal baby is born.

An abduction report which preceded the Hill encounter, and which by contrast became widely known only among UFO investigators, was the 1957 Villas-Boas case.[5] In this Brazilian incident, Antonio Villas-Boas, a twenty-three-year-old farmer, was plowing a field by moonlight one night when a football-shaped object flew over him and landed near his tractor, coming to rest on three supporting legs. According to his account the tractor's electrical system failed and he was seized by three of the UFO's occupants. He was taken inside the craft, undressed, sponged with a clear fluid, and then a blood sample was taken from his chin. He was put, alone, in a small room which soon began to fill with a grayish vapor of some kind. Villas-Boas said that at first he thought he would suffocate, but a moment later he became so intensely nauseated that he vomited.

Shortly after this a small "woman" with large, slanting eyes entered the room—naked. He described her as being very white-skinned and as having almost white hair, high cheekbones and barely visible lips. But suddenly —and under the circumstances, inexplicably—he found himself sexually aroused, and an act of intercourse followed. Just before the "woman" left the room she pointed to her belly and then, looking directly at him, pointed to the sky. The meaning of all this to Villas-Boas was that she had been impregnated.

The Brazilian investigator who worked on this bizarre case, Dr. Olavo Fontes, claimed that there was extensive medical evidence to support Villas-Boas's account, and that he had been unable to shake the man's story in any way. (The young farmer's experience was "naturally" recalled; hypnosis was not employed.) My impulse, when I first learned of the case sometime in the later nineteen-sixties, was to dismiss his story out of hand as a sexual fantasy, pure and simple, except for one nagging detail. Villas-Boas's description of vomiting copiously just before the female's appearance did not seem to cohere with anyone's freely invented sexual adventure—especially not that of a presumably macho young man. Villas-Boas represented himself in the story as having been subdued and stripped of his clothes by three small men and then somehow being induced to vomit, before an odd-looking female made her appearance and evidently had her way with him. It was just not an ordinary, garden-variety macho fantasy, and many of its peculiar details had an unmistakable aura of truth —all apart from the fact that his recollections of the ship and its occupants fitted patterns that we have come to recognize from many later cases.

In my early investigations I occasionally ran across details suggesting that sperm samples had been taken from certain male abductees. Yet something inside me wanted to ignore, or at least bypass, such intimations. A number of female abductees I've worked with recalled operations, similar to Betty Hill's, which suggested a laparoscopy-like procedure, and again I put these descriptions on some back shelf of my mind. But as these apparently "reproduction-focused" cases accumulated I realized that the issue could not be avoided. The Copley Woods affair has been crucial to my awareness of what I now believe to be a central purpose behind the UFO abduction phenomenon.

As the cases have slowly accumulated, the patterns have become clearer. Over the past six years I have worked with four male abductees who have described encounters very similar to Villas-Boas's abduction, and three others whose incomplete accounts strongly suggest such an event. (Personal hesitation and embarrassment operate as strongly here, it would seem, as the effects of amnesia.) The female side of this equation, which we will examine later on, is more complex. It should be pointed out, however, that I know of *no* case in which a female abductee has ever reported an act of intercourse. Above all, in none of these cases involving either men or women do we have what can be called a basically *erotic* experience. The descriptions are invariably of a detached, clinical procedure instead, even if some of them result in a more or less involuntary ejaculation.

Now all of this leads to the unwelcome speculative inference that somewhere, somehow, human beings—or possibly hybrids of some sort—are being produced by a technology obviously—yet not inconceivably—superior to ours. And if that possibility is not enough to induce paranoia in the heartiest, consider this: With our own current technology of genetic engineering expanding day by day, is it not conceivable that an advanced alien technology may already have the ability to remove ova and sperm from human beings, experimentally alter their genetic structure, and then *replant* altered and fertilized ova back into unknowing host females to be carried to term? Ova that can be removed can also be replaced, even by our own present-day medical technology.

In the speculative paragraph above I used the word "alien" to describe the UFO phenomenon for a very precise reason. The word "alien" defines negatively; it says what something is not, rather than what it is. It means, basically, "other than," foreign, different. Whatever the nature and origin of the gray-skinned UFO occupants—and there are many exotic theories—they are not us. They are not short humans, like midgets, dwarfs, or the members of certain African tribes. They are physically, culturally and technologically different from us, *alien*. They have been called angels, demons, robots, space-travellers from another solar system, "ultra-dimensionals," "time-travellers" and so on, but there is one essential fact—they are not us. They are alien. And as such their purposes and goals—even their mental processes—are possibly unknowable by us humans. However, from what I know about *our* physical makeup, *our* anatomy, I can infer that if human sperm and ova have been taken as the evidence implies, then human beings are possibly being produced in an alien context. But at that point "safe" speculation must stop; we simply cannot guess at the purposes of such a program within an alien culture. And having said all this, I also admit that none of it allows me to sleep any better at night.

Kathie's description of her November "dream" seemed to me more like the drowsy, half-drugged fragments of memory one has in the recovery room after surgery than it does the memory of conventionally disconnected dream images. And in the context of Robbie's tale of the bedroom visitor, Tommy's nosebleed and Kathie's physical problems—including the mystery of how her underwear ended up off her body and on top of the bed—I felt almost certain that she had been abducted yet again. If so, Kathie's abduction so soon after her visit to New York left me with an ever deeper sense of powerlessness than I had before.

With the Christmas season approaching, the earliest I could plan to fly to Indianapolis was in the latter part of January. I was very eager to go there, to meet Kathie's family and to see things for myself. In the meantime Kathie and I communicated by telephone, and to no one's surprise, more odd events rose to the surface. I will offer one example, an incident that has not been investigated beyond a few personal interviews. The man in question, Kathie's brother-in-law, simply does not want to undergo hypnosis, nor does he wish to explore the matter in any depth. Kathie's original letter to me described a missing-time UFO experience that occurred to her older sister Laura as a teenager. Laura went on to marry a fine man I shall call Johnny, and they are now the parents of four children. Over the years, Johnny had heard his wife tell about her UFO sighting, and by the fall of 1983 he was aware of the marks in the Davises' backyard and my investigation of the case. Johnny is something of a "good ol' boy," a Southerner with a calm I-got-to-see-it-to-believe-it attitude towards the world. He would seem to be the last person in the world able to tolerate a strange UFO experience, so his reaction was understandable; when it happened to him he was as confused as he was frightened.

In November of 1983—that same busy month—Johnny and two friends of his went on a hunting trip near Spencer, Indiana. They were staying in a small cabin they own together. Johnny awoke early, before dawn, and walked into the living room. Through the window he could see a bright beam of light shining down onto a nearby wood, but he could not make out the source of the light. It moved this way and that, soundlessly, as if searching for something. A moment later he noticed two figures standing outside near the cabin, and he assumed that they must be his two hunting companions. He decided to call to them, to direct their attention to the strange light, but here his memory of that predawn period ends. The very next thing he remembers is standing in the living room after the sun had already risen, watching his friends prepare breakfast. He told me later that for some reason he felt he should not mention the peculiar light to them, nor his confusion about the missing hour or two, but the experience had obviously and deeply unnerved him.

A month later he had a second unusual experience, this one more overtly upsetting. Johnny owned a pickup truck which had a double cab; its backseat was somewhat like a sedan's. The truck, according to both Laura and Kathie, was his pride and joy. In December, on his way to work about 5:30 A.M., Johnny slowed to a stop before pulling out onto the main road. Almost automatically he glanced up into the rearview mirror—and saw a man sitting in the backseat. Unbelieving, he turned his head and looked over his right shoulder. The figure, apparently a normal man, was wearing what Johnny later described as somewhat resembling a big western hat. He appeared solid, darkish, clearer in silhouette than in surface detail. Johnny panicked, pulled on the brake and jumped out of his truck. He ran twenty feet or so and then turned around. As one might have guessed, the truck was empty and the surrounding open ground provided no cover for a running figure. Johnny sold his no longer beloved truck the very next day. When I interviewed him, he told me that he thought the events in the woods and the sudden appearance of the man in his truck were somehow connected. Whatever the objective reality of the figure in the backseat, Johnny's reaction is an index of the effect of the first event on his traditional state of skeptical calm. And he steadfastly refuses to explore these events under hypnosis.

But the UFO phenomenon, whatever it is, reserved even more terror for this good and gentle man. I will not discuss this later event in any detail, but in the spring of 1984, after a mysterious problem with his new truck, Johnny found himself confronted on a dark road by two very small men who seemed "to just appear there." He remembers that they spoke to him without making sounds, and that subsequently he lost a period of more than *six hours.* This experience so frightened and confused him, his wife told me, that he apparently found it difficult to remain anyplace by himself. For days after, when Laura left the room where she had been sitting with him he would get up and follow her. She said he acted as if he were afraid to be alone in his own house, even for a moment.

When I finally flew into Indianapolis on January 22, 1984, it was almost seven months after the original incident in the Davises' backyard, and three months after Kathie's first visit to New York. She was there to meet me at the airport, smiling her now-familiar quizzical smile. It was a grin that seemed to say, "Do you know what the hell we're doing here, 'cause I sure don't." As Kathie drove me to her home she told me the latest family news and any bits of information about "the case" that I might not have heard. Robbie and Tommy were dying to meet me, she said. They'd been excited for days.

Both boys lived up to their billing. Tommy, who at that time could speak very little, was a plump, energetic, lovable three-year-old. He was very hard to keep out of your lap. I would sit down at the kitchen table, pad in hand, to interview Mr. Davis. Almost subliminally, I would become aware of some wriggling going on, and when I glanced down, there would be Tommy's beaming face about a foot from mine. I would suddenly understand why there was a strange weight in my lap. He was irresistible, and I began to see him, in his silence and his very physical presence, as a kind of infant Harpo Marx; I wanted to buy him a tiny horn to beep.

Robbie, a year older, was more thoughtful and less physical. He has a wonderful imagination and his own strange sense of humor. In order to interview him about his bedroom encounter and any possible emotional fallout it may have caused, I chose a circuitous route and inquired about his dreams. He told me that last night he had a really funny dream. "I was with these babies," he said, "and another baby came in and said 'goo goo ga ga,' and we all laughed and laughed." "What was so funny about that?" I asked. Suddenly serious, he said, "Don't you know? That's a baby's joke."

Over the years I have developed a special interviewing method to use with small children in UFO cases, and Robbie's wonderful dream helped me formulate this technique. On the one hand an investigator must be careful not to trigger suddenly a child's semi-forgotten traumatic memory, and on the other, he must find a way to separate real experiences from dreams and fantasies. Both of these problems are difficult enough with adults, but when four- and five-year-olds are the subjects, the problems escalate. In a recent case, the father, an abductee, reported that his seven-year-old son described a "dream" in which he said "little men" came into his bedroom, lifted him up and floated him out the door into the living room. They kept telling him not to worry, "everything will be all right, you won't be hurt." He was floated out the front door and into the yard, where he suddenly ascended up into the sky. Later he awoke in bed, thoroughly frightened. His father wanted me to interview him, but as circumspectly as possible. I spoke with the boy for a while, and then I told him I liked to hear about dreams. "What's the funniest dream you've ever had?" I asked. He thought a bit and then sort of made one up, something funny he'd seen on TV, perhaps, which permitted a bit of creative alteration. Then I told him a funny (made up) dream of my own. After a bit we moved on to scary dreams, and I went first with a not very scary one of my own invention. He followed with a conventional scary dream of his, which seemed to have a certain degree of familiar movie content. Then I asked him if he'd ever had a dream in which he was floating. "Oh, yes," he answered enthusiastically, and repeated almost verbatim the "dream" he had told his father about the little men who floated him out of the house. "Dreams can be all mixed up," I told him. "I bet you dreamed you were in a different, mixed-up place when the dream began." "Oh, no," he said. "It was my bedroom in the country, just like I was there." I replied that some dreams feel crazy and some seem real, and asked about this floating dream. "It seemed real," he answered, "like I was really floating out of my room."

Since that afternoon when we talked together about our dreams, this case has been thoroughly investigated, with extensive interviews, hypnosis, and psychiatric and medical involvement. Like the Copley Woods affair, it has turned out to be an example of an apparent UFO "family study" of at least three generations. The boy, his father and mother, his aunt and his grandfather all seem to have been abducted, and there is every reason to believe that his father, like Kathie, has had many such experiences dating back to his early childhood.

During a later conversation with Kathie's son Robbie, perhaps a year after he told me his dream about the baby's joke, he brought up another, more recent dream. He had seen the movie E.T., and wanted to tell me that he'd dreamed E.T. had come into his room. I wasn't sure whether that meant he'd had another UFO experience or just a normal dream about what one can consider the Walt Disney version of an extraterrestrial. (The charm of Spielberg's E.T. is that it looks like a turtle without its shell. Every child loves turtles, which seem—unlike the "E.T.s" of actual UFO reports—slow and cute and nonthreatening.) I asked Robbie if E.T. was the man with the big head and the invisible mouth, that he had told me about before. "No. He's different. I dreamed E.T. came in my room. He didn't look like that man. He looked like E.T." And to show me the difference he made a drawing (see illustrations) that shows *both* E.T. and the little man with the big head in his room at the same time. Robbie tried to explain that one was a dream, but the other really happened. He even showed me the place in his room where he thought the "man" came through the wall. I wondered if he hadn't recently invented the pleasant E.T. dream to somehow defuse the fear he had about the man with the invisible mouth who "came into my room and wouldn't let me move."

My first trip to Indianapolis in January of 1984 was by far the most crucial of the four visits. It led to the uncovering of a number of other apparently UFO-connected recollections by the Davis family and several of their friends and neighbors. Any investigator knows that memory and perception can easily mislead, but I came back to New York certain of one thing: that I could trust the veracity, the inherent honesty, of Kathie and her family. During the six days I spent with the Davises, I interviewed Kathie and her mother and father separately and together, upon numerous occasions and with reference to many different events. I interviewed Robbie and Kathie's sister Laura, as well as Laura's husband and two of their children. I interviewed three of the Davises' neighbors and seven of Kathie's friends who were, in one way or another, witnesses to some aspect of this complicated series of events. At no point did I find the slightest reason to doubt any part of the Davises' various accounts. On the contrary, I heard many details that Kathie had never related to me before (one doesn't, after all, remember everything)—details that only buttressed her account.

By the end of my January visit, four months after I'd received Kathie's original letter, I knew that the Copley Woods affair was the strongest as well as the most complex UFO case I had yet encountered. But the night before I left, it took on another dimension. Kathie and I were talking about her family. It was dusk, and we had just pulled into her driveway. I told her how wonderful I thought her boys were, how lucky she was to have Tommy and Robbie. As she stopped the car she looked directly at me. "Budd, you know I have a daughter, too." I sat there in silence, not knowing what she was trying to tell me. "I don't know where she is," she continued, "and I never gave birth to her, but I know I have a daughter."

After a moment I collected my thoughts and asked the obvious question. "How do you know that, Kathie? What makes you think that?" She looked at me steadily, seriously, more seriously than at any time since we first met. "I know I have a daughter. I think I've even seen her. I know what she looks like."

I was still silent, still confused. I had no idea of how to reply, but I knew Kathie was telling me her deepest secret. There were tears in her eyes when we walked towards the house. She spoke once more, just before we opened the front door. "And I know something else. I'm going to see her again. I know it."

5

The Camping Trip and Other Adventures

My mind was filled with new information, some of it crystal-clear and some of it hopelessly opaque, when I flew back home to New York. My first visit to the Copley Woods opened up more issues than it resolved, and Kathie's cryptic, obviously heartfelt remarks about a lost child were only one example of the territory awaiting exploration. But while I was there I had looked into other accounts, interviewed new witnesses, and explored certain other newly recollected events, so I had a vivid sense of the expanding complexity of it all. One of the most interesting stories to surface was the account of Kathie's trip with her girlfriend Nan, in 1975, to Kentucky's Rough River State Park.

It was the July 4th weekend. Kathie, sixteen at the time, traveled with Nan's family—her parents, her younger brother, and Nan's boyfriend Sam —to a cabin in a remote area of the park. There was a lake, boating, fishing, and the other usual natural amenities of such a place. When Kathie and I first talked about her UFO-related experiences she said nothing about this trip; it was Nan herself who reminded Kathie that something very unusual happened there.

During one of my earliest phone conversations with Kathie I had asked about any recurring dreams she might remember. One dream that re- mained vividly in her mind involved her sitting in a truck at night, talking to someone over a CB radio. Suddenly the lights in the truck blink off and the radio goes dead. She looks up and sees four lights descending, spinning like pinwheels. Terrified, she crouches down under the dashboard. In the last image of the dream she is clutching the microphone and asking, "Who are you . . . what's happening," and there the dream ends. I asked if she could recall ever literally being in such a truck, speaking over a CB radio, and she then dimly remembered Nan's father's Chevrolet pickup, which in fact did have a CB radio. The trip itself, to Rough River Park, was less clear in her memory.

Shortly before I began to look into this incident, Kathie talked to Nan about her father's truck, and Nan had refreshed her memory with many details Kathie had forgotten. "Don't you remember the boys who turned up that night, who we had been talking to on the radio . . . especially the blond boy who liked you so much? They came over and we had a party." Kathie told me she was astounded when she suddenly remembered; she had practically fallen in love with that blond boy. It had been very strange. "The boys said they were camping in a particular place, and when we went there the next day to look for them there weren't any campsites anywhere around there. It sort of didn't make any sense . . . We could never figure out how they found us in the first place, either, because when we were talking to them on the CB we never told them how to get to where we were. There weren't even any names for the roads around there, so I couldn't have explained it even if I wanted to. They just showed up, as I remember, in a kind of clunky old car with hardly any lights on it."

The second day of my visit with the Davises, Kathie and I went into this experience in detail. On that day in 1975 she had been sitting in the truck along with Nan, Nan's brother and her boyfriend Sam, talking to "these four guys. They wanted to come and see us, and I told them if they could find us they would be welcome. We'd make a party out of it. We were just talking and fooling around on the CB, and finally Nan's brother and Sam got tired of it and went back in the cabin. A little bit later Nan went in, too, and then I was out there alone. I was having a great time. I remember seeing these lights coming down the road real slow, and the boy said on the CB, 'I see you,' and then they got out and I got out of the truck and kinda met them halfway. And we went in the cabin. There were three of them. The blond guy said there had been four, but one of them didn't want to come. The blond one was real cute, and I got the idea he liked me.

"When we went in the cabin it was really late, maybe midnight or so, and I thought Nan's parents would be asleep, but they were up. Everybody was up, even her little brother. I kinda thought they were mad or something, but the blond guy started to talk and everything went really well. We had some beer and talked. I think we even went outside and built up the campfire. It was fun, and they stayed a long time."

I asked what their names were. "You know," Kathie said, "I don't think they ever told us their names. They were all wearing blue shirts, and they told us they were part of a band. I told him I liked music, and he asked me what kind, and I said rock 'n' roll, and he said they played that kind of music. He asked me who my favorites were and I named some groups and he said they played music like those groups." Kathie had described the blond but had not mentioned the other two, so I asked about them. "I don't really remember them. I think they were tall and skinny, and I think they looked alike. But they never said anything. The blond guy did all the talking."

I was curious about what happened when they came into the cabin. "Well, Nan's mother asked them what they wanted to drink, and they asked what she had, and she said beer and Cokes and coffee. They asked what she had most of, and she said beer, so he said they'd have beer." I wanted to know what else they talked about. "You know, I don't remember what we talked about. We were having fun, though, I remember that. They were there a couple of hours." I asked if they all sat down in the cabin and talked when they came in. "I don't think so. I think the other two guys just sort of stood there. One stood by the door. I don't think they ever said anything at all." "Not even their names?" I asked. "Didn't the blond guy ever say these are my friends George and Bill, or anything like that?" "I don't think so. I don't think they ever spoke," Kathie replied, leaving us both a little puzzled.

Earlier I had asked Kathie for a chance to meet Nan and Sam—now husband and wife—and the evening of this interview they came over to the Davises' house. Sam is a quiet young man, the father of two children, and rather conservative in bearing. Nan is a slender and pretty woman who seems both intelligent and a bit withdrawn. At the time of this interview her father was seriously ill, and their mood was decidedly not frivolous. I asked them about the incident, and they described it very much as Kathie had. The most interesting thing about their recollections was what they *didn't* remember. Neither Nan nor her husband could recall anything whatsoever about the other two men, except that they were tall, skinny and wearing very similar clothes; neither could remember hearing them speak. Each, however, could easily describe the blond boy. Sam said that he was "kind of short, stocky, wearing blue jeans and a matching blue jeans jacket over a yellowish shirt."

I asked Sam and his wife what they remembered about the evening's conversation; each recalled what Kathie had already told me, that the boys were in a band, camping nearby, and so forth, but not one word or idea or even simple social exchange beyond that. Yet they were certain the visitors had been there for hours. Sam had an interesting observation to make, however. He said that the two men (who never spoke, who were never introduced by name, and whose appearance no one could remember) stood "sort of like guards while the blond guy ran things."

Kathie, Nan, and Sam shared essentially the same memories of the evening—and the same peculiar gaps in their recollections. When I later interviewed Nan's mother and her younger brother, this situation was compounded. Nan's mother remembered "how nice and polite the blond boy was. When I asked him what he and his friends wanted to drink, he asked what we had. I told him we had Cokes and coffee and beer, and he asked which we had most of. I said we had more beer than anything else, and he said, 'That's what we'll have.' " I was curious to know if he ever asked his two friends what *they* would like to drink, but she said she doesn't remember either of them talking at all. I also wanted to know if she had any idea of why the three had come to their cabin in the first place. "I guess they wanted to meet Kathie, since she'd been talking to them on the CB, and I guess they were just looking for a party. I know they stayed real late, but I don't remember much of what they said, except that they were part of a band."

The day after my conversation with Nan and her husband, Kathie and I decided to try hypnotic regression to further explore this strangely suggestive event. At the outset, Kathie describes sitting in the parked truck with her friends, "talking to some guys on the radio." One by one her friends go inside until she is alone. "Joe [Nan's brother] wants to go in . . . he's not too thrilled about these guys . . . he's getting bored 'cause there's no chicks on the radio. Nan and Sam are gonna go in, but I want to stay." After a pause she continues:

KD: I'm not really tired. I'm gonna play on the radio. *(Pause)* This guy wants me to talk with him some more. *(Long pause, and then, slightly disturbed:)* . . . I didn't remember that . . . like that . . . I'm having that dream . . .

BH: Describe it to us, Kathie.

KD: *(Somewhat alarmed)* It got real light out, like it was day. And the . . . radio still works, but there's no voices on it, just static . . . and something's flashing off the hood of this truck, and it's all over the truck . . . so I looked up in the rearview mirror, and I saw it . . . it's real bright and it hurts the eyes . . . I shut my eyes and I can still see it coming through my eyelids. It looks like pinwheels and there's four of them, and there's something sparkly in the light, like sparklers or something . . . *(Alarmed)* . . . and I'm really getting scared . . . *(Pause)* I jumped down and hid my face under the dash, and then I wasn't scared anymore. I looked again to see if it was still there, and it was still day out . . . I picked up the radio and I asked them who they were and what do they want from me. And the guys were still there and said they wanted to see us. When I heard them talking, when they started to talk to me, everything was normal. *(Pause)* They said I had to be pretty close, and I told them they could see me, but I wasn't gonna tell them where I was, that they had to find me . . . That one guy that I talked most to, he was real nice. And he said, "Look down the road," so I did, and he said, "I think I see you." And there was a car coming up the street real slow, and they pulled in and shut their lights off before they pulled in the driveway, though. When they got to the front of the house they got out and I got out, and I walked halfway to meet them, and they walked to meet me. The blond was in the front and the other two were behind him, one on each side. They walked up real slow . . .

I next asked Kathie about their car. Her description includes details which subtly suggest the vehicle was no ordinary compact car. The dirt road to the cabin was extremely bumpy and full of potholes, but Kathie said the car "glided along without bouncing . . . its light was very steady and even and didn't go up and down as it went over the bumps." There was something else a little unusual about the car's lights. "I think one of their headlights is out, that's why I saw a little light like side ones, you know, but I think I only saw one white light, like they had a bright light on, but I think one of their headlights was out . . ." Later in the session, Kathie described how the car left: "They started going down the street . . . I could see a light in the front of them and the sides, but they didn't have any taillights . . . I thought, Uh oh, they don't have any taillights. The taillights on the car are burned out."

Kathie goes on to describe their meeting:

KD: He's just smiling at me. He didn't say anything. I said "Hi" . . . and he said "Hi" back. I thought he was cute. He didn't look like he sounded on the radio, though . . . he looks cuter . . . He told me . . . he was the one who wanted to see me. He asked where Nan was, and I said she's in the cabin. He said, "Can we go see her?" And I said sure, follow me. So we went to the cabin and went in. The other guys didn't even say "Hi." Then we walked in and they were all awake. I thought everybody would be in bed, asleep, 'cause it was so late, but they're not. Nan's dad is sitting on the couch. Her mom is in the kitchen, standing in the doorway watching, and my head started to feel funny around my eyes and between my eyes, and I remember that 'cause I was getting dizzy . . . Her brother was there, her and Sam were sitting on the couch but the TV was off. I don't know why they were all in there. *(Pause)* The blond sat down but the other two never sat down. One stood by the door and the other stood on the other side of Nan's mom. I can't remember what they looked like . . . they were taller than the other guy . . . I didn't look at them much, and they didn't say anything.

BH: Did they introduce themselves with their names?

KD: No . . . no, they didn't. They never did. I . . . I thought I knew the blond's name, but no, they never did tell us their names.

BH: Did they tell you what their band was called, or anything about themselves?

KD: No. They already knew our names from the radio.

Now it seems to me that one of the first things a rock 'n' roll band leader would do would be to tell his teenage hosts the name of his group and where it has played—even possibly embellishing its credits a bit—but it was becoming clearer by the second that this was no simple group of musicians. Kathie's further recollections only underlined the one-way nature of the conversation.

BH: Can you remember what you talked about?

KD: About the CB and the cabin and why we were there and the Fourth of July and the fireworks, and, uh . . . music that we liked and where we were from and what we did there.

BH: Did they talk about their music and what *they* were doing?

KD: No. Not really. They asked me what kind of music did I like, and I told 'em I liked rock 'n' roll and I named off some of the bands, and they said that they did rock 'n' roll and that they did

some music from those bands that I named off, and that's really,
just, you know, all they talked about. That. He had on a blue
jeans jacket, I remember that, because when I got back from
Kentucky I went and bought me a blue jeans jacket just like
that.

BH: What did he look like?

KD: He was about my height and he was about my size—I was a lot
skinnier then—chubby but not fat fat. He had a round face and
blue eyes, real light, light brown, like blond, hair . . . wasn't
yellow-blond, but it was blond. Curly down to his collar, not
tight curls, just lots of wavy curls, just cute.

After this observant description of the leader, I was curious to know
what the other two looked like. "They were taller and skinnier. I can't
remember their faces. I can't, really . . . I think . . . both of them had
blue shirts on, but I can't remember their faces. They weren't like him,
though." Several things about Kathie's descriptions—her exact choice of
words—have interested me in retrospect. She said that the two silent
companions "weren't like him," rather than that they didn't *look* like
him, a choice of language that suggests—perhaps unconsciously—more
than just superficial differences. This suggestion takes on more weight
when one considers how clearly and consistently everyone remembers the
blond leader, and how consistently everyone draws a blank on his companions. But I realized another bizarre aspect of Kathie's description of the
blond leader: She describes someone who could be her brother, even her
masculine twin: "My height, my size, a round face, blue eyes, shoulder-
length curly dark blond hair." Other remarks she made both before and
after this hypnotic session support this feeling of special closeness: "I had
feelings for this man like an obsession. It took a week to get over it." "Just
before he left he kissed me on the cheek and I felt real funny, nice, but
funny." "I couldn't stop thinking about that guy. He looked at me a lot,
maybe because I was staring at him all the time. He smiled . . . he was
always smiling at everybody . . . and I thought he really, you know, liked
us and liked me . . ." I asked Kathie if she felt she'd ever seen him before
or since. "Someone like him, yeah, since. I don't know, I think I saw. I
think I felt I already knew him, but I don't know where. I guess you do
that with some people. But I feel like I met somebody like him since that
time. Their eyes were the same, and the way they smiled at you with
them." I asked, "Smiled with their eyes?" "Yes. Made you feel warm and

good." It was a phrase I'd heard before, in other UFO cases: "Their mouths never moved. They smiled with their eyes."

After I brought Kathie out of the trance state she mentioned to me how strange everyone looked when she first took the three visitors into the cabin. "I was sure some of them would have been in bed, since it was late, but they were all up, just sitting there or standing, and the TV wasn't even on. But Budd, they were just *still*, you know, not moving, like they were hardly awake, and not saying anything. And my head started to feel funny, between my eyes, and then the blond guy spoke and everyone kind of came to life, and began to move and talk. It was really weird, like they had been asleep or something." In the Betty Andreasson affair, documented by investigator Raymond Fowler in his book of the same title, there is a similar scene. Betty has been taken from her home and into a landed UFO. After an extended series of events she is returned by her captors and brought into the living room. She is startled to find her entire family sitting or standing there completely mute, looking like statues, completely unaware of her. Betty, in a hypnotic trance, describes the scene: "They're still all sitting there motionless. [My daughter] Becky's . . . there and she's smiling and grinning. She seems to be awake! She seems as if she's up, standing up, just smiling at me . . . Just standing there . . . Her expression isn't changing now. She seems to be frozen in that smile . . ."[1] This disturbing tableau—so similar to what Kathie saw when she entered the living room of the cabin—ends peacefully as Betty's captors lead each of her "sleeping" family members up to bed, and then restore Betty's conscious memory after they leave.

As we have seen, one of the basic patterns in UFO abductions, part of the modus operandi, is the ability the abductors have to "shut people off," as it were, for as long as the particular operation lasts. This procedure can be seen as a way of eliminating potential witnesses, less drastic in its consequences than the Mafia's basic method. This state of "suspended animation" has been reported by UFO investigators in widely differing situations, and with varying numbers of abductees involved. In a Florida case, for example, two people were abducted from an automobile while three other passengers were apparently "switched off." In a 1975 North Dakota case, two were abducted while the third was maintained in the suspended state. The details may change but the method remains the same.[2]

So what really was the purpose of this visit to the cabin in Rough River State Park? Even under hypnosis Kathie did not recall anything suggestive of a conventional UFO abduction experience. The focus of this strange event seemed to be her relationship with the apparently normal blond man who so resembled her, and their "conversation" together. But there is something of a sequel to this encounter involving not Kathie, but her friend Nan.

One evening during the winter of 1982, Nan and Sam, now married and parents of two small children, were at home watching television. During a commercial Nan went into the kitchen for a drink of water. She pulled the cord on the fluorescent ceiling light but it did not go on immediately. She was standing at the sink, facing the kitchen window, and suddenly she went cold with fear. Only a few feet outside stood a tall figure, staring at her. He was dressed in a kind of long, tight-fitting coat, and on his feet he wore what Nan referred to as "moon boots"—heavy, rounded plastic footgear. He simply stared at her, unblinking. After a few seconds the ceiling light went on and she could no longer see the man. She raced into the living room in something close to panic, and she told me that it took her a few moments to get words out to inform Sam of the man standing right outside the kitchen window. At that time Nan and her husband owned a beagle which notoriously barked at any sound or movement, however faint. The backyard was completely fenced in with high mesh broken only by two conventionally squeaking gates: The dog never made a sound. Sam rushed outside with the beagle. There was fresh snow on the ground, but no sign of either the intruder or any footprints. Nan later told me that the man seemed to be looking at her from close to eye level, which would have meant that he was either phenomenally tall or was not on the ground at the time. Naturally, one does not know what to make of a bizarre report such as this; it happened so quickly that I suppose Nan's eyes could have played tricks on her, as they say. I don't know what to think except that I believe she was genuinely terrified. "Budd, I called the police, I was that scared. And I've never called the police before in my life." When I visited her house for a reenactment of the incident, it appeared to me that the figure was only perhaps seven or eight feet away from her, as she stood nearly paralyzed with fear at her kitchen sink. Other things Nan has said to me suggest that there may be a few more experiences like this in her life, experiences of which she has so far only the barest of memories. A question, then, arises: were Kathie and her best friend Nan perhaps *both* central to the purposes, whatever they were, of the 1975 visitation at Rough River State Park?

One of the main reasons for my various trips to Indianapolis was to interview anyone who might have been a witness to the original June 30, 1983, UFO landing on the Davises' property, the incident which led Kathie to contact me in the first place. Joyce Lloyd, the next-door neighbor who had described the flash of light from the direction of the Davises' backyard and the subsequent power outage and other attendant events at her house, was someone I was especially eager to meet. Joyce turned out to be a very attractive young woman who seems quiet and reserved, with a somewhat anxious undertone to her general behavior. I was able to interview her on several occasions. A few of the experiences she recalls have been explored in some depth, with hypnotic regression, but several have not. The essential point, however, is that Joyce seems almost as deeply embedded in these strange events as the Davis family itself.

Joyce has a round, scoop-type scar on her leg extremely similar to those on Kathie's and her mother's legs; the origin of this scar, which dates from her childhood, is unknown. In 1981, Joyce was driving home from a visit to her mother's, and though the route was familiar she found herself becoming confused and disoriented. She remembers pulling off the road, but there her memory ends. She knows that when she finally arrived at home her phone was ringing; it was her mother, frantically worried about her. Whenever Joyce left after a visit her mother routinely called around the time her daughter should return home; this time she was over an hour late, with no explanation for the delay. There are still other very odd experiences in Joyce's background, but one in particular is of interest here, in the context of Kathie's camping trip encounter.[3]

In that 1975 Kentucky experience, Kathie described her three visitors arriving in a vehicle which had decidedly unusual lights. When I interviewed Joyce on one of my later visits to the Copley Woods, she told me about a strange experience she'd had in the summer of 1984. She had wakened in the middle of the night upside down in bed, alongside her normally positioned and peacefully sleeping husband. Her bare feet, which rested on her pillow, were wet, and the clothes she was wearing were also damp. She was cold, and felt very strange. She thought she had been dreaming, because she recalled lying a moment before in a field next to an automobile. She recalled that she had just seen a light rising straight up at the edge of this field, and "a second later" she awoke back in her bed. The experience had been confusing and upsetting; it had seemed very real, yet she knew it must have been a dream. But there was another problem; she did not remember having gone to bed that evening. And so, eventually, we began a hypnotic regression session to try and find out exactly what was dream and what—if anything—was literal reality. Joyce turned out to be an excellent hypnotic subject. Kathie and Joyce's sister, who was visiting, witnessed the regression which could be called, among other things, the metamorphosis of an automobile.

JL: I want to remember . . . why I was upside down in bed. It was odd.

BH: Let's go back to then, when you wake up upside down. Tell me exactly how you feel as you wake up upside down in your bed. What you're wearing, whether it's cold, how your body feels. How do you feel?

JL: I feel excited . . . and very anxious. *(Pause)* I had on a pair of shorts and a T-shirt . . . My body's damp and cold. My feet are wet. How . . . what am I doing here? I don't remember going to sleep, and I don't know why I wake up, except that . . . the dream . . . it had to be a dream . . .

BH: Tell us about the dream.

JL: All I remember is . . . I don't remember going to sleep, but I was laying in a field . . . and there's a car . . . there's a car . . . and it's silver. It has funny markings on it. I don't know whether it's a car . . . I think it's a car. I feel pinned to the ground. Laying on the ground.

BH: What are you wearing?

JL: My shorts and my shirt. I don't feel afraid.

BH: What are these markings on the car?

JL: Can't see . . . Black. Silver? It's very round, and long. I think it's a car.

BH: Is there a driver for this car?

JL: I don't see any people. *(Pause)* I don't know why I'm here. I'm not afraid. I know I'm dreaming.

BH: I want you to look at that field. What do you see? Long grass, weeds, what?

JL: It's dirty in the middle, like there's been a lot of traffic. The grass is kinda burnt . . . from the sun. There's tall weeds on both sides. There's tall trees, but they're far away. There's a clearing and a hill. And I see a light. All I remember is looking at the light. I see the light go away. And then I wake up in my bed upside down. I don't know about the car. *(Sighs)* This car has funny markings on it, and I don't understand why there's just me and the car . . .

BH: Or how you got there . . .

JL: I didn't worry about that, 'cause I think I'm dreaming. That's why I'm not scared. I know it has to be a dream.

BH: Well, maybe there's more to the dream . . .

JL: I don't know . . . I can't remember.

BH: We'll try a little experiment here. There probably is more to the dream that happened before the part with the car. You're going to see that part.

At this point in her hypnosis I suspected that there were other images and events which Joyce was reluctant to describe. This unwillingness to see is something I frequently encounter in hypnotic regression sessions, so I have had to develop a way around the problem. I ask the subjects to imagine a thick, black curtain, a two-section theater curtain, right in front of them. This curtain gives them safety, concealing them from whatever exists on the other side. I ask them to feel the double-thick black velvet, to experience its weight and texture. Then I tell them I will count to three, and at the count of three they will open the curtain a crack and peek out very quickly, closing the curtain immediately afterward. The device has worked just about every time. At one the subject reaches out and grasps the velvet; two, the grip is tightened and ready; and three, the curtain is quickly parted and closed. I used the curtain method at this point and at the count of three Joyce pulled it open and took a peek. I asked what she saw.

JL: Uhmm. (Sighs nervously) I don't know about the car. I think I want to see a car.

BH: What do you really see?

JL: (Long pause) I don't think it's a car. I haven't seen a car like that . . .

BH: Is it the same size as a car?

JL: Just bigger than a car. Not a lot bigger than a car.

BH: Silver, like cars are silver?

JL: No, it's kinda flat. It's not real shiny.

BH: Taller than a car, or about the same height, or shorter?

JL: It's longer. It's rounder. I didn't see the door.

BH: (Who is nothing if not persevering) Does this car have a driver?

JL: (Who is nothing if not stubbornly unleadable) I didn't see a driver.

BH: Is this car on any kind of road?

JL: It's on dirt, where there aren't any weeds or grass.

BH: Is this place close to where we are now *(in the Copley Woods)* or far away, or where?

JL: I don't know where this place is. I've never seen this place before. I'm not scared, and I don't want to know about the car.

BH: You said it had markings on it . . .

JL: I think that's why I think the car was painted with black mesh. It has a . . . it's hard to see it . . .

BH: Does it have windows, like a car has windows?

JL: No. The windows are high.

BH: How big is it in relation to a car? You said it's bigger. Is it twice as big as a car; half again as big?

JL: Maybe four times as big.

BH: How about the height . . .

JL: About three times . . .

BH: Three times higher. How do you feel you got out to the field by this thing?

JL: I want to think I dreamed it . . .

BH: Well, in this dream how did you get there? Did the dream just start there, or do you remember dreaming getting out there?

JL: Well, what about the dream I don't understand is I don't remember going to sleep . . .

BH: In your dream . . . you're just suddenly out there?

JL: Yeah. *(Surprised)* I don't remember going to bed!

BH: Let's take another tack. You're lying next to this object . . . how does your body feel?

JL: I feel kinda cool.

BH: Does any part of your body feel different? Unusual?

JL: My neck hurts.

BH: The back, the front of your neck?

JL: Along my spinal column.

BH: A sharp pain or an ache or what?

JL: It just aches. My eyes hurt. Like short, stabbing pain, like when you look at a light.

BH: How about the rest of you . . . your face?

JL: No. Everything's O.K.

BH: How about your chest?

JL: Feels heavy. I feel like I'm glued to the ground . . . like I couldn't move if I wanted to.

BH: Can you feel the coarse grass under you . . . is the ground right against you?

JL: I think it's just dirt. I just feel a hard surface under me. Just hard underneath me. It's dark. I remember seeing a light. I had to get here, somehow, though. I don't think I want to remember that. I don't think I want to remember how I got here . . . I feel anxious when I want to remember that. It's not logical. It doesn't make any sense.

BH: *(Reassures her: You're safe, etc. You can remember what you feel easy about remembering, and you don't have to remember anything you don't want to.)* About how you got there, you were either taken here or you came here of your own accord.

JL: I remember before . . . I remember walking in the hall . . . it was before . . . a different time. I remember seeing a fluorescent light. I remember thinking I saw something in George's *(her stepson's)* room. I remember seeing a face. But it wasn't a little person . . . It didn't have features like a person. There were eyes and a face . . . It was real bright. The body was luminous . . . the head was shaped funny, but it wasn't out of proportion . . . kinda square at the top and the nose was kinda . . . there were patches of shadow on the face, but the suit was luminous. And it was tall, like a person, and I'd seen the face before.

BH: You'd seen the face before?

JL: I think I had . . . and . . . have you ever felt something's watching you? I had that feeling. It was like a dream. I didn't want to believe it . . . I told myself "no."

BH: Why did you connect that face with the car?

JL: I don't know.

BH: Do you think that face was connected with the big thing in the field?

JL: I don't know. I'm not sure. I know I'm frightened of it. I don't understand it . . .

BH: *(Prepares to bring her out of the trance with reassurances, etc.)*

JL: There really aren't people like that . . . I don't understand . . . There really aren't people like that . . .

BH: Like the figure you saw in your hallway?

JL: People like this . . . are there really people like this? It doesn't make any sense . . .

BH: *(Reassures her again)*

JL: I'm not afraid of them . . . but I can't understand . . . I can't understand . . .

BH: *(You're safe, you're with your friends, you're a strong person who has come through this, etc. Pieces of this puzzle will come together and slowly you'll understand, etc.)*

I brought her out of the trance state, with these and other posthypnotic reinforcements, and then asked how she felt. "I'm O.K.," she said, appearing both relieved and puzzled. "Now I know what bothers me in not understanding it. It doesn't make logical sense to me, so I can't accept it . . ." This is a point of view I have heard dozens and dozens of times from people who have been through the same sort of experiences: Though it seems like it really happened, it doesn't make any sense. How can I believe it? And yet, how can I deny that it happened?

Tracy Tormé is a young man who has been involved with me in the investigation of several UFO abduction cases, including the Copley Woods affair. Tracy—whose father, the singer Mel Tormé, once told me of a very interesting UFO sighting of his own—has several questions he routinely asks in such situations. First, he asks the abductee if he or she feels he was selected—hand-picked, as it were—for the abduction. Every abductee he has spoken to has answered this question with a definite "no." "I feel like I was just in the wrong place at the wrong time," or some such, is the typical answer, though most abductees feel that any subsequent abduction experiences they have had are deliberate, as if they had been somehow "tagged." Next, Tracy asks if the abductee, having explored his or her experiences, understands the purpose of the operation—has any idea why these abductions are occurring. Again the answer is a unanimous "no." Regardless of the specific images and quasi-medical procedures the abductee has recalled with or without the aid of hypnosis, no one seems to understand what it all means. Abductees like Joyce or Kathie almost always ask us, the investigators, to tell them what it all means, why it is going on. And I always have to confess the truth—I have no idea of the ultimate purpose of it all. Tracy's third question is the key one: He asks the abductee if he or she isn't somehow secretly glad the experience happened, isn't proud of the unusual status the encounter bequeaths. Every abductee answers more or less the same way: "I would give anything that this had never happened to me. It's caused me a great deal of fear and anxiety and uncertainty. And I don't really know what it means." Tracy's final question is the most ominous. He asks if the abductee feels, now that his case has been explored to a certain extent, that the experience is over, that he or she will not be again subject to an abduction. The answer here is a unanimous "no." Every single abductee I've ever worked with is sure that it may happen again. "If they want me, they can get me," is the general sentiment. One young man said to me that if his father were president of the United States, and he lived in the White House, guarded by the Secret Service, he would still feel that "if they wanted to pick me up again they could."

The truth that emerges from these answers is a simple one: Abductees are not "believers" in some religion of outer space, they are not seeking publicity or other rewards, and they are, at heart, confused and frightened by their experiences, which they regard more as a profoundly unsettling problem in their lives than as any kind of advantage. These abductees are neither paranoid nor suffering from delusions of grandeur; they are honest people who have suffered traumatic experiences they do not understand. A skeptic who knows next to nothing about the evidence (the two conditions seem to go hand in hand) once said to a friend of mine that "people who take UFO abductions seriously are cultists. It's really nothing more than a cult." I thought about that and appreciated his remark because it points up an extremely interesting fact: Cults, as for example the Reverend Moon's or Father Divine's or whatever, are all beliefs and no miracles. The UFO situation is the polar opposite: all miracles and no beliefs. The events happen, the landings take place, the soil is altered, people are taken, floated out of their homes or cars, incisions are made, samples are removed. UFOs have been photographed and tracked on radar; pilots and astronomers have seen them and various government agencies have investigated these "miraculous" events. But what are the beliefs, the doctrines of this "UFO cult"? What is the faith of a typical abductee? I quote Joyce Lloyd, after she describes her experience: "I can't understand . . . It doesn't make logical sense to me, so I can't accept it . . . I want to think I dreamed it." In this strange, topsy-turvy world the skeptics, with their ideologically rigid ideas of what is and what is not possible, are the "true believers." The abductees, the people who have actually had these frightening experiences, sound like the true, baffled skeptics.

Joyce Lloyd's memories of lying paralyzed beside the large craft-like object in the middle of the field, her memories of the ascending light and the strange figure she saw in her son's room—all of these have echoes in other UFO abduction reports. When she first awoke and found herself with her feet on the pillow and her head at the foot of the bed, she wakened her husband and asked him what was going on. He had no explanation, as one might imagine, and asked her to turn around and go back to sleep. But the situation reminds one of other cases in which this sort of thing has happened. On October 16, 1973, "Patty Price" and, apparently, four of her seven children were abducted from their house and taken into a landed UFO. In Coral and Jim Lorenzen's account of this event, hypnotic and normal recall by three of the principal abductees details what happened that night.[4] Relevant to Joyce Lloyd's situation, however, is one particular detail: Three of Patty's children awoke in the morning to find themselves in different locations than they had been in when they went to bed the night before. No one was literally upside down, but it is clear that when the Price children were returned by their abductors there was a certain degree of carelessness about who was put into which bed.

The damp condition of Joyce's shorts and shirt, suggesting that she had indeed been lying down outside on dewy grass, and her wet feet, which suggest she had walked there, have their parallel in the Sandy Thomas abduction I described in Chapter 2. Sandy recalled what she—like Joyce —hoped at the time was only a realistic dream. She remembered that a tube of liquid had been inserted in her ear as part of what seems to have been an implant operation, and when she awoke, she found that her hair and neck were inexplicably wet—wet enough to have dampened her pillow. Her husband, like Joyce's, confirmed these odd physical details. For that matter, Kathie's UFO "dream" experience apparently involving a gynecological examination had a strange physical aftermath—she had gone to bed wearing her panties, but in the morning found them lying neatly outside the covers on top of the bed.

The reader may by now feel somewhat overwhelmed by the different cases I've alluded to, by the different names and locations and experiences I've mentioned, a reaction which is both understandable and almost unavoidable. But the pattern I've been dealing with in this chapter is rather simple. Two people besides Kathie are the central figures—her best friend Nan and her next-door neighbor Joyce. As detailed in Chapter 2, Joyce was involved in Kathie's original June 30, 1983, backyard experience as a witness; she saw the the flash of light from the Davises' yard when the UFO presumably took off, she heard the sounds, suffered a power outage at her home, and was apparently prevented in some way from calling the Davises to see if they were safe. (Her hypnotic recall of this experience is offered as Appendix C). So Joyce is both peripherally involved in one of Kathie's abductions, and apparently an abductee in her own right. Nan, Kathie's best friend, shared with Kathie the 1975 Kentucky cabin incident with the three mysterious visitors, yet with the staring figure in her backyard, Nan also seems to have her own personal involvement with the phenomenon. Kathie Davis may be the hub of this complex series of events, but even away from her, her friends and neighbors are far from immune from contagion.

One of the many variants in UFO abduction accounts is the degree of amnesia one finds among the witnesses. The spectrum is as broad as one can imagine, ranging from some people who remember nearly everything at the time, the way one remembers a mugging or an accident, to some who remember almost nothing. Hypnosis, our most useful technique for breaking through these memory blocks, also varies from case to case and individual to individual in its strength and efficacy. Psychologists have noted how often the human mind seems able to deal out traumatic recollections a little at a time so that consciousness is not swamped by too many suddenly disturbing memories. This built-in self-protectiveness is something I've noticed frequently in UFO abduction cases. My feeling is that Joyce Lloyd's obviously fragmentary recollections of her experience in the field with the large craft-like object are a case in point. She was more comfortable not remembering any people—figures—"drivers" for the "car," nor any other events that night, nor, for that matter, understanding why she associated a strangely luminous face in her house with the experience. Lately Joyce's general health has been rather precarious, and I have no desire under the circumstances to press her into further recollections. The well-being of the abductee is of far more concern to me than the accumulation of yet more information. Moreover, I believe that Joyce has probably had a number of UFO encounters over the years, and when she feels strong enough and curious enough they can be looked into. And one thing is certain in the meantime—her memories are not going to go away.

6

The Saddest Day

Kathie's first conscious recollection of seeing a UFO—a flying something that neither she nor her friends could identify—was in the late winter of 1977, around the time she met her husband-to-be. As recounted in the first chapter of this book, Kathie told me that she and her friends "Dorothy" and "Roberta" had once and possibly twice sighted a strange flashing, darting light as they "drove around out in the boonies." Dorothy's boyfriend sometimes offered rather lame excuses when he broke dates, so every now and then she drove out to the countryside where he lived to see if his car was actually there in the driveway, or if something was going on that he might be concealing from her. Teenagers do things like this. I did, myself, when I was that age. It's an activity that lies somewhere between checking out one's paranoia and providing a teenager with something quasi-important to do to pass the time.

On my first trip to Indianapolis I met and interviewed Dorothy. She remembered one night in particular when they stopped the car to look at a dipping, leaping light that eventually seemed to come down to the ground. Kathie did not recall its ever having seemed to land, and in a few other respects the two women's memories did not quite agree. However, both were sure that on this occasion their friend Roberta hid on the floor in the backseat, too frightened to look up at the strange light, and both remembered that it was unusually late when they finally went to Dorothy's house to spend the night. But the clue that I should have noticed immediately was the fact that in retrospect both women felt the experience had been not only odd but for some reason very, very unsettling. One should always be attentive to any apparent disparity between cause and effect, between a seemingly innocuous *sighting* and an overly emotional reaction to it. Such disparities often indicate that the sighting was only the consciously remembered portion of a longer, possibly traumatic encounter.

It was not until Kathie's second visit to New York in February 1985 that I thought about looking into her experience "driving around out in the boonies with Dorothy and Roberta." So many other recollections seemed more important that for sixteen months I completely neglected this potentially significant three-witness event. On February 25 we decided to explore the first of what Kathie had come to feel were two or possibly three successive encounters in the late winter of 1977 and early spring of 1978. At the beginning of the hypnotic session Kathie describes driving with her friends, seeing nothing but cornfields all around, and then noticing a small, moving light. I ask how she feels as she drives along.

KD: Well, I'm not afraid, 'cause Dorothy and Roberta are here. But I don't really like this. It feels funny. It's just so dark and there isn't anybody else around, and it's just kinda spooky. I feel kinda creepy . . . but it's not . . . it's just sorta . . . in the back of my mind. We're talkin' about Tommy . . . just trying to think of what we're going to do after we cruise Tommy's house and see if he's home . . . where he should be. So it's a little after two o'clock in the morning and the places we can go to are closed, and we couldn't get into a bar . . . and we don't have any money, but we'll find something to do. I just keep lookin' around . . . I look out the window . . . watchin' . . . I'm watchin' this. They're talking and I just watch . . . *(Long pause)*

BH: What's happening now, Kathie?

KD: *(After a long pause)* I don't know . . . I . . . I . . . *(Sighs deeply)*

BH: Tell me what's happening.

KD: Nothing . . .

BH: Are Roberta and Dorothy still talking?

KD: No . . . Just drivin' real slow . . .

BH: Tell me how you're feeling as you drive along.

KD: I don't know. Tingly. I tell Dorothy, "Look at that thing," and

Roberta looks at it . . . she leans over the seat. It's kinda to the east but now it's sorta ahead of us . . . sorta to the right. It looks like a . . . I told Roberta it's a UFO. Then me and Dorothy are giggling 'cause Roberta got all spastic. I don't . . . I feel fine . . . I feel excited about something. I feel all tingly and . . . anxious. I want her to stop, so we both can look. No one's around. I'm not scared. Just feel excited. I don't feel creepy anymore. *(Long pause)* We're just wheelin' down the road, driving along . . . real slow. Dorothy rolled her window down and she's sticking her head out . . . 'cause that thing is all over the sky now . . . It darts from east to west and west to east, right over us . . . and it gets bigger, but . . . it disappears . . . like a strobe light. First there's a flash in the east and then it flashes again, and it's west, and then it flashes again and it's right ahead of us, and it just passes over us, and it's getting bigger, and I'm . . . I thought it was an airplane with the strobe things on it, at first . . . 'cause it was far away, but it's not. I'm not . . . I'm not scared. I think it's . . . weird . . . but I'm excited over something . . . I don't know what. I want to get out and look at it. *(Sighs, then jumps as if startled)*

BH: What just happened, Kathie?

KD: I couldn't see anything. I don't know. It was like something lit off a flashbulb in the car, and now I'm really, really cold . . . and we're not moving anymore. And I'm . . . I can't *see* anything. I know I'm still in the car . . . I can feel it . . . but Dorothy isn't here. I can't see. Everything's just black . . . and I'm still not afraid. It just surprised me. I want to get out of the car, but I can't. My hand is on the door latch, but . . . I wish I . . . I want to get out. I can feel the plastic and the stitches on the plastic [upholstery] . . . but it won't . . . it won't . . . *(Long pause)* It's like I'm in the car but everywhere it's dark. Outside I can see the . . . cornfields and the sky. And I can't get out. *(Frightened and almost crying, then a long pause)* My . . . my back feels so stiff and I want to get out, and I can't get out . . . I can't move my arms, I can't move my legs, I can't get out. I can't move . . . I can feel . . . I can feel everything. I can breathe . . . I can see . . . I can think . . . and feel, but I can't move. My arms and legs feel cold and stiff . . . heavy. My hand is still on the doorknob and I can't get out. *(Speaking firmly)* It makes me mad, 'cause I want to get out! I don't want to sit in here by myself! I want to know where Dorothy is, and I don't know if

> Roberta's here or not, 'cause I can't turn my head to see if she's
> back there. But I can see from my side that Dorothy isn't here.
> I don't even know if I can talk. But I'm not afraid, I'm just mad.

During this part of her experience Kathie seems to be in the switched-off state of suspended animation that is so frequently encountered in UFO abduction accounts. Her rather precise description is extremely similar to literally dozens of others. For example, in a 1975 case alluded to earlier, two people were abducted from an automobile while the third was held in a state of "suspended animation" in a field nearby. Under hypnosis the young woman described her experience this way: "Something . . . was holding me back . . . a force . . . it wouldn't quit holding me. It wouldn't let me move . . . I'm just stuck there . . . just an invisible force." She was asked what she could see around her as she stood paralyzed. "Just open space . . . I was standing in a field and I couldn't move . . . I just stayed there until they let the force go," and she added, "I was alone."[1] Like Kathie, she could see, she was conscious on some level, but she had no freedom of movement. She had been effectively neutralized.

From what follows, as well as from remarks Dorothy made to me during our interview, I assume that both women were abducted that night—taken aboard the now landed UFO—and that they were taken separately. My guess—and it is only a guess—is that Kathie was taken first, perhaps moments after the flash of light inside the car, and then was returned to the car and frozen in place. At that point Dorothy was abducted and later returned to the road. Consciousness was reinstated for both, and Kathie got out of the car to look at the now disappearing light. There is no reason to believe that Roberta was taken, since she apparently has never had troubling memories about that event, and in fact barely remembers it at all. Perhaps she lay on the floor in the backseat of the car through it all, maintained in a slightly deeper state of suspended animation than either of her friends. Kathie's hypnotic recall continues after a pause:

KD: I can see. Cornfields and sky.
BH: Are you looking through the windshield?
KD: Yeah. *(Sighs)* I get out of the car.
BH: You can move again?
KD: Yeah. I'm gonna get out of the car and watch. It's just standing there, and I ask Dorothy if she can still see it, and she's telling me it's gone.

BH: What is "it"?

KD: It's a light.

BH: Kathie, I'm confused. Has Dorothy been standing outside? Where is she when you get out?

KD: I get out and she's standing by the front of the car, in the road, and she's just watching the sky. I come up and stand next to her, and I asked her if she could see it, and she said it was gone. So we got back in the car. Roberta gets up out of the backseat, and she asked if it's gone, and we told her yes. We just drive . . . and I'm feeling funny . . . watching the sky.

BH: What time is it, Kathie?

KD: I . . . the next time she looked at her watch we were in town and we'd probably driven ten minutes, and it was about four-thirty. It was about fifteen after four. Huh.

BH: What's that mean?

KD: 'Cause when we looked at her watch she said, "Time flies when you're having fun." I don't know . . .

BH: Didn't you tell me it was two-something a short time ago?

KD: Yeah, 'cause we'd just come from the pizza shop, and she got out at one, and we were going to see if Tommy was where he was supposed to be. I don't know . . . I don't know why I sat up so long . . . It didn't seem so long . . . It only seemed like about five minutes. We're not tired . . .

At this point in the hypnosis I suggested that we backtrack to the moment when Dorothy first stopped the car to look at the UFO. I told Kathie to concentrate on that time, as she watched the darting, strobe-like light.

KD: I was doing what you said and it was darting around, and . . . I don't know, I saw something black. It was funny . . . right over the top of the car . . . The sky was dark but this was darker, and it was big and long . . . and it . . . I can't describe it. I've never seen anything like that before.

BH: Is it as big as the car?

KD: Yeah. It's bigger.

BH: Does it have a particular shape to it?

KH: No. It was just . . . it was like a black cloud. Kind of rounded, curving . . . puffs or something, I don't know, I can't describe it. It's just real big and looks like a black cloud that's kind of curved.

BH: Do you have the feeling that Dorothy, when she looks up, can see it too, or is it just you? Are you looking up through the windshield or are you looking out through the window?

KD: I'm looking up through the windshield, but I don't have to go very far up. I just grab hold and lean forward, 'cause it's kinda coming up towards the car from ahead of us, over the top of us. And it's so fast. It's just all black . . . and it's not light anymore.

BH: You said before that you felt a tingling and felt that you had trouble moving. Is that part of what's happening now, or hasn't it happened yet, or what?

KD: It hasn't happened yet.

BH: Let's continue with this. Does the black cloud come towards the car from the front? Am I right about that or wrong?

KD: Right.

BH: So now what happens?

KD: There's a flash.

BH: Is that the flash you said was inside the car? Like a flashbulb?

KD: *(Softly)* Yes.

BH: It wasn't from outside?

KD: No.

BH: Inside the car. I'm trying to keep the details together so that I can follow the story. What's happening now, Kathie?

KD: It's . . . *(Moves around as if in pain)* I don't like it. I just don't want . . .

BH: *(Calms her: You're very safe, etc.)*

KD: *(Crying)* I just don't like it. It makes my stomach hurt.

BH: What makes your stomach hurt, Kathie?

KD: I don't know. I don't know. I just . . . I can't move, and it feels like I'm being squeezed, and I just don't want it. *(Moans in obvious pain)* It feels like my legs are being pulled off my body . . . from the waist down.

BH: Are you sitting in the car while this is happening, or . . .

KD: I don't know. Yes. No. *(Moans)* I'm laying down . . . *(shivering, moaning)* . . . I'm laying down but my legs are floating. I feel like I'm being pulled really hard. And I just . . . I don't like it . . . I feel like I'm just being pulled. But it doesn't hurt . . . it's just too . . . weird. *(Sighs)*

BH: What's doing the pulling?

KD: I don't know. Nothing's touching me. It's just like my legs are . . . all metal, and a big magnet's pulling me. I can feel the pull everywhere . . .

BH: It doesn't hurt?

KD: No, but I don't like it.

BH: What can you see while this is happening?

KD: Black.

BH: Are your eyes closed?

KD: Yes.

BH: Do you want to see?

KD: No! If I don't look I won't be so scared . . . I'm hot from the waist down and cold from the waist up, and my . . . *(Sighs, moans "Ooh")* I feel like I have . . . *(moans)* . . . I feel like I'm getting one of those gyno- . . . those . . . somebody . . . I got the cramps really bad . . .

BH: All right, Kathie, that will pass. That will pass. It's in your gut?

KD: In my . . . where my uterus is, down low, like I'm going to have my period . . . *(Moans)* It's hard, it hurts. It's like a toothache . . . a lotta pressure . . . Oh! . . . oh, it feels like someone's pushing on me *real hard* . . . wiggling and pushing, right in there. *(Sighs in pain)* Ooh!

BH: When you say it feels like somebody, do you feel hands or do you feel just a general pressure, or what?

KD: It's like a finger.

BH: A finger. On your abdomen or in you?

KD: It's . . . it feels like it's in me. *(Groans)*

BH: In your vagina, or where?

KD: No. In my . . . real low. *(Sighs)* . . . Right above my . . . bladder and stuff. Just right in there. *(Sighs)* It feels real tight. *(Now whispering)* I can't move.

BH: What position are you in while this is happening, Kathie?

KD: I'm laying down. It's just . . . it stopped.

BH: You said you were cold from the waist up and hot from the waist down?

KD: Yeah. Kinda burning sensation from the waist down. Can't move.

At this point it is evident that the gynecological part of the examination is over, and whatever caused the pressure in the area of her uterus—the "wiggling and pushing right in there"—has been withdrawn. The only remaining discomfort in that area is a generalized burning sensation. I ask Kathie what kind of clothing she is wearing during this ordeal, and after a moment she replies that she doesn't know but she can describe how it feels: "Soft . . . silky . . . slippery is a better word . . ." I ask how about her general condition, now that the pressure has stopped. She sighs and says, "I feel real flat."

But suddenly there are new sensations:

KD: Now I feel the same thing in my side . . . and on my chest. Under my right breast, a little further right . . . a sucking sound, a vacuum, I can hear, like a straw at the bottom of a glass.

BH: Do you feel it or hear it?

KD: I feel pressure on my side, but I hear that. I don't feel any pain. *(Sighs)* . . . Very vague . . . *(Sighs deeply)*

I was very interested in finding out what Kathie could see in this situation, though she was still unwilling to open her eyes and look around. It seemed an ideal time to employ the curtain trick, so I explained what we were going to do. At the count of three Kathie pulled the imaginary curtain open and took a peek. I asked her what she saw.

KD: A room.

BH: Tell us some of things you see . . . Is there any furniture in the room, doors and windows, lights? You got a good look. No one saw you . . .

KD: I don't know what you call them. I don't know what they are. A railing . . . with stuff on it. I don't know . . . I don't know. *(Sighs)*

BH: Railings are often connected with balconies and stairs and things like that. Are there any stairs or balconies there?

KD: Sort of like a balcony, but I don't know what it is. The railing has . . . handles . . . I don't know. They look like handles, and a hole in the wall with a thing that sticks out of it and smooths down to where you stand, and . . . *(Sighs)*

BH: Are you alone in this room or do you see your friends, or what?

KD: I don't know. I'm sitting on something, now. There isn't anybody here but me . . . It's light, but I don't see any lamps. I think there's a doorway but it doesn't have a door and it just kinda curves . . . out into something else . . . It's kinda weird . . . I'm just getting real tired. I want to lay down. *(Long pause, sigh, agitation)*

BH: What's happening, Kathie? Something happened. Tell me what it was. You're safe here with your friends. Tell me what's happening . . .

KD: *(Softly)* Someone talked to me. There's somebody in here besides me, and I don't want to look. If I don't look I'll be all right.

BH: You're all right now, Kathie, you're safe.

KD: No. I'm not safe.

BH: *(Calms her)* Tell us about whoever this was who came in there
with you.

KD: I think they were there all the time and I just didn't see 'em.

BH: What did they look like? Who are they?

KD: I don't know! I don't want to . . . I don't see 'em. I heard 'em.

BH: What's happening, Kathie?

KD: I'm just lying there with my legs up . . . they're just up on a step.
I'm lying down.

BH: But your legs are on a higher level than your body?

KD: Yeah. Feels good. They just told me to rest. *(Sighs deeply)* I'm
done.

I ask Kathie what she means, and she just repeats the sentence "I'm
done" with the implication that some sort of physical operation is over
with, finished. I ask her to describe the people in the room with her, and
again she refuses to open her eyes and look, and so again we use the curtain
device. After she peeks out I inquire about what she sees. "It's just him
. . . It's the same face." As she will explain when the hypnosis is over, it's
the same gray-faced small figure she'd seen before, but right now she
wants to wake up and end the session. She sighs deeply, and when I ask
what happened she answers, "Nothing. Go ahead. I don't want . . . any
more . . ." Her voice is sad and resigned as I begin the countdown to bring
her out of the trance state.

Usually when I conduct a hypnotic regression session I try to have a
third person present as an observer, and in this case a woman named
Rosemary—an abductee herself—was there watching the proceedings.
After Kathie was out of the trance state, she talked with the two of us
about her recollections. She had felt very "crampy" and was sure that
something had penetrated her uterus. Having another woman present—
and Rosemary is a good and sympathetic listener—made it easier for
Kathie to speak about her experience. There was nothing pleasurable
about it whatsoever, nothing erotic. She had been penetrated by a probe
of some sort that she felt had gone deep inside her. The pressure she felt
was very real, as were the burning sensations. She had no idea what to
make of the experience except that she had no intention of ever undergoing such an operation again, either in reality or in hypnotic recall. It had

been very unpleasant. Reviewing what she remembered, this seems to be the sequence of events: First there is the flash of light and she finds herself lying down on some kind of table or platform. Her stomach hurts and her legs are being pulled away from her body. Refusing to open her eyes, she next describes a kind of gynecological operation that causes cramplike sensations and a firm, probing pressure in the region of her uterus. The pressure comes from something with a fingerlike diameter, but it is apparently removed to be followed by a burning sensation "from the waist down." Next, shifting higher up her body to her chest, she feels a similar pressure and hears the sound of suction, "like the sound of a straw at the bottom of a glass." The arena in which this is happening is an evenly lit, relatively featureless place with some kind of railing around it. She lies back feeling very tired, with her legs elevated above her body, and at the end sees a small, gray-skinned figure with big eyes, perhaps the same one she remembers from other encounters.

One of the things I had been doing in researching Kathie's ongoing series of strange experiences, whether overtly UFO-connected or not, was to keep a chronological record of these experiences as they might intersect with other significant events in her life. According to both Kathie's and Dorothy's reckoning, this particular UFO encounter occurred in late 1977, around the time that Kathie, at age eighteen, started to date her husband-to-be. Thus the date of her first pregnancy and the date of this UFO experience are within the same narrow time frame. As recounted in Chapter 3, Kathie discovered that she was pregnant in early 1978, and as a result the date of her wedding was moved up from late spring to April. Pregnancy was confirmed by both urinalysis and a blood test; there was no doubt about that fact in either her mind or the mind of her doctor. But then, as the reader will remember, in March Kathie had a completely normal menstrual period, underwent a second pregnancy test, and discovered that she was no longer pregnant. She was distraught, and her doctor was clearly somewhat mystified. "I don't know what happened," he told her. "I think we'd best just forget about it."

Kathie told me one afternoon about that discovery. "I had a normal period, not even as heavy as I sometimes have. I *knew* I'd lost the baby. My mom said that sometimes you do have a light period or spotting or whatever and can still be pregnant, but I *knew* I wasn't. Dorothy was going to Planned Parenthood that day to get fitted for a diaphragm, and I went with her. They have free pregnancy tests. When she went in, I went in to have the test, but I knew what it would show. Roberta was with us. I got done before Dorothy came out, and when we got in her car I got in the back, and I couldn't stop crying. I kept saying, 'They took my baby . . . they took my baby,' and I cried so hard they didn't know what to do with me. But I knew somebody took my baby."

I was aware that Kathie felt she had had at least one other UFO experience during that same time period, but I looked forward to exploring it with a certain amount of dread. She mentioned one day that she had had some very strange feelings one time when she was baby-sitting for her sister Laura. As frequently happens with subjects once they begin the process of hypnotic regression, Kathie's buried memories began coming to the surface consciously, spontaneously, without hypnosis being necessary. Often these memories were only fragmentary, but they nevertheless provided new information and specific areas for more in-depth hypnotic exploration. It was not until October 1985, however, during Kathie's third visit to New York, that we decided to act upon her intuitive feelings and explore the possibility that something had happened to her one night early in 1978 while she was at Laura's house. Hypnosis revealed a crucial, personally tragic event in Kathie's life.

As we set the scene, Kathie described feeling nervous and apprehensive. She was pregnant and not at her best to begin with, and the isolated, rural location of Johnny's and Laura's house always made her uneasy.

KD: The kids are asleep in bed, and I'm in Laura's room watching TV. I was talking on the phone to Eddie *(her husband-to-be).* I kept thinking that I . . . I never really saw anything but I had the feeling that somebody was watching me through the back window. And I was afraid it was a prowler in the house or something, and I got real nervous. *(Long pause)* I got real nervous and had to leave the room. I went and lay down on the couch and watched TV some more. I didn't feel it there in the living room—just in that bedroom. *(Very long pause)*

BH: After you go into the living room to watch television, does the feeling go away?

KD: Yeah.

BH: What do you watch on TV?

KD: *Bob Newhart Show.* Then *Mary Tyler Moore.* Reruns.

BH: *(Asks how her body feels, tells her she can experience her feelings exactly, etc.)* At the end of the evening, how does your body feel? How did it feel earlier?

KD: Tired. And heavy. *(Pause)* And tender. *(Very long pause)* I feel like someone's touching me. My eyes are shut. I'm still on the couch. It's really nice, in a way. *(Sighs. Nervously:)* Just when I first started to feel it I jumped but I never opened my eyes. And after a moment I wasn't afraid anymore. It's real nice.

BH: Where are you being touched? What part of your body?

KD: My face, stroking my face and my shoulder, real gentle.

BH: Like a caress?

KD: Just on and on. Feels good. Real tender. *(Long pause)* And they rub, somebody rubs the small of my back real easy.

BH: Did they turn you over, or did you roll over on the couch, or how does that work?

KD: I'm on the couch on my side. Facing the back of the couch. And they came up behind me, and then I jumped at first, but then I . . . in a moment I wasn't afraid. *(Long pause)*

BH: What's happening now, Kathie?

KD: Nothing.

BH: Being touched still?

KD: Unh-huh. *(Pause)* Feel kinda funny, but not bad. Peaceful, but tingly all over. Real warm and nice. Real tingly. Just . . . O.K. My legs feel funny. *(Long pause. Sighs deeply)* I feel like I'm being pulled apart. But it doesn't hurt.

The description Kathie gives so far closely echoes the beginnings of other abduction experiences she has undergone—the warm, comfortable feelings followed by a general tingling, and then, as in the 1977 "gynecological" experience, the sense that her legs are being opened. As in that hypnotic session, I ask a series of deliberately leading questions to see if Kathie's recollections have any connection with typical sexual fantasies. She resists my attempts to lead her in that direction; the experience seems, again, purely objective and clinical, a puzzling and real event rather than an erotic fantasy. I inquire if Kathie is still lying on the couch in Laura's living room, and she answers by saying she doesn't know.

KD: I can't move my legs. I feel . . . half numb . . . I can feel . . . something . . . big . . . too big . . . but it doesn't hurt.

BH: Where do you feel it, Kathie? The thing that's too big?

KD: *(Sighs, in obvious discomfort)* I feel like a flower opened up. *(Sighs)* It doesn't hurt. It doesn't hurt. No, not at all. I'm just . . . *(Pause)* It's too weird, it feels wide open . . . Too much . . .

BH: What feels wide open, Kathie?

KD: Me.

BH: Is it your torso, or a particular part of your body? What part of your body feels wide open?

KD: *(Sighs, followed by a long pause)* All my female stuff . . . It doesn't hurt. I can feel it, but I can't feel pain. It feels real . . . it feels good, in a way. It's strange.

BH: Does it feel exciting?

KD: No . . . just pleasant.

BH: Is there any sensation at your clitoris, that you're being touched there in any way?

KD: Not there.

BH: More outside, or more inside, or where?

KD: More inside.

BH: You feel like you've been opened up?

KD: Unh-huh.

BH: Do you feel like there's anything in you?

KD: Something very large.

BH: Does it feel like a part of a person, or an instrument, or what does it feel like?

KD: I don't know.

BH: Does it feel hard, or does it feel pliable, or what? How does it feel?

KD: It's just hard.

BH: Do you feel it way up inside you, or down near the mouth of your vagina, or where?

KD: All through it. Everything.

BH: While this is going on can you see anything?

KD: No.

BH: Are your eyes open or closed?

KD: I don't know. I don't know. I just can't see anything.

BH: Is anything said?

KD: No.

BH: Do you say anything?

KD: No. It's just so . . . unusual . . . it feels so strange.

BH: Kathie, you've had pelvic examinations. Is it like that? Or is it different? Or is it partly alike and partly different?

KD: Sort of . . . like when the doctor puts the thing in and spreads it real far. Only a lot wider. A lot more.

BH: Do you feel any kind of stretching from that?

KD: Yeah, my whole hips and everything . . . but it doesn't hurt a bit. I can feel . . . it's so odd . . . almost pleasant. *(Long pause)*

BH: When you feel this opening, in an almost pleasant way, do you feel there's any kind of movement, or anything that changes about it? Or does it stay exactly the same for a while?

KD: Stays the same for a while. *(Long pause)*

BH: Kathie, would you describe the feeling as sexual feeling, the way you feel when you're touched in a nice way, sexually? Or just more neutral, the way you might feel when you're getting your shoulders rubbed? Is there any way you can describe your feelings?

KD: *(After a long pause)* Slow. Gentle-like. *(Long pause)*

BH: Do you have any idea why it's happening, what the reason is?

KD: No. I don't really care.

BH: Are you still lying on your back on the couch?

KD: *(Voice very quiet, as if half asleep)* I don't know. *(Very long pause. Then:)* Something's not right.

BH: What makes you say that, Kathie?

KD: I don't know. My back is starting to hurt.

BH: Your spine?

KD: No. *(Groans, suddenly very upset. Starts to shake and then begins crying.)*

BH: Tell me what's happening, Kathie.

KD: No!

At this point I tried to calm her, telling her that the sensations would diminish, ebbing gradually away, but she was writhing about in deep and obvious pain. I asked her what was happening, where the pain was located, etc., but she was beyond words. It was a frightening moment, the worst experience she had yet had under hypnosis. Finally she regained her composure somewhat and answered my question about what she was feeling.

KD: Like I was being squashed . . . my stomach . . . *(Sighs)*

BH: Was it a sudden feeling?

KD: Yes.

BH: It was very painful, I guess.

KD: Even my ribs are sore . . .

BH: *(Calming her, saying the pain will ebb away, etc.)*

KD: *(Sighs, then moans softly)* It's . . . it's . . . it's . . .

BH: What were you going to say, Kathie?

KD: *(Softly)* I just want to scream.

BH: Scream from the pain?

KD: No.

BH: *(Sensing her agitation)* Why? What makes you want to scream? You should tell me, Kathie, right now, why you want to scream. You'll feel better later if you tell me what your feelings are . . .

KD: *(Suddenly, in a high, wailing voice)* No! *(Sobbing)* It's not right, it's not fair! IT'S NOT FAIR! IT'S *MINE! IT'S MINE! (Sobbing)* I *HATE* YOU. *I HATE YOU!* . . . IT'S NOT FAIR!

I guessed what had happened, and shortly after I brought Kathie out of the trance she confirmed it. They had taken her baby. I tried to comfort her, telling her that what they had done was cruel, that they had no right to do it, that she had every reason to feel deeply angry. Talking to Kathie at this moment, trying to calm her and yet helping her to vent her feelings, was as difficult as anything I've ever done since I first began to explore this bizarre and, by our standards at least, sometimes cruel phenomenon. Kathie continued to sob helplessly, her shoulders shaking and tears flooding down her cheeks. I began to speak about her sons Robbie and Tommy, and what lovable children they were. I tried to remind her that she would be going back home very soon, and that it would be especially wonderful to see her boys again. There was little more I could do but let her feelings take their course. When she had calmed down somewhat, I asked if they—those who had done this to her—ever told her why, ever offered a reason? She answered in a coldly angry voice: "No." I asked if she ever said anything to them, ever told them that it was cruel, that they had no right to take her baby. She spoke to me almost in a whisper, calmly furious: "I screamed it at them." Then, in a sad, ironic mix of incomprehension and profound personal loss, she added this: "And the fucker looked surprised."

7

Other Women, Other Men

There is no way for me to convey in these pages the emotional authenticity of the hundreds of letters and phone calls I've received and the interviews I've conducted over the past six or seven years of UFO research. I cannot attempt to do justice to the mystery and the pain and the confusion that I have heard from so many different people whose accounts are, at heart, so very similar. This book is being written partly out of this frustration, in the hope that in at least one instance the particular mind and voice and physical presence of an individual like Kathie Davis will somehow take on reality. But there are hundreds, perhaps thousands, of men and women like her who have also been through these bizarre, un-asked-for encounters. Each abduction presents a special and discrete mystery, and to some extent at least each is a personal tragedy.

A few months after the emotional moments I lived through with Kathie, witnessing her private horror and loss, I received a letter from a woman in upstate New York. Most letters or phone calls I receive are from stable, articulate individuals who almost always begin with an apology: "There's probably nothing to this story, but . . ." or "I hope I'm not wasting your time, but when I was about seven years old I had a strange experience I've never been able to get out of my mind . . ." Typically, one woman wrote with the hope that I or someone could help her lay to rest a particular dread. "I'm forty years old," she said, "and otherwise a normally happy wife and mother. But I've had to sleep every night of my life with a hundred-watt light on in my room ever since a recurring childhood dream about some small gray-skinned figures . . ." And so on. Some letters—very rarely—come from obvious psychotics, who are generally easy to identify, and whose stories rarely bear even a superficial resemblance to the basic UFO abduction scenario.

Occasionally I receive letters from those I believe are normal people who have had genuine UFO experiences—abductions—but who have been too overwhelmed to handle these experiences with any degree of balance or calm. Most of these writers, I feel certain, are sincere and essentially sane, but are now teetering on the rim of mental breakdown, trying to hold themselves together in the face of radically disorienting traumatic experiences. The letter I received in June, 1985, from the young upstate woman falls into this category. She seemed like a sane person on the very edge; a woman who had been through devastating experiences, but who was trying desperately to hang on and to find out what had happened to her. The letter had a powerful, pleading quality. She wanted —needed—help immediately.

"Andrea" had read my book *Missing Time*, and wanted to tell me about several "dreams" she remembered from her childhood which closely echoed incidents reported in the book. I called her that night and we talked, making arrangements to meet a week hence. She seemed sad, and honest, and deeply frightened. She said over and over again, "Please believe me, I'm telling the truth. You've got to believe me." In fact everything she told me seemed plausible, and firmly within the patterns of the UFO phenomenon as I had come to recognize them. Andrea had never been hypnotically regressed, but she remembered several childhood encounters as well as one very vivid recent incident, the pretext for her letter. About six weeks before she wrote to me she "dreamed" that she awoke in her bedroom with a small, gray-skinned figure standing beside her bed. The man she lives with was asleep next to her, but she was unable to move to alert him in any way. She was floated out of her bed, across a field behind her apartment, and into a UFO. Then, as she sat paralyzed on a table, the small figure pressed a long needle up into her nostril, causing her pain as it broke through at the top of her nasal cavity. Her memory ends there, but she woke úp in the morning with blood on her nightgown and the bedclothes from a nosebleed she had suffered sometime during the night.

Andrea also told me about a long, straight scar she has had on her chest ever since childhood. She recalled being very young, perhaps six years old, and lying on a table in a small, round room lit by an odd pinkish light. Her memory of this was not absolutely clear, but she recalls a small man doing something to her chest. These and other detailed recollections suggested to me the standard pattern of UFO abduction experience, though she found it more comfortable to refer to them always as dreams. In keeping with her desire for immediate help and my belief in the buddy system I have described earlier, I put her in touch with a young woman about her age, an abductee whose case had already been investigated. "Louise" spoke to her on the phone, and a few days later the two of us made the nearly three-hour drive to Andrea's upstate home.

She is a small, slender, pretty young woman who is obviously suffering from acute anxiety. Louise and I tried to calm her, to assure her that she was safe and that she should seek some kind of therapeutic help. It was clear that for Andrea to be able finally to talk to people who took her account seriously was of definite benefit, and she was noticeably calmer when we left than she had been when we arrived. Andrea is somewhat shy, so I left the room for a few minutes to give Louise a chance to talk to her as one woman to another—and also so that she could examine her scar. It is horizontal, about two inches long, and is located just below her left breast. In the course of their conversation, Andrea mentioned that in her recent "dream" a little gray-skinned man with shiny black eyes had also done something to her back, something that caused pain right along her spinal column. Louise asked her to hold her blouse up so that she could take a look, and was surprised to see a thin, red cut that ran for perhaps three and a half inches straight down the center of her back. It was faint but still visible, as if it were a recent wound that had almost healed. This cut—of which Andrea had been unaware—was, of course, a new and unexpected piece of evidence that helped support the accuracy of her other accounts.

I have been digressing here from the Copley Woods affair and Kathie's various UFO experiences for a very important reason: to suggest to the reader some of the other abduction cases I have looked into which also bear upon the theme of genetic experimentation. When I first began investigating the Kathie Davis case I assumed it was more or less one of a kind, but these later accounts effectively established it for me as all too typical. During my first phone conversation with Andrea I brought up the subject of her physical health. I asked about any anomalies, any odd, unsolved medical problems, and as I often do, I dragged a few red herrings across the trail. I mentioned heart and respiration and other deliberately misleading topics, but then I asked about any unusual circumstances involving pregnancy. We had talked quite a while before we arrived at this subject, but Andrea quickly announced that something odd had happened to her when she was thirteen. "Budd, I got pregnant," she said, "but I hadn't had anything to do with a boy at the time. I didn't even know much about sex. I was only thirteen. I just dreamed this man was in my room, and I was having sex with him. He was real funny looking. He didn't have any hair on his head and he had real funny eyes, not like mine." I asked if it felt like normal sex, and if they touched one another. "No," she said. "I couldn't touch him. I couldn't move. I just felt something in me, something sharp, and then my vagina felt like it was on fire, like my stomach was going to explode. I felt like I was flooded. And in the morning my underpants were all wet, and the bed was wet, and I felt all burning.

"And after a while my stomach started to grow. My mother took me to the gynecologist, and I was pregnant. I couldn't believe it. My father was furious and asked who did it to me, he wanted to get even. I told him it was a weird man in a dream, with funny eyes and a big head. And you know, Budd, the gynecologist said I was still a virgin. I still had my hymen." I asked how the situation was resolved, and Andrea said she had had an abortion. The year was 1971 and no one suspected anything but an all-too-normal misadventure, so undoubtedly the fetus was not examined. Dr. John Burger, director of gynecology and obstetrics at New Jersey's Perth Amboy Hospital, has been serving as my consultant in such matters, and he has told me that it is unlikely extensive medical records still exist. Fifteen years ago when this unfortunate incident occurred Andrea was only a thirteen-year-old child; obviously neither her physician nor her parents would have felt a strong need to preserve much information about this unhappy situation. At the present time Andrea is hesitant to bring the subject up either to her parents or to her former—now relocated—physician.

What is most significant in this context is the similarity of Andrea's description to Kathie's 1977 "impregnation" experience, an event that happened the night Kathie went driving out in the "boonies" with her friends Dorothy and Roberta. (See pp. 113–17.) Inside the UFO, Kathie described lying down with her legs elevated while something "finger-thick" was pushed into her vagina and on, it seems, into her uterus. Andrea felt that the probe penetrating her was long and hard and obviously of a diameter thin enough not to tear her hymen. Kathie reported feeling extreme discomfort from the waist down and a burning sensation; Andrea felt as if her vagina was flooded and "on fire." Both Kathie and Andrea sensed that they were paralyzed and unable to move throughout the early part of their experiences. Each recalled the presence of a man with "big eyes and gray skin" ostensibly responsible for the operation. Neither woman reports anything that can remotely be described as erotic or pleasurably sensual; the weight of both accounts suggests a straight medical procedure, an artificial insemination the purpose of which we can only guess. The basic difference between these two situations, it would seem, lies in the fact that the fetus in Andrea's case was aborted by a physician before it could be removed by UFO occupants during a second abduction.

A third related account came to my attention in 1985. An artist friend of mine introduced me to one of her closest friends, a psychotherapist with a flourishing practice in a midwestern city. Susan Williams, as I shall call her, is married to a surgeon and is the mother of two children. She is highly intelligent, attractive and refreshingly self-aware. Susan had had a classic missing time encounter as a young woman in 1953, when she was a college student in Austria. Her memory jumps from the recollection of a huge light almost filling her field of vision but beneath which she could see the form of two booted feet, to a moment some time later when she arrived at a youth hostel feeling confused and frightened and unable to recall what had happened in the interim.

I met the Williamses at a small dinner party given by Jane—my artist friend—and her husband. Jane had read *Missing Time* and was struck by the similarity between the story Susan had told her years before about the light, and the events recounted in my book; thus she planned the evening for us to meet. Dr. and Mrs. Williams arrived late, and it was immediately obvious that Susan was extremely nervous. Though she had not read *Missing Time* Jane had told her its thesis, and it had obviously stirred up old memories. After drinks had been handed round and the requisite period of small talk had run its course, Susan began to tell me her story in detail. She looked as tense as one can be, and as she arrived at the point in her account when she first saw the huge light, she suddenly burst into tears, jumped up and fled the room. She returned a few minutes later, having composed herself, and finished her account. When I inquired about other earlier events that she might connect with this she told me about an incident that happened when she was about sixteen and living in Vermont. She had been driving one night alone on a country lane when she stopped her car and got out to watch a strange darting light. She is not sure how long she was out of the car, nor of how the sighting ended, but in answer to my question she said that she remembered getting home later that night than she should have.

This first meeting with Susan and her husband has led to an extended exploration of these experiences, both of which have turned out to be UFO abductions. So far we have conducted eleven hypnotic regression sessions which have helped fill in these two complex encounters (and two other previously unremembered experiences) in fascinating detail. The incident that concerns us here, however, is Susan's memory of what happened when she was sixteen years old and stopped her car to watch the strange, darting light. After the first few moments of wonder and surprise she began to sense a kind of communication between herself and the UFO, as if it were as aware of her as she was of it. And then to her utter surprise she felt herself rising vertically off the road, floating upwards in a gradually curving trajectory until she came to rest on her back on a table inside the UFO. She was relaxed and unafraid—a familiar enough detail by now—as a physical operation of some sort was begun. There were two occupants in the ship, slightly different from one another in both appearance and function. Suddenly Susan's hypnotic account became vividly physical as she described feeling two small clips being attached to her labia, spreading them apart, and then a thin probe moving up into her. She could not move, but she could sense the probe at or in her cervix, apparently snipping or cutting. There was no pain, only an odd sense of discomfort. She does not recall feeling any uterine contractions, but she somehow knows what the thin, double-bladed tool looked like, and afterwards made a sketch of it.

Susan recalled this operation during a hypnotic session I conducted when she made a visit to New York in 1985. A few days later she reported two significant new pieces of information. The year this abduction experience occurred—1949—she was dating a Vermont boy with whom she still occasionally corresponds. She decided to call him and ask if he remembered her telling him about her UFO sighting that summer. He said that he didn't recall her mentioning it, but he then reminded her of a UFO sighting they made *together* that same summer, which he discovered *she* had completely forgotten about (another apparent non-accident of memory). As he described the circumstances of this incident and what they saw together, some of the details began to come back, though vaguely, to

Susan's conscious memory. But most significantly, Susan told me that after her friend talked about this forgotten UFO sighting she had a dream about a thin probe being pressed up into her vagina, an experience that seemed entirely new and different from the earlier, hypnotically recalled "snipping" operation.

Because of this new dream's possibly symbolic content, it was important to know if Susan at sixteen, and her friend a year or two older, had had sexual intercourse that summer, and the answer, from a very honest, very liberated, very self-aware psychotherapist, was an unequivocal "no." The content of the dream was apparently not erotically connected with her boyfriend; instead, it seemed to have been triggered by her memory of their shared UFO sighting. Susan was a virgin at that time, and remained so for a number of years. Like thirteen-year-old Andrea, she was using tampons, so she could easily have been penetrated by a probe thin enough to remove a tiny fetus without tearing the hymen.

I realized that the time they both witnessed a UFO it was possible that Susan had been abducted along with her boyfriend and artificially inseminated during the encounter. If she subsequently missed a period or two she would not have been alarmed in the slightest, since she could have no reason to believe she was pregnant. Evidently many adolescent girls experience menstrual irregularity during the early, post-puberty years. Three more hypnotic sessions in the spring of 1986 confirmed my suspicions. There were in fact *two* 1949 abductions—the one we had previously explored in which Susan was taken alone, and another in which she and her boyfriend were simultaneously abducted. Though I have not yet established to my satisfaction that this joint abduction did in fact precede the one in which Susan recalled the "uterine cutting," her recollections of this experience suggest that it did.

In August of 1986 I finally met and interviewed "Al," the man who had been with Susan during their shared 1949 experience in Vermont. Three successive hypnosis sessions revealed the details of an abduction that took place while the two young people were on a hike from Stiles Mountain to a shelter near Griffith Lake.[1] A number of these details, such as Al's recollection of what seemed to be a jointed, metallic section of the UFO's landing gear, precisely repeated the description I had earlier received from Susan. She had associated their dual abduction with this same Griffith Lake shelter, and their accounts of how the experience began and ended, where they were standing when they first saw the craft coming down, and so forth, all dovetail perfectly. Their recollections diverge somewhat once they describe what happened inside the craft. Apparently they were dealt with separately, an aspect of joint abduction accounts that has been reported as far back as the Betty and Barney Hill case.

I must again make the point that details from this experience were not passed from Susan to Al in advance of his hypnosis. Nor in any of the "reproduction-focused" accounts we have been examining have the women exchanged information. None of the women have ever met or spoken to the others. Neither Kathie, Andrea or Susan has ever had a miscarriage, and apart from Andrea's experience as a thirteen-year-old, none has ever had an abortion. Kathie and Susan, as I've mentioned, each have two children, while Andrea, the youngest, is childless. Andrea recalled her impregnation as a "dream," but both Kathie and Susan only discovered their gynecological experiences when they underwent hypnosis. Dr. John Burger has listened to the tape recordings of Kathie's and Susan's hypnotic accounts and has assured me that everything they report —their descriptions of specific sensations and apparent medical techniques—seems clinically plausible and appropriate.

It is important to state here—though the evidence will be considered in detail later on—that all three women have either had "dreams" or normal recollections of having been shown, at later times, tiny offspring whose appearance suggests they are something other than completely human . . . that they are in fact hybrids, partly human and partly what we must call, for want of a better term, alien. It is unthinkable and unbelievable—yet the evidence points in that direction. An ongoing and systematic breeding experiment must be considered one of the central purposes of UFO abductions.

Early in 1985, through artist and UFO investigator Richard Thompson, I met a young woman named "Pam" who had had an interesting missing time experience when she was a teenager, driving to California with her mother and older sister. The details Pam recalled under hypnosis, when put beside her mother's and sister's suggestively ambiguous memories of the incident, form a substantial and coherent whole, an abduction case that has just begun to be investigated. Pam and her older sister recalled that their car had somehow overheated or otherwise broken down somewhere and her mother had left them inside while she went to get help. From then on their recollections get hazy, but under hypnosis Pam described a low, silver-gray vehicle arriving and at some point she is inside a round space; her memories then become those of a typical UFO abduction. But the details of this California experience and a childhood abduction that occurred when Pam was only five years old are simply too complex to go into here; the only reason I've brought up her case is because of its relation to the pattern we've been considering.

Pam was born in 1957. Currently divorced and childless, she is a slender, very attractive dancer, her profession apparently taking precedence over thoughts of marriage and family. I have said that whenever I interview someone I have reason to believe is an abductee I always make it a point to ask about that person's dream life, especially any recurring dreams from childhood that may have a bearing on the subject of UFOs. Pam told me that in 1980, when she was living in New Mexico with her husband, she had a series of nightmares including a recurring dream of a "silver train" coming down to get her, to pick her up and take her away. They lived at the edge of a golf course, rather far from other houses, and the isolation for some reason always made her nervous. The fear I sensed in her voice when she talked about that house and her dream of the big silver train, as well as certain other of her glimmering half-memories, made me feel that she may very well have been abducted at that 1980 location as well. Later in the interview I inquired about her health, asking the usual cover questions and then bringing up the subject of pregnancy: Had she ever had any unusual experiences in that area? Her answer was immediate. She had had an odd thing happen during the time she and her husband lived in the house by the golf course. For both personal and career reasons she was practicing birth control, but she missed a period and inexplicably found herself pregnant. Both urinalysis and blood tests were positive, and at that point she chose to have an abortion. When she went to the clinic for the operation she had been pregnant for about two months, and afterwards the doctor came to her with a worried look. He had found no fetal tissue, no sign that she had been pregnant. Not knowing what to make of the unusual situation he insisted that she go back to her gynecologist for further testing and examination, suggesting that perhaps she had had a tubal pregnancy. Pam told me that the doctor's demeanor made her quite uneasy, so she did as he suggested. All tests were negative; she was just not pregnant anymore, and yet there was no sign that she had had a miscarriage.

I am aware, of course, that odd things happen during pregnancy. People as well as animals have false pregnancies; in fact it is far from uncommon with farm animals. Ironically, according to Sigmund Freud's biographer Ernest Jones, even Freud's dog once had a false pregnancy! Yet physicians claim that urinalysis and blood tests, when paired and properly administered, cannot be wrong. Pam evidently missed two periods, and only later, after her abortion, did she have a normal menstruation. Her situation, seen beside Kathie's, Andrea's and Susan's, is at the very least highly suggestive. But as we shall see there are even more profound similarities.

So far we have been dealing with this issue as it relates to the female sex, but men have been far from exempt. In November of 1985 I received a letter from a Wisconsin man I shall refer to as Ed Duvall. He had read my book and felt that perhaps he had had a missing time experience in the early 1960s. On the face of it the incident he related seemed insignificant, but the tone of his letter nevertheless suggested a great deal of buried anxiety. Ed was a roving mechanic at a mine and often worked the night shift. After his first few hours of duty, when most of the routine work was finished, Ed would customarily drive off to an isolated area to park and catch a wink or two of sleep until he was needed next. Since there was a two-way radio in his truck he was accessible to anyone who called. Wisconsin winters are extremely cold, so the motor had to be kept running if the heater was to work. The truck drivers all knew they should park headed into the wind so that any exhaust fumes would be blown away; that way they would not be endangered by carbon monoxide asphyxiation while they slept. Ed described his strange experience in this way: He had been napping in his truck when

> I awoke completely paralyzed. I was wide awake, but the only thing I could move was my eyes. My first thought was that the wind had shifted and I'd gotten carbon monoxide in the cab. My second thought was to try to reach over for the radio mike to call for help. It was within easy reach but I couldn't move. It seemed like I lay there for a long time, but it probably wasn't more than a couple of minutes. The paralysis left. I got out and suddenly had an extreme urge to get away from there. I jumped back in my truck and hurriedly left that area. I never slept in that area again. To this day I don't think I've ever been back to it. This incident happened in between spring of 1961 to the spring of 1963. I had no headache or any nausea that you'd get from carbon monoxide. I'd completely forgotten about it until I read your book. Even now, to write about it makes my stomach uneasy.

That last sentence, in an otherwise calm and understated context, carries a great deal of emotional weight. My initial guess was that Ed's situation was like so many others I've known—an apparently insignificant surface recollection is accompanied by a very deep sense of anxiety and fear. As cause and effect they simply do not add up. Reading between the lines, I made a decision to phone him and talk a bit about his experience. Ed ended his letter by pointing out that he very easily "could have been away for two or three hours. If no one called me on the radio then no one would have known I was missing. I have slept in running trucks for many years and I can never ever recall being paralyzed like that any other time. I would like to find out if anything did happen."

I called him later that week, and found him to be a very ingenuous, very open man who seemed curious only about that one incident. When I asked him about any childhood experiences which he might remember in this context, he insisted there was nothing else—just this one odd recollection. However, he told me that he and his wife had once had a very interesting nighttime UFO sighting—a very dark, very large object at treetop height shining down beams of light at regular intervals, as if seeking something. On another occasion he and two friends watched at close range as a small silver sphere maneuvered near them in bright daylight. Both of these sightings, he pointed out, occurred after the truck episode, the one incident that really bothered him.

Ed insisted that he had no clear-cut periods of "missing time," no scars of uncertain origin, or any other sign of earlier UFO encounters. These negative claims are, of course, indications of his inherent honesty. If he had merely been interested in pleasing me he could have "remembered" a few odds and ends to make his situation more intriguing. Almost anyone can dredge up a mysterious scar or a half-recalled humanoid dream if one wants to impress an investigator. For this reason it's often worthwhile to pay out some line, raising one suggestive issue or another, just to see what gets taken. Ed took nothing. He was an obviously honest and straightforward man, and there was real emotion connected with his experience. He told me later, when we met, that because of the parallels he sensed between his experience and those described in *Missing Time* he had had trouble reading the book. "Several times," he said, "I had to stop reading and go into the other room because the tears came to my eyes and I didn't want my wife to see. The book really upset me."

A fortuitous invitation to appear on a television program in Minneapolis provided me with the chance to meet Ed only a few weeks after I received his letter. I was able to interview him at length and also to conduct two hypnotic regression sessions about his experiences. Ed is a handsome, gray-haired man in his fifties, and he's been married to his equally attractive wife for thirty years. They have children and grandchildren, and a very stable, conservative home life. He is still employed by the same company as he was over twenty years before when the truck incident occurred. Our regression sessions took place in the Minneapolis hotel where I was staying, and they were unexpectedly dramatic. In the first hypnosis, January 5, 1986, with his wife in attendance, we went back to the episode Ed had written me about. I set the scene and we began.

BH: Can you see the truck?

ED: Yes, I can see it.

BH: What color is it?

ED: Green.

BH: Tell me a little about the weather.

ED: Overcast . . . a little overcast.

BH: What do you do . . . where do you drive?

ED: I just go away from where all the action is so that nobody will bother me. And I don't want to be followed. *(Very long pause)*

BH: Tell me what's happening now, Ed. Have you stopped the truck or are you driving along?

ED: I park the truck into the wind. I get comfortable. The light . . . *(Begins to tremble, breathing rapidly. Extremely frightened)*

BH: *(Comforts him: You're safe now. It happened many years ago, etc.)* Just tell me about the light.

ED: It's just such a real brilliant light . . . *(breathing quickly, obviously terrified)* . . . real bright . . . it shines . . . right down on the truck. Just on the truck. Just . . . everything else is black.

BH: *(Comforts him again, assuring him he's safe)* What color is the light?

ED: Just a very, very bright, real brilliant, bright white light. I got out of the truck . . .

BH: Where are you standing when you get out of the truck?

ED: Right by the truck. I don't need . . . I wasn't afraid at the time. I was standing there looking at the light . . . *(terrified again)* . . . and all of a sudden I'm lifted up. I grab for the truck door but I missed it, and it's already too late. I'm too far above it, and I'm weightless . . . I'm floating up . . . *(Terrified and in tears)* I can't stop . . .

BH: *(Calms him, assures him he's safe, and that he can end the hypnosis anytime he wants)* What's happening now, Ed?

ED: I float. I float right up. Up to the light. The light's blindingly bright. I can see the truck clearly on the ground. I still . . . still the light shines on it, but everything else is black.

BH: *(Again calms him: You're feeling better now, etc.)* What are you seeing, Ed, what's happening?

ED: The door opens and they let me in. I only see two of them. *(Pause)* They help me over to a table. I lie down.

There was a long pause and I took the opportunity to tell Ed he wouldn't have to see anything for a while, that I was just interested in how his body felt. I instructed him not to answer right away, to concentrate on parts of his body as I named them, and to say "normal" if they felt normal, and to describe any differences if he felt any. I often use this technique when the subject appears frightened and confused at what he is seeing. It provides an interlude of relaxation—with his eyes closed, as it were—and it connects him with the reassuring presence of his own body. It also frequently leads to more information about the events he is experiencing. I began with his feet, and he answered "normal" to everything until I reached his torso, whereupon he said, "I'm sick. My stomach is sick." When I asked about his arms, he said, "Heavy," and said the same thing about his face, though individual features, eyes, ears, etc., were normal. After this somewhat calming line of inquiry I returned to more visual matters.

BH: Would you like to tell me, Ed, what these people look like? You said there were two of them . . . ?

ED: Not big. Small people. Shaped like people. Little. Round heads . . . pretty round. Slim-featured. Some kind of belt around their middle . . . around their waist, like a belt. I don't see any pockets.

BH: And there were two of them?

ED: Yes.

BH: *(Tells him to get a good look, because he will remember their appearance)* At some point, Ed, you get off the table. Does anything happen before you get off the table, or not?

ED: There's a bright light on the ceiling. I'm still on the table. They're just, they're examining me, I guess. I don't know what they're doing. They've got all my clothes off. They're looking at me all over. Ears, eyes, mouth, they look my body all over. They look at my genitals. They look at my feet. They look at my hands—how scarred they are. They turn me over. They look at my back. They look at my rectum. They look at my calves, on down to my feet. *(Pause)* It's cold in there. I feel chilly.

BH: Do they pay more attention to one part of your body than another, or is it all pretty even?

ED: They look at my hands. They're scarred and callused.

BH: Do you say anything or do they say anything?

ED: They don't talk. Not yet. They haven't said anything yet.

At this moment all of Ed's fear suddenly came flooding back, if anything more powerfully than before. I tried to comfort him, assuring him that he was safe, but he continued to shiver and hyperventilate as the tears flowed down his cheeks. I felt an enormous sorrow and a deep undercurrent of anger at whoever or whatever would subject a man to such terror. I asked him what was happening, and he answered, "I . . . I . . . I can't . . . can't . . . I can't . . ." He would not, or could not, tell me what was taking place. It was so profoundly disturbing that he simply could not describe it. I told him that if he wanted to, he could tell me about it later. At that he seemed somewhat relieved, and whispered, "Maybe later . . ."

After a few more words of comfort, I asked him to tell me what happens next. "They put my clothes back on. I'm all dressed. They tell me not to be afraid. I guess in a way it's not voice communication. I guess it's a . . . a mental communication. I don't think they move their mouths when they talk." A long pause ensues, and then Ed continues. "I'm back in the truck. I'm laying on the seat. I can't move. I want to open my eyes and I can't move." After another pause, he says, "That's it. I guess I'm all right now." And so I began the countdown and brought him out of the trance.

Our conversation afterwards—the debriefing—was lucid and fascinating. The first thing Ed said was, "There's something I can't talk about," so I knew that for the time being I would not question him about it. Significantly, he also said that at the beginning of his ordeal he had thought "not again," as if he were somehow familiar with this kind of experience. He told me that when he first saw the light and got out of the truck for a better view, he was amazed and curious. "It was too bright to look at. And I looked a second time and had to shield my eyes again, and all of a sudden, poof! I was weightless. I made a grab for the truck door and I missed it. Then I panicked. I started looking for tree branches but of course there weren't any there." I asked how fast he rose. "Not rapidly. The thing was only up fifty feet or so. Fifty or sixty feet." I recalled that he had mentioned a door . . . "An opening. It just opened up on the bottom as it sloped up the sides—a hatch. Two heads, two beings were waiting for me to come up through the opening." I asked if they said anything when he came in. "I don't think they talked to me at all. No movements or communication like you and me. The communication was like mental communication. It just doesn't seem to me that they cared much what I thought, what I wanted to know or anything. They just did what they wanted to do and then put me back in the truck."

I asked what they looked like. "They were about four and a half feet tall, I would say, and slight, slimly built. Seventy pounds, maybe, sixty pounds. Skinny. But the heads were disproportionately bigger than the bodies. And funny-looking hands." I asked about their skin color. "I don't know. I think they wear some kind of a . . . some kind of a covering over them. It didn't look like skin. I don't know what it looked like." Ed's description of their eyes was very familiar. "It looks like if you took the bottom of a black glass and put it over your eye . . . they had weird eyes, with no pupils. You can't see any white, any blood vessels. You can't see anything in the eye except that black thing looking at you. You can't really see into it."

I inquired if he remembered their undressing him. That harrowing part of the scenario is usually not recalled, a detail which suggests that the abductee is actually unconscious during the process. Ed's answer conformed with the pattern. "I don't remember them taking my clothes off and I don't remember undressing." "But you were suddenly naked and then later suddenly dressed?" I asked. He replied somewhat nervously, "I'd like to delve into that another time . . ." The final question and answer encapsulated my suspicions. I asked if there was any part of his body, other than his hands, that his abductors seemed specially interested in examining. His reply was immediate and succinct: "They had more than a reasonable interest in my genitals."

After Ed and his wife left to return to their room for the night I made a few notes, one of which said simply that a sperm sample was probably taken during the abduction. Ed's nervousness, his inability to discuss an obviously disturbing or humiliating feature of the experience, was something I had seen before in other cases in which that kind of sample was taken.[2] I sensed that he wanted to talk privately, and so I was not surprised when, after breakfast the next morning, he suggested to his wife that she should take some time off for shopping. He told her that he wanted to discuss with me certain other details he had recently recalled. Since she had expressed an interest in buying a few things for her family there was no problem, and the three of us made plans to meet later at the hotel for lunch.

As soon as Ed came into my room and sat down, I could see his profound uneasiness. He said that there was something he had to tell me, something that seemed impossible to believe. He spoke softly with his eyes lowered, and I sensed that he was having trouble deciding how to begin. "Budd, I never believed that a man could be raped. Functionally I don't think it's possible . . ." "But it happened?" I asked, knowing in my heart that this was the issue he refused to discuss the night before. "Apparently," he said as he sat slumped in his chair in an attitude of complete dejection. I still wasn't sure if by "rape" he meant a mechanical procedure of the type I had encountered in other abduction cases, or an actual act of intercourse. So I asked rather uncertainly, "Did it happen with a . . . figure or a person or a . . ." He replied quickly. "A female of the species, but she wasn't exactly like them. She was taller. She was built more like a human being. She had mammaries, but she didn't have any body hair at all. Her head was larger than a normal woman's would be." I asked what her head looked like. "It was bigger and rounded. But she had absolutely no hair. She didn't have any pubic hair, either." I inquired if she had a vagina, and he answered with a simple yes.

He was obviously relieved to be able at last to talk about his virtually unbelievable experience, so I decided to try to ease his mind further by showing that there was, in fact, a precedent for such events. I gave him my notes of the evening before in which I stated my guess that a sperm sample had been taken by artificial means. Ed lowered his eyes and said almost in a whisper, "It wasn't artificial." I asked exactly what took place. He answered confessionally, in short phrases, as if the whole distasteful subject was something he wanted to get through with as quickly as possible. "They had her in a different compartment of the ship. They brought her out. She didn't say anything. I was laying on my back on this bench and I didn't have any clothes on, and somehow they made me erect and she mounted me. It was very perfunctory." I asked if she ever touched his penis. "I don't recall her doing it unless she just inserted it. She rode me and she was on top of me until I orgasmed, and then she got off and left the room and the two guys, they took little spoons and scraped the leftover semen off my penis and took it in a sample in a bottle and kept it. I never could move. She or they came and just took what they wanted."

Ed paused a moment and then went on, trying to understand what had happened, trying to make sense of his unimaginably bizarre recollections. "At that time in my life my hair was thick and coal black, and I don't know if they told me or I just had the impression that they liked my coal-black hair, and they liked my . . . they like our features. They like our skin, and they like our eyebrows and they like our hair. Maybe they're trying to upgrade their own species . . . 'cause I think their species are ugly . . . but maybe they think we're ugly, too, but I don't think that. I think they think we're attractive, and they're trying to upgrade their own."

I inquired about the differences between the female and the two small figures. "She was at least a head taller. Her legs were thinner than us, but she had calves like a human. Her arms were fairly well developed and she had nice mammaries. But she had a narrow chin. If . . . if this is part of their attempt to change their species they're doing it gradually." "So she could be half and half," I said, and Ed replied, "Conceivably. She had a fairly nice . . . I don't know if she had a nice mouth or not. She had a mouth. She never smiled, she never said anything." He said that she had ears, though he didn't remember seeing ears on the two smaller figures. "Her eyes weren't like our eyes, either. But they weren't like the men's eyes. She had eyes like we have in the sense that we have eyeballs and pupils and the white. But the shape of them was different. They were rounder, like when your eyes are wide open. Yet she wasn't unattractive. I wouldn't call her pretty but she wasn't ugly. And I remember her breasts looked like any other. She was well endowed—she definitely had mammaries."

I wanted to know exactly how, under these bizarre circumstances, Ed had become excited enough to achieve an erection. Was the process mental or physical or was it unclear? "God, this is preposterous, but it seems they stuck like a vacuum device on my penis." He paused, and then spoke very softly. "I never thought I'd be able to talk about this, about being . . ." But he couldn't finish the sentence for the tears and the remembered helplessness.

A few minutes later Ed looked up and revealed a surprising irony about the situation. "You know, Budd, I'm sterile. They didn't even get any sperm. I'd had a vasectomy a couple of years before this." The previous night, just after he came out of the hypnotic trance, he mentioned that his abductors had seemed angry at him, and now I understood why. If anything about such a traumatic, horrifying experience could be considered even remotely humorous, this was it. They had abducted a man apparently for the purpose of using him for procreation, but the man they picked was sterile. "You said you felt their anger at the time," I said. "Do you think that they knew right away that you had had a vasectomy?" Ed answered instantly. "They knew before they put me out."

But our conversation now took another turn. There was something else he wanted to tell me about. He said that last night, just before he fell asleep, he recalled another peculiar image from his past. A few years prior to the incident in the truck he remembered a particular time when he had not been able to sleep, and for some reason he got out of bed in the middle of the night and wandered out to the backyard. He didn't know why he had done this or when he returned, but his behavior, he felt, was very uncharacteristic. He remembered standing there in his pajamas as if he were waiting for something. I explained that hypnosis had apparently opened his mind to still earlier repressed memories, and that this process was normal. I said that there might be more recollections, and that there may in fact be more to this particular memory. I told him that we should at least try to explore it under hypnosis. He was willing to try again, so that afternoon we had our second regression session.

I will not go into detail about what we learned. This earlier backyard experience took place in the late nineteen-fifties and was another abduction. The abductors emerged from the woods behind Ed's house; he could not move, though he wanted to try to fight them off. He was taken into the UFO, which had landed in a nearby clearing, and was placed on a table. A suction device of some sort was put over his penis and a sperm sample was taken. This procedure was very painful. Ed apparently did not have an erection, and there was no spontaneous ejaculation. The specimen was taken into another part of the craft, and after a few moments the small, gray figures returned and took a second sample. Ed begged them not to do it, his pain and humiliation movingly evident. His captors did virtually nothing to ease his suffering, and even returned for a third sample. Ed was left with a deep, aching sensation in the region of his pubic bone. His anger at his captors' apparent indifference to his suffering was consuming. "They take what they want whenever they want it, regardless of anything," he said. "They don't seem to care how we feel."

Remarkably, this same hypnotic session provided details of yet two more abduction experiences. One occurred when Ed was a teenager, and an even earlier encounter took place when he was a child about five years old. Since Ed was born in 1934, that means he was first abducted about 1939, years before the World War II "foo fighter" sightings and the famous "original" UFO wave of 1947.[3] There is an interesting coincidence involving this sequence of events. Susan Williams, the psychotherapist whose abduction I described earlier, was born in 1933. Chronologically, the first of Susan's several UFO experiences apparently occurred in 1938, when she, too, was five years old. Her second remembered abduction, the one described in this chapter, took place when she was sixteen, in 1949. Ed's teenage abduction he feels happened the same year—1949—when he was fifteen, so there are distinct similarities between their experiences, all apart from the fact that both seem to have been used in some kind of genetic or reproductive experimentation.

One of the major findings described in my book *Missing Time* was an apparent program of systematically repeated abductions of the same individuals over many years. The analogy mentioned earlier that comes to mind is our program of zoological study in which wild animals are captured and tranquilized to allow the permanent attachment of small transmitters or even simple tags before they are released back into their natural environments. The transmitters allow scientists to track their movements and thus to learn the species' migration patterns, grazing habits and other useful information. This analogy is obviously anthropomorphic, but it is nevertheless suggestive, especially since there is evidence that tiny implants are put in place in UFO abduction cases, as we have seen.

The transcript of Ed's childhood abduction contains many details which help to underline the authenticity of his entire account, so I will present it here. In Chapter 4 I described the childhood abduction of an Ohio woman I called "Margaret Bruning," an event that took place when she too was five years old, and which parallels Ed's descriptions and reactions very closely. One of the most interesting features of both is that each adult relived the experience with words and emotions appropriate to a frightened but intelligent five-year-old. Neither, at the time of the abduction, had any idea of UFOs, and so neither child had terms to describe the craft itself. At the outset of the hypnotic session dealing with an adult abduction experience, Ed said that it had happened before, so I asked him if he could remember when.

ED: I'm small. Real small. *(Very frightened)* About five years old, maybe. Real small. *(Breathing heavily. Very frightened)* I'm scared. I don't know who they are. They look awful. They're ugly. They're homely. I'm afraid of them. They're several of 'em. It's daylight. I don't know where my mother is. *(Crying)*

Can't find my mother! I call for my mother but she doesn't answer me. *(Sobbing)* Momma! Momma, where are you? Nobody answers. *(Crying)*

BH: Where are you, Ed?

ED: I'm just in the backyard, playing. They take me into the woods. *(Breathes nervously, and then speaks from his adult perspective)* It's the same guy! It's the same darn guy, that did it before. Now I remember him. *(Crying and shifting now back to the child's perspective)* Leave me alone! Leave me alone! Get away from me! Get away from me! I don't want you to do that to me. Leave me alone. Get away from me, I don't want you to do that to me. My momma'll be mad at you.

BH: *(Comforts him)* There's a happy ending, you came back in the house. *(Ed continues crying, unconsoled)* What are they doing to you, Ed?

ED: They took my clothes off and they looked at me *(crying)* and I don't know why they're looking at me. I don't know . . . I don't know where I'm at . . . I don't know where it is. I want to go home. I don't want to be here. I want 'em to leave me alone. I'm afraid *(sobbing)* and I want my momma.

BH: *(Again tries to comfort him)* She was there when you went home, so it's O.K. It's O.K.

ED: *(Sighs, somewhat relieved. He slowly gains control of his emotions.)* I tell my momma, but she doesn't understand. She doesn't believe me, she says I was dreaming. She says, "You had a bad dream." *(Crying)* I had a bad dream. She holds me and pets me and comforts me. I had a bad dream.

BH: Do you think it was a bad dream?

ED: It was a bad dream. It's all gone now. And the little men, they're gone. It was a bad dream.

BH: And you're feeling better, having your mother comfort you like that. You're feeling much better, much better.

At this point I could see that Ed was becoming more calm, so I decided to ask a few questions. I was curious to find out if the little men said anything to him when he asked them what was happening. I also wanted to know if they ever told him where he was, or if, for that matter, they told him anything at all. His answer was the same I have heard over and over from people describing childhood abduction experiences. "They told me to behave. They told me they wouldn't hurt me. They told me they'd bring me back to my mother when they were done. They told me not to be afraid."

I decided to check out any possible physical aftereffects, and in doing so unexpectedly recovered a significant new piece of information.

BH: Does any part of your body feel funny, or hurt, besides your nose? *(This remark reveals some confusion on my part. When Ed had relived his teenage abduction experience only minutes earlier he had described something being put up his nose and causing pain. I confused the two incidents, but immediately explained to him what I had done. His answer, however, led in a different direction.)*

ED: I cut my leg on the barbed wire.

BH: Where was the barbed wire?

ED: By the garage, in the backyard.

BH: How did you happen to cut your leg on the barbed wire?

ED: I don't know. *(Puzzled)* I don't know how I cut my leg.

BH: Where was it cut, Ed?

ED: On the lower left leg, above my ankle, on the back.

BH: I see. Does it hurt a lot?

ED: No.

BH: How do you know you cut it?

ED: It's bloody.

BH: Does your mom notice it?

ED: Yeah. She says, "You cut your leg, how did you do that?" I said on the barbed wire. She said, "I'll have Daddy take the barbed wire down and throw it away."

Knowing what he had just been through, and judging from past experience that barbed wire probably had nothing to do with his wound, I couldn't resist an ironic question about the cut on the rear of his leg. "Did you back into the wire, Ed?" He answered simply: "I don't know." I inquired about any other physical problems. After a pause, he said, "My nose is all plugged up." I mentioned the fact that that was to be expected because he had been crying. "I know," he said. "But it was all plugged up then, too. It hurt. They looked at my nose. They . . . they stuck something in there when I was little. They made my nose hurt." It had been a very long and emotional session, and I felt at this point that it had gone on long enough. And so, after a few more reassuring words, I began the countdown and brought Ed out of the trance.

The reader will by now recognize many details linking these experiences to other abduction accounts. But in this context there is one very interesting fact that should be mentioned. Ed, of course, had read *Missing Time* and after our hypnotic sessions he asked me a rather striking question. "Budd, I don't remember anything in your book about anyone just floating straight up like he was weightless into a UFO. I also don't remember anything about anybody reporting intercourse with one of them, like I remember. Most of what I remembered is kind of different. Have you ever heard of these things?" Good, honest man that he is, Ed was disturbed at how these central details of his account diverged from what he had read. I assured him that I had come across these two details in a number of cases. I reminded him that I had written my book years before, and since then had investigated many other UFO abductions. But I was naturally very pleased that Ed was not simply handing back to me exactly what he could have learned from *Missing Time*.

And then there was the business of the cut on the back of his calf. As I stated earlier, when I first talked to Ed on the phone I asked him if he had any perplexing, "unresolved" childhood recollections, periods of missing time, odd, recurrent dreams, and so on. I specifically asked, since he obviously knew about this aspect of abduction accounts from having read my book, if he had any noticeable scars on his body, the origins of which were mysterious, unexplained, and so forth. He had said no to all of these questions, and yet under hypnosis he remembered the cut on the back of his leg, a wound which had arrived painlessly and under suspicious circumstances. "Do you really have a mark on the back of your leg?" I asked him. "Not that I know of," he answered. "Can we take a look and see if there's anything there?" I asked. He raised his ankle and pulled up his trouser leg. And there it was, a thin, vertical, hairline scar, about two inches long, perfectly straight and regular, a mark neither he nor his wife had ever noticed before.

Just before I left to fly back to New York, Ed and I had a final conversation. He told me that it had been extremely important to him to have found out what happened the night he was taken out of his truck and into the UFO. It explained a personal mystery. "You know, Budd, I've had a good marriage and it's all gone very well, but there was a time there, around the time that happened, when my sex life went downhill, and I began to drink a little bit more than I should. I never understood what was wrong with me. It bothered me. But now I know." I told Ed that he had every reason to feel good about himself. Though he was a basically conservative, live-and-let-live working man from a small town in Wisconsin, he was demanding enough to insist on finding out what had happened to him all those years ago, and to resolutely search out the cause. It was a privilege to have become his friend.

Ed is not the only man who has had such an experience. So far I have been involved in the investigation of four UFO abduction cases in which men have described acts of intercourse with apparently "alien" females.[4] One of the quartet is a police officer, another a farmer, one a factory worker, and Ed, of course, is a mechanic. I have reason to believe that three other abductees I've worked with, a writer, an Air Force officer and a government lawyer, have also had such experiences. But the natural ability of the human mind to censor such sensitive material, to guard against humiliating recollections, may mean that these three, along with certain other men whose cases I've investigated, have simply not allowed that aspect of their UFO experiences to come to the surface.

In February of 1985 I received a letter, forwarded to me by my publisher, from "Dan Seldin," a factory worker near Cleveland, Ohio. His letter was not a flowing, literate production. It was, instead, a simple, desperate, impassioned plea for help. "Dear Mr. Hopkins," he began,

> This is very difficult for me to write about. It's like a great big mental block sets in for words. I and six other people some years back had a close encounter. I have reason to believe there was a time lapse . . . It seems also that I am remembering little things as time goes by. Let me tell you, sir, I feel like I'm going crazy at times and I get scared. Real scared! I don't like what I remember. Mr. Hopkins, please help me if you can. It gets harder to cope with . . . I've tried so many times to sit down and write someone who knows about these things . . . Something happened to me and six other people on a clear summer night. Two of these people I've looked up in the last two years seem to think there was a time lapse, too . . .

Dan's letter continued, pleading for me to reply and to help him. It ended on a truly desperate note. "I don't know what to do. Please answer me. This godamnned thing's been haunting me since I was about seventeen. I'm nearly thirty-two years old now and it hasn't been put to rest. It just increases. I'm really scared sending you this. Please help me if you can. I want my mind to be at rest with this. Please forgive my handwriting. I think it's the best I can do right now. I'm crying like a baby."

At the end of his letter he gave his address and phone number, and added a postscript asking for the matter to be kept confidential. "Please write or call. Something." He signed his name and at the bottom of the page wrote the single word "Please," underlined twice. I called him that evening. The incident he wrote me about is an especially intriguing one because of the number of people involved. It occurred, apparently, in the summer of 1969 in a rural area near Cleveland. Dan and his friend "Jeff," another seventeen-year-old, had taken an after-dinner hike into the woods with four young girls and one adult, the mother of two of the girls. On their way back, as it was getting dark, a huge light suddenly appeared at treetop height above a small clearing where they were walking, and at this point everyone's memories begin to fade. "Mrs. Warren," the adult on that outing, explained to me in a later telephone interview that the light was as big as a baseball diamond, that it was motionless above them, and that she never saw it either go out or leave. She is aware that somehow there is a period of missing time. One of her daughters had left the group and had gone on ahead to their house. As it grew later and later and the others did not return the girl became alarmed, and when they eventually arrived her questions underlined the fact of the time lapse. Mrs. Warren told me that the light had "lit up the whole woods." She had been so curious that the next day she returned to the clearing, looking for an explanation, and discovered a huge circle on the ground where the grass was "all dry and brown." She knows that that night "we seem to have lost an hour or so," and that ever since then she has been afraid to walk in those woods alone.

When I first talked to Dan by telephone, I found him to be a shy, intelligent, gentle person, and far more literate than his ragged letter style had suggested. He became the fourth person to come to New York to stay in my studio for the purpose of exploring his UFO experiences through hypnosis and personal interviews. He arrived in the middle of April 1985, only about two months after Kathie left New York to return to Indianapolis. Since another abductee visited between their trips for the same purpose, the studio hide-a-bed scarcely had a chance to cool.

Dan is a tall, handsome man, and the father of a young daughter. He has been divorced for several years and lives alone in a small apartment. His abduction experiences, which date from early childhood, turned out to be many and complex, and deserve fuller treatment than I can provide in this account. I will discuss here only those aspects which parallel the events in Ed Duvall's encounters. The 1969 experience, involving his friend Jeff, Mrs. Warren and the young girls, was the first incident we explored through hypnosis. It begins with a description of the hike and then the appearance of the huge, solid-looking light. Dan is the farthest away from the clearing, but he can see the others standing there as if transfixed, staring up at it. He feels paralyzed himself, and then he de-

Photographs of ground traces.
1. View of Kathie Davis's lawn taken about six weeks after the June 30, 1983, UFO landing.
2. January 1984, seven months after the landing. The melting snow clears first over the affected soil, which in its "baked," dehydrated state will not hold moisture.
3. June 1984, one year after the event.

4. August 1983 view showing the long swath from the presumed line of take-off. The night of the landing, Kathie and her friend Dee Anne walked along the gravel path at the far right on their way to the swimming pool. Dee Anne's daughter, Tammy, walked to their left, stepping on the affected swath. She reported that the ground was still warm and her bare feet tingled (see Chapter 2). 5. Contrast between control soil at left, taken from an area several feet from the landing sight, and the affected soil itself, right. Note the lighter color and hard, desiccated appearance of the affected soil. 6. The soil sample lab report shows the difficulties the testers had trying to turn the control sample into the pale, hard, desiccated chunks of the soil from the landing area. Both samples are the same chemically, verifying the fact that they originated in the same general area. Thus the changed color and texture of the affected soil was apparently caused by the application of some sort of heat or other energy, rather than by chemical action. To duplicate the affected soil, sample B had to be heat-treated at 800 degrees Fahrenheit for six hours.

PHYSICAL LABORATORY REPORT

Mobay Chemical Corporation
Inorganic Chemicals Division
Pemco Products
5601 Eastern Avenue
Baltimore, MD 21224

P— 2387

Material   Two soil samples
Sample A affected area
Sample B unaffected area

Analysis No. 6869
Date 6/5/85
Type of Analysis XRD + SPEC

Submitted to Mr. Cullen Hackler   Project

Two soil samples were submitted for evaluation; one was from the affected area (A) and the other was soil from an adjacent unaffected area (B).

X-Ray Diffraction analysis showed no significant differences in the crystalline structures of samples A and B.

The visual color of sample A was lighter than sample B. Additionally sample A was more dense / less fluffy than sample B. Heat treating a portion of sample B for 6 hours at 800's produced a visual color similar to sample A but did not duplicate the density of sample.

Spectrographic chemical analysis (see attached report) showed no significant differences. Further and larger sample quantities of the soil samples would be required for additional analysis.

Vernon L. Srebe

6.

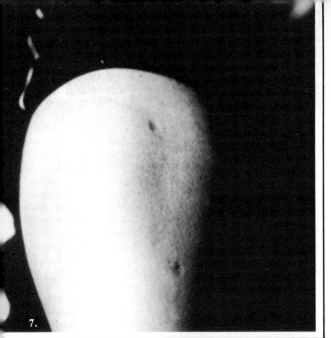

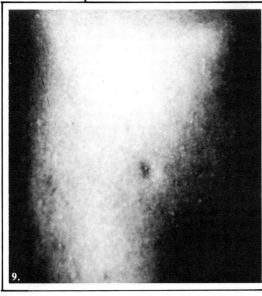

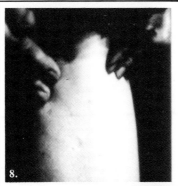

7. Kathie's leg showing scars received during two childhood abductions (see Appendix A). **8.** Kathie's mother's leg showing scar apparently received during a childhood abduction (see Appendix A). **9.** Scoop-mark scar on the back of "Nick," received during a childhood abduction in Brooklyn, New York (not discussed in the text).

10. Finished drawing by UFO investigator Gayle McBride, based on a North Carolina abduction case. **11.** Finished drawing by Kathie Davis of the UFO occupant she has observed on a number of occasions. **12.** Finished drawing by "Rosemary," an artist abducted one night in 1972 from an apartment rooftop within the New York City limits. Note the wrinkled or mottled skin of the lower face, an unusual feature but one that has been reported in a few other cases.

12.

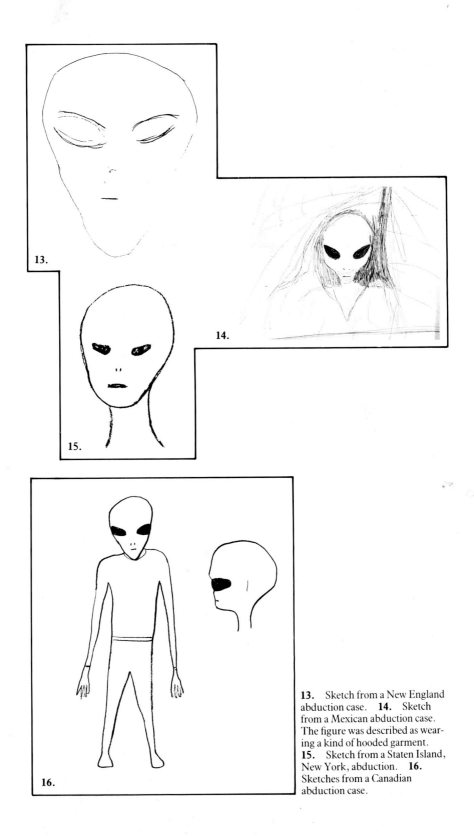

13. Sketch from a New England abduction case. **14.** Sketch from a Mexican abduction case. The figure was described as wearing a kind of hooded garment. **15.** Sketch from a Staten Island, New York, abduction. **16.** Sketches from a Canadian abduction case.

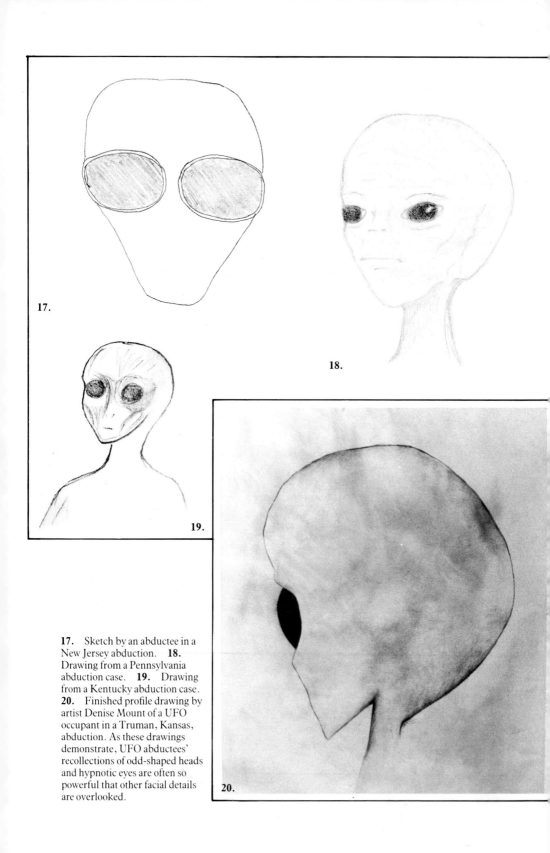

17. Sketch by an abductee in a New Jersey abduction. **18.** Drawing from a Pennsylvania abduction case. **19.** Drawing from a Kentucky abduction case. **20.** Finished profile drawing by artist Denise Mount of a UFO occupant in a Truman, Kansas, abduction. As these drawings demonstrate, UFO abductees' recollections of odd-shaped heads and hypnotic eyes are often so powerful that other facial details are overlooked.

21.

21. A sketch by Kathie's son Robbie of his bedroom, drawn when he was four years of age. At the top of the drawing, Robbie explained, is "E.T.," whom he dreamed came into his room. He told me that it was a nice dream, and E.T. is drawn with some accuracy and charm as the movie depicts him: turtlelike and very long-necked. Down below, however, is the "scary man with the big head and the invisible mouth" who Robbie explains "really did come into my room." He makes a very clear distinction in both his drawing and his recollection between the dream and the reality (see Chapter 4).

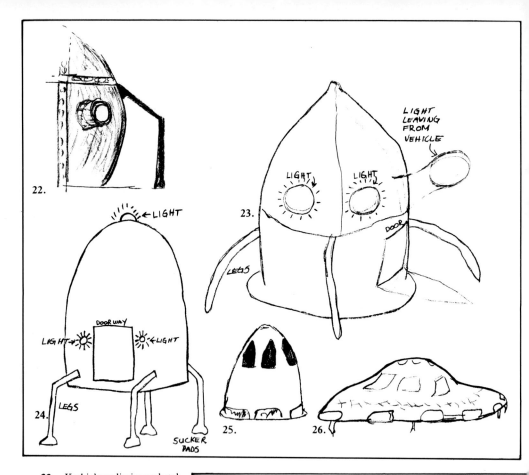

22.

LIGHT LEAVING FROM VEHICLE

LIGHT

LIGHT

LIGHT

23.

DOOR

LEGS

LIGHT

DOOR WAY

LIGHT→ ←LIGHT

LEGS

24.

SUCKER PADS

25.

26.

22. Kathie's preliminary sketch of the landed UFO glimpsed through her garage door on June 30, 1983. Note the light and the jointed landing gear leg (see Chapter 2). **23.** Kathie's more developed sketch of this eightfoot diameter object. **24.** Sketch of a similar object involved in a Mindalore, South Africa, abduction investigated by Cynthia Hind. Note the similar position of the door, the jointed landing gear and the external lights. **25.** Sketch by Joyce Lloyd of an object she saw near her house on another occasion. (This incident is not discussed in the text, though the object is similar to the UFO Kathie recalls.) **26.** Joyce Lloyd's sketch of the vehicle she encountered in an open field (see Chapter 5). **27.** Kathie's full-length sketch of Emily. This drawing was made immediately after her first hypnotic recall of the presentation incident.

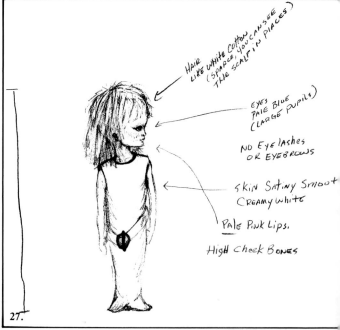

HAIR LIKE WHITE COTTON (SPARCE, YOU CAN SEE THE SCALP IN PLACES)

EYES BLUE PALE (LARGE PUPILS)

NO EYE LASHES OR EYEBROWS

SKIN SATINY SMOOTH CREAMY WHITE

PALE PINK LIPS.

HIGH CHEEK BONES

27.

scribes the arrival of several small, frightening-looking, white-skinned figures. Shortly thereafter he is taken into the UFO, along with Mrs. Warren, Jeff and the three remaining girls. He is separated from them and led into a large, brightly lit, circular room where he is suddenly aware that he is naked.

Right in the middle is this metal table . . . kinda shiny, in a way . . . I . . . they want me up on the table. It's like they're helping me and I'm getting up myself. There's something to put my feet on. And there's something above besides all this light. The whole ceiling's light. It's got a pattern, but there's something seems like it's hanging down. I'm getting scared again. *(Breathes nervously)* He's standing at the end by my feet. I don't understand this. It's a funny table. It seemed solid before, but now it seems like it's spread open. I don't understand this. He's . . . gonna do some experiments . . .

Dan explained to me later that the table remained in one piece from his hips to his head, but below it split into a Y, moving his legs into a spread position. He asks again, firmly, what they are doing. "They don't say nothing. He's not even paying any attention to me . . . One of them is to my left . . . He says, 'Be calm.'" Dan shivers and sighs, again appearing to be very frightened. I try to calm him, and then ask what happened. Though I have deleted most of my questions, the following transcript covers the next few minutes of his experience.

The one on the left touched me . . . on my left shoulder . . . the fingers are smooth . . . like a reptile's . . . cold . . . not that cold, but they were cold and kinda clammy . . . moist . . . soft . . . The other one put something . . . on my genital area . . . It looks kinda clear . . . a conical shape . . . it covers up the whole area . . . There's a sensation, a vibrating. It didn't hurt. I just feel that vibrating, and it seems like a shock. I don't know. Kind of like a pleasant shock. This time the one on my left moved his hand to my upper arm. He's pulled this thing down over my head. *(I ask if he thinks he did or did not have an erection while the vibrating object was over his genital area.)* I'm not sure. It seems like both . . . I could feel it touching the end of my penis, and right around the whole area. It felt kinda cold. Then they put this thing over my head . . . They did it at the same time. While one was putting this thing on [my genitals] the other pulled this thing down over my head. It's clear. It has little holes in it . . . and very bright light . . . and . . .

Dan suddenly jumps and begins to shiver. Tears come to his eyes and he is obviously very frightened. I ask what happened, what he felt. He answers very softly, and I have to ask him twice before I can make out the single word of his answer: "Electricity." I ask if he feels it through his whole body. "Just the head." I ask if the clear, conical thing is still on his genital area while this is happening. He answers in a soft, bewildered voice. "I don't know. I don't know. I just see a bright light above me. I don't know. I don't understand it."

There is a great deal more to this experience, but as Dan acknowledged afterwards in this part of his encounter a sperm sample had been taken. The surge of electricity that he felt at his head while his genital area was covered by the clear conical object suggests to me some kind of artificial neurological trigger for the sexual release, though this is only speculation. Steven Kilburn, an abductee whose account was dealt with in *Missing Time*, also described having a clear plastic covering placed over his genitals. He felt a vibration, the sudden rush of orgasm, and then the sense that his semen had been taken as a sample.[5] He had not described this under hypnosis; the hypnotist was a woman, Dr. Aphrodite Clamar, and the experience was so humiliating and disturbing that Steve relived it in silence. (The idea that someone in a hypnotic trance has no will, no choice about what he or she wishes to report, is one of the more common misconceptions about hypnosis. One can remain silent or comment garrulously, depending on one's feelings at the time. Hypnosis is simply a very relaxed state, not a helpless sodium pentothal-like "truth serum.")

Dan stayed with us in New York for nearly a week, and we explored a number of earlier—and later—UFO experiences. In two incidents prior to this 1969 abduction, he recalled other sperm sample-taking operations. Many of his recollections were conscious, and hypnosis only helped us recover more detail. All were disturbing for Dan, as he realized how deeply these traumatic experiences had affected his life. When he understood that semen specimens had been obtained on three separate occasions, he had a sudden flash of self-awareness. "You know," he said, "when I got married and our daughter was born, I was so happy. I immediately went and had a vasectomy. I knew that once I had a child I could have myself made sterile, and I did, right after she was born." When I think about this issue myself, I can't really imagine two men less obviously likely to have this operation than Ed Duvall, in a small town in Wisconsin in the 1960s, and twenty-seven-year-old Dan Seldin, the new father of an only child. And yet, considering their unconscious memories, the humiliation and the sense of being used, taken—farmed as it were—their decisions are understandable.

During one of our extensive conversations, Dan told me about a "dream" he had had only a few months before he came to New York. The recollection involved his waking up in bed and seeing three of the large-headed, black-eyed creatures standing in his room, perhaps twenty feet away, looking at him. Then he recalls the image of a woman's face close to his, a woman with the same dark eyes, whose black hair is swinging to and fro. There are other details which follow, but these, for Dan, are central, vivid images. He felt that the experience was totally realistic and yet dreamlike at the same time. The incident seemed a logical subject for hypnotic exploration, so on April 15, 1985, we went back to his dream. The following excerpts begin about ten minutes into the session.

DS: I can see the three of them. It's like they're talking among themselves . . . I can see their whole bodies . . . They're dressed in black.

BH: Do you have the feeling you know what they're talking about?

DS: *(Pause)* Me.

BH: Can you hear it?

DS: No.

BH: And what's the next thing that happens?

DS: The girl . . .

BH: How does she come into your vision?

DS: She's just there . . . her head . . .

BH: *(A purposely leading question on my part, turned aside easily by Dan)* Is she dressed in black, too?

DS: All I see is her head. She looks evil, but she looks pretty, too. Her eyes make her look evil. Ugly eyes.

BH: Do you know why she's there? Is there a connection with the other people?

DS: *(Pause)* The only thing that comes to mind is . . . she was sexy-looking, except for her eyes. They were pretty horrendous-looking eyes . . . all black and shiny. But she was pretty . . . Ugly eyes. Blacker than hell. *(Pause)* I'm feeling aroused. Hm . . . I'm feeling that right now . . .

BH: Well, you said she was a sexy-looking woman . . .

DS: Except for the eyes. They're . . . Her eyes are ugly, like they had their own . . .

BH: *(After a pause)* Is there a body to go with the face in this dream?

DS: All I can see is the face, and her hair, like it's blowing or in motion or something. She doesn't have any teeth. She has her mouth open but there are no teeth.

BH: Does she seem real or does she seem like something out of a dream?

DS: *(Firmly)* She was real. Connected with them . . . Those eyes . . .

BH: Now, Dan, in the dream she is there, in front of you. What happens in the dream, the very next thing that you see or feel or whatever? Dreams have sequences. What happens next?

DS: I'm not sure. I think that what I'm thinking now isn't real. *(Pause)* I'm starting to feel aroused . . .

BH: Just tell me what you remember. A dream is a dream. Dreams are not real. You don't have to decide what's real. I'm just interested in what you remember. We all have dreams. We all get aroused in dreams . . .

DS: I'm getting scared.

BH: Tell me what you're feeling . . .

DS: She's over me.

BH: What position are you in that she's over you? Are you standing and she's higher up?

DS: No, I'm lying on the bed . . . Covers are down . . . she . . . It's like I'm laying there, and she's . . . *(inaudible)*

BH: She's what?

DS: *(Softly, in a whisper)* She's . . . screwing me . . .

BH: Dan, tell me, does it feel like it normally feels when you're having sex with somebody? Does it feel the same?

DS: *(Softly)* Yes . . .

BH: Does she feel the same?

DS: Yes.

BH: Can you embrace her? Do you hug her?

DS: No. It's just like I lay there.

BH: Where are your arms? Are you touching her?

DS: No.

I was deliberately asking leading questions here, trying to suggest that he touched her, because I wanted to see if he could be led. I suspected, of course, that he was not leadable, would not embellish his account, and that he was most probably unable to move.

BH: Why aren't you touching her?

DS: Don't know.

BH: Is this happening in your bed?

DS: Yes.

BH: As you look around can you see your room? Does it look normal or does it look strange or what? Does the room look like a dream room, or what?

DS: It seems like my room.

BH: How about the light in it?

DS: Normal light.

BH: Can you see her body?

DS: Yes.

BH: What's her body look like?

DS: Like a regular woman. Pretty body . . .

BH: Did she do something to arouse you?

DS: No. It's like she gets on top of me, and she's got her hands down by the tops of my shoulders.

BH: She does the whole thing?

DS: Yes.

BH: And you don't move?

DS: Right.

BH: Do you do anything to her or does she do anything to you?

DS: No. *(Pause)* He's standing over there.

BH: Who's he?

DS: Him. The white-headed figure. Over in the corner. Just watching.

BH: Does anybody say anything?

DS: They're in the corner by the rocking chair, just watching.

BH: Do you feel you know why this is happening?

DS: No. Just a blank. Just don't think anything.

BH: But you feel normal sensations?

DS: Yes.

BH: Did she do anything to arouse you with her hands?

DS: No. It's just like she got on top of me.

BH: So you were already aroused?

DS: Yes . . . Just looking at her . . . Her eyes. They're ugly, but they're . . .

BH: How do you feel about this experience? Do you feel pleased or displeased or . . .

DS: Excited. Puzzled.

I tried several times to test the validity of Dan's recollections by attempting to lead him down various pathways. I asked questions designed to provide him with an opportunity to embellish his encounter with erotic detail, yet he passed up these chances and maintained the simple, spare, puzzling outline of his experience. I gave him opportunities to editorialize, to provide reasons and a meaning for the encounter, but these too he rejected. And now a familiar irony reveals itself in the closing moments of the hypnotic session. Dan begins to laugh, softly, privately, but with real pleasure.

DS: I fooled them. *(Laughing)* I'm just thinking I fooled them. They can't get what they want. I'm not some stud bull . . .
BH: Because of the vasectomy?
DS: Yes.
BH: Do you think they wanted sperm?
DS: *(Softly)* Yes. Sometimes I get afraid they're going to heal it back up. I don't want them to heal it. *(Pause)* They're stupid. They're stupid.
BH: Do you feel there's any possibility that the woman is feeling sexual pleasure?
DS: No.
BH: How do you feel about that? What do you think she's going through?
DS: Just like it's something she has to do. For whatever purpose. *(Pause)* She's cute from the back . . . without those stupid eyes looking at you.
BH: How do you see her from the back?
DS: When she gets off. Starts to walk away. And that guy looks at her, and they're just gone . . .

There is more to this incident, as there is, naturally, to everything so far described in these pages. I have deliberately withheld certain details in many of these cases in the hope that later investigations may turn up specifically corroborating information. As an example, in this encounter, Dan seems to have been told the name of the black-eyed woman who so perfunctorily mounted him in his own bedroom. It would be interesting if this name turns up elsewhere in related abduction accounts. But in the meantime there is no way for me to convey the depth and the coldness of Dan's anger and hatred for his abductors. With some abductees there is curiosity and even occasional feelings of warmth and closeness for these strange, unknowable "alien" creatures who have become so intertwined with normal people, people who never asked for—or even imagined—such bizarre involvements. But with Dan the issue was simple; he felt only loathing for them.

Earlier in this chapter I alluded to still other cases I have investigated in which male abductees describe this same kind of sexual experience. One of them involves a New York City police officer, and I will only mention the harrowing hypnotic session, conducted by Dr. Clamar, in which these details emerged. The subject was so frightened, so repelled by the experience, that he found it difficult afterwards even to begin to describe what happened. The police officer, "Mr. J.E.," was at the time in his twenties, happily married, and the father of a young child. Like Ed and Dan, he was placed on a table or bed, immobilized and somehow aroused, and then mounted by an apparently nonhuman female. In this case, however, the female was considerably less human-looking than were the others. "They put this thing on me," he said, "like a woman, but it wasn't a woman. It was gray and it had a face, but I couldn't look at it. It didn't really feel like a woman. It was horrible. It had to have been a dream." J.E.'s eyes are dark and intense and deep-set. He turned to me with a pleading look in those deep-set eyes, a haunted and desperate look that I will never forget. "It was a dream, wasn't it, Budd? It had to be a dream. Things like this can't really happen, can they? This can't be real, can it?" I told him that he was right, that it must have been a dream, that things like this just can't happen. It didn't help much, but at that moment I would have told him whatever he wanted to hear. And as I spoke there were tears in his eyes, and in mine, because we both knew the truth.

8

The Presentation

In the quarter century since the Betty and Barney Hill case first brought the issue to international attention, the UFO abduction phenomenon has had a complex and baffling history. What I consider to be the most important abduction event in this long, bizarre history took place sometime during the dark night of October 3, 1983, in a rural area outside of Indianapolis, Indiana. As recounted in Chapter 3, it began when Kathie Davis was floated out of her room as she slept. She was then subjected to a physical examination inside the UFO. Yet the ultimate meaning of that experience only came to light months later when Kathie recalled, little by little, through natural recollection, details of what followed the examination: a profound confrontation, simultaneously as human and as unearthly as one can conceive.

I was informed of this event during Kathie's second trip to New York, in January of 1985, some fifteen months after it happened. On the evening of the twenty-sixth, as we sat in my living room, chatting about this and that, I sensed that there was something important Kathie wanted to tell me. She seemed nervous and hesitant, and I noticed that there were tears glistening in her eyes. "Budd, you remember when I said that I knew I had a daughter?" She paused and cleared her throat. "Well, they showed her to me. I've seen her." As she continued with her story, I was too moved and surprised to think about setting up my tape recorder. At some point I remembered that my friend Tracy Tormé planned to drop in to meet Kathie, so I decided that when he came I could ask her to repeat her account, and I could record it then. By the time he arrived an hour or so later she had collected herself somewhat, so the following taped version is less emotional and more formal in tone than her narrative earlier that evening.

It was the ending of some kind of scene. It was like a dream or something, before I woke up in bed. But it was too real to be a dream . . . Something had happened before, some kind of test. Someone had talked to me . . . I was in this place and it was all white. It was like I was getting ready to go back to where I came from . . . like they were essentially finished with me except for one thing. And there was a whole bunch of these guys in there in the big room . . . little gray guys, and there were several of them around me. One of them, I seem to remember . . . it's almost as if he had his arm around my waist . . . very comforting. I was standing up. And they were all around me and one of them touched my shoulder. Everyone seemed very pleased with me, and . . . I didn't know why. I wasn't afraid at all.

At this point Kathie begins speaking slowly and more softly—almost confessionally—as if the undercurrents of emotion were suddenly closer to the surface.

And then . . . a little girl came into the room . . . escorted by two more of them. And she stood in front of the doorway . . . She looked to be about four. She looked about Tommy's size. He's four, and she didn't look like them, but she didn't look like us, either. She was real pretty. She looked like an elf, or an . . . angel. She had really big blue eyes and a little teeny-weeny nose, just so perfect. And her mouth was just so perfect and tiny, and she was pale, except her lips were pink and her eyes were blue. And her hair was white and wispy and thin . . . fine . . . real thin and fine. Her head was a little larger than normal, 'specially in the forehead and back here . . . The forehead was a little bit bigger . . . but she was just a doll. And they brought her to me. And they stood there and looked at me. Everyone was looking at me. And I looked at her, and I wanted to hold her. She was just so pretty, and I felt like I just wanted to hold her. And I started crying . . . and I was crying when I told Budd earlier tonight . . . This is the only part of any of these weird things that really gets me emotionally. There's no emotion left for any of the other. Maybe I'm afraid sometimes, but I'm more or less . . .

Tracy had been listening intently to Kathie's obviously painful account, but he interrupted here to ask if she had recalled all of this through hypnosis.

No. It was almost like they let me remember this part. They held her hands. Each one was holding a hand and she was almost like she was timid, like a very timid bunny rabbit, and she almost was afraid of me. She turned towards one of them and reached out to her. And then she looked at me from the side, and when she did her lip quivered, and she almost . . . it was kind of like a smile, on one side. It was like she was really interested in me, but she was a little bit afraid of me. And it was so sweet. And I think I was even crying, actually, then. I know I woke up crying, and I cried when I told Sue, and I cried when I told Budd. I can almost cry just thinking about it . . . I don't know, it was just . . . it wasn't sad, but . . . I wanted to take her with me . . .

I don't know what any of them said to me, but one of them said something or told me something that I can't remember. I just know everyone was happy with me, and there was a very good feeling . . . it was a very satisfying feeling, yet it was very sad for me . . . I'm pretty sure somebody told me I should be proud. Her eyes were so blue and huge, and her pupils were so blue, and she blinked them at me . . . it was like a blink, but it wasn't. It was almost as if her eyes rolled up. Her skin was creamy . . . it wasn't gray. She was pale and soft and creamy . . .

The three of us talked for a few moments about the fact that Kathie had remembered so much normally, without hypnosis having been employed, but she offered a possible explanation.

It's almost like someone felt sorry for me 'cause I was so emotional over the child . . . it was like a little piece of her they left with me 'cause they had to take her away. I know I'm going to see her again.

They told me so. But I wish it was going to be sooner than I think it probably will be . . .

Kathie was willing, now, to undergo hypnosis on this event, just for the joy of reliving the experience of being with the little girl. Her little girl. I set the scene, instructing Kathie that we will return to the place she has just told us about, involving "a wonderful memory or dream experience." She describes the room as having a happy feeling. A happy room. "There are four people with me, and another across the room at the doorway." After more description there ensues a very long pause. Then she speaks so softly and slowly and with such wonder that her voice is a mere whisper. "Look . . . at . . . that! She's beautiful . . . *(Almost inaudibly)* I want . . . to hold her." Kathie cries very quietly, and whispers, as if to herself, "She's mine."

A long pause ensues, and then the "man" she's seen so many times before says to her that she can't take her with her, that the child would not be able to live. "You wouldn't be able to feed her. She has to stay with us." The disappointment in Kathie's voice as she relates these words to us is palpable and profound. She continues, quoting the small gray figure.

KD: "A father . . . a father has to take care of his children."

BH: He's the child's father? *(Kathie sighs, and there is a long pause)* Does he explain how she was conceived?

KD: No. *(My question is disposed of quickly, and Kathie returns to what is for her the central issue)* I don't want them to take her away.

BH: Tell me what she looks like.

KD: She's . . . gorgeous. She looks like an angel. She's tiny. Thin. *(Speaking slowly, as if lovingly and systematically observing her features)* Her skin is creamy. Pale. Her face is shaped like a heart. She has a tiny, tiny little mouth. Perfect lips. Blue eyes. White hair . . . not a whole lot of it. *(Kathie later told me that the hair was sparse and unevenly distributed on her head, and that patches of scalp were visible here and there through it. It hung down in something of a tangle, "as if," Kathie said, "they didn't know what to do with it.")*

BH: Can you see her ears?

KD: She has really tiny, little tiny ears, but they're lower on her head than they should be. Than mine are. Forehead is a little big. Eyes are big. Pretty. She's so tiny. She makes them look big. You

could hold her in one arm. She probably doesn't weigh more
than twenty-five pounds. Thirty.

BH: What's she wearing, Kathie?

KD: *(Speaking softly)* It's white. It's like white silky stuff, kind of
shiny. Goes over her head, a hole cut out to pull over her head.
Drapes around her shoulders and down to the floor.

BH: What are her feet and hands like?

KD: Can't see her feet. Hands are really tiny. Thin. Her thumbs
. . . are not as close to the palm side as mine. It looks like they're
more to the side of their hands when she reaches for that guy.
But they look normal, mostly. She's just so cute.

BH: Does she know you're her mother?

KD: *(Softly, after a pause)* Yes, but she doesn't understand
"mother." She's too young.

BH: How old is she . . . may she be?

KD: I can't tell. She could be . . . really old, or she could be an infant.
I don't know. In some ways she looks like a midget grownup,
and in other ways she looks like a baby. She's about as tall as
a three- or four-year old. Like Tommy. Maybe not quite as tall
as Tommy.

BH: How does she look at you?

KD: That's what bothers me, too. *(Sadly)* She looks at me almost like
she's afraid of me. Not afraid enough to run away, but afraid
enough to turn to them.

BH: Are there any women there, too?

KD: Yes. The females are the ones that have her.

BH: How are they different from the males?

KD: Physically, not really at all. But in the way they think, the way
they speak to you.

BH: Can you tell by looking at them?

KD: If you look at their eyes . . .

BH: How many are in this room?

KD: Two with her, four with me. And one standing in the doorway.

BH: Do they understand that you want to take her?

KD: *(Firmly)* Yes! But he's right. *(Softly)* It's better this way.

BH: Do they explain anything to you, Kathie, about how this happened, or why?

KD: He just said she was a part of me.

BH: Did he say there were others like her?

KD: Didn't say.

BH: Did you ask?

KD: No.

BH: Is there just one little girl in there? Do you see anybody else?

KD: I only see her . . .

BH: Do they explain why they made her?

KD: No. Why should they?

BH: Do they say where she's going now?

KD: With them.

BH: Do you know where that is?

KD: No.

BH: Did they tell you you'll see her again?

KD: They *promised* me.

BH: Did that seem like it would be soon?

KD: *(Sighs)* No.

BH: Do you think that she can understand your thoughts when you're looking at her?

KD: Yes, because I thought to myself she was beautiful, I wanted to hold her, and she smiled at me. And I knew she could hear me.

BH: Take a good look at her, Kathie, and you'll be able to make a drawing of her later on. You'll remember her for your whole life . . .

KD: *(Very softly)* I will.

BH: We'll come back to her again. But I want you now to tell me how this scene ends, how it comes to a close.

KD: *(Pause, sighs)* Everybody's leaving. They're going out the door.

BH: Do they leave you alone in the room?

KD: Just me, and him.

BH: Do you talk to him?

KD: I ask him why they were taking her . . . He said she was safe, and always would be. I asked him again if I could ever see her again, and he said yes. Said it was time for me to go. If I stayed much longer I would get sick.

BH: Do you feel ill at all?

KD: Not really.

BH: So what happens?

KD: He takes me over to this . . . platform . . . it's round. *(Pause)* Holds my hand. *(Pause)* I feel all kinds of things. It's funny, I don't . . . he doesn't say anything to me, but he just holds my hand, and I look at him, and I feel all kinds of things . . . sad, and warm, and care, and distance . . . and goodbye . . . and lonely . . . I feel lonely, too. All at the same time. Makes me want to cry. It's not really bad . . .

BH: So you're together on a platform?

KD: Just me. He's not on it. It's not much higher . . . about an inch. This looks different from the rest of the floor. Different color. He lets go of my hand . . . steps back. The whole room starts to . . . starts to shimmer . . . like firelight . . . heat . . .

Kathie suddenly jumps, her breathing rapid and unsteady. I ask what happened, and she says that her chest hurt suddenly, for a moment. I ask if the pain is inside or outside, and she says that it was inside, "like pulling, from the inside out . . . in my chest." I wondered if she had just passed through some sort of airlock, from an environment with one kind of air pressure to another with a different one, but I did not remark upon it. I did inquire if she was still on the little round platform. "No. I'm lying on the grass." She was in the backyard near the swimming pool, clad only in her pajamas and feeling a little chilly. Apparently the UFO was leaving. She said, "I can see it, but now it's gone . . . a light . . . like a headband with little lights on it . . . a barrette."

The next problem is that Kathie is locked out. "I'm tired and I want to go to bed." She calls for her mother, who, as if still under some kind of external control, comes down and lets her in. Neither speaks to the other, no questions are asked, and both climb the stairs to their bedrooms as if everything is perfectly normal. This seemed a natural place to end, so I prepared to bring Kathie out of the trance state. Considering the momentous nature of what had transpired, I realized that I must provide her with the most positive kinds of posthypnotic suggestion. I praised her inner strength, her love for her children and her family. I stressed her ability to endure such a powerful emotional experience and yet carry on her life at home as usual. I assured her that she would see her little girl again, and that she would never forget her. Then I began the countdown and brought her out of hypnosis.

We sat for a few moments in silence. Neither Tracy nor I wanted to break the complicated mood of wonder, of sadness and joy that Kathie's account had established in all of us. But then the questions raised by her experience suddenly insisted upon answers, and our posthypnosis conversation began all at once. Kathie was the first of us to speak. "That man," she said, referring to the small gray figure whom she had seen so many times before, "just can't be the father. Maybe he donated some cells or something. Maybe that's what he told me." She insisted that she had never had any kind of sexual experience involving him, and that the very idea was upsetting—"gross" was her word. But she went on to remark that "when he said something like that to me, that he was the volunteer donor or something, I got the impression he was telling me that because it was the only way that I could understand it . . . I always felt that they treated me somewhat childlike." And then she added, modestly, "But then again, maybe they have a right to.

"I think that my emotions really touched them. And when he . . . held my hand, and was looking at me . . . I was looking at him, his face, his eyes . . . He didn't say anything, and I got this burst of all these kinds of emotions . . . real confusing . . . all at once. Maybe he was trying to feel something." I asked Kathie if she felt these emotions were coming from him, were his emotions. "Yes. He was trying to make me feel something, or trying to make me understand that *he* was trying to understand *me* . . . my feelings."

I remarked that this put a new twist on things. It meant that when an abductee reported what might seem to be inappropriate emotions, such as sadness or loneliness at the end of a traumatic UFO abduction experience, that these emotions might actually be *coming from the abductors* rather than from the abductees. Kathie responded quietly and introspectively, as if she had only half heard my observation. "You know, when he looked at me and held my hand I got this rush of emotion that I didn't know where it came from. It was lonely and sad and sorry, but love and caring and happiness and satisfaction—and guilt—all at once. I didn't think it was coming from me. Why would I feel guilt?"

I told her that it must have been his guilt, that she certainly wasn't guilty of anything. "Yes," she responded. "It wasn't my guilt. He felt sad and lonely, but he felt satisfied and happy and he cared, about me, as a living thing. He was going to miss me as much as I was going to miss her.

"But he felt guilty! He felt guilty about how sad I got when I had to leave her. He didn't want me to feel like that. He wanted me to be happy at the success like he was, and he felt guilty that I felt that way . . . I was saying goodbye, and all of a sudden there was just this burst of emotion hit me inside, and it was love and sadness and guilt and happiness and all these things just all jumbled up . . . it was like somebody who wasn't real used to feeling all these things . . ."

I pointed out that I could understand the aliens' loneliness. We have a rich planet with greatly varied life forms, and by contrast their world might be very sterile. Tracy mentioned the fact that UFO occupants are usually described as not having any emotions, but Kathie had an immediate reply. "They have them, but they don't use them much." She added, ironically, "I guess we bring the worst out in them. You know, emotions can cloud scientific thought."

Kathie was certain, however, that they reacted positively to her feelings when she saw the child. "I think they were surprised, but I also kinda think it's what they wanted." Tracy asked if there was any interaction between the little girl and the other people in the craft, if Kathie noticed any kind of affection. She said that there seemed to be a relationship of some kind with the two "females" who cared for her. "She clung to them." Tracy was curious to know if Kathie thought the child could grasp what was going on. "Did she have an infant's mentality or was she able to understand what was happening?" Kathie's reply I think demonstrates her objectivity. Our questions were rife with every possibility of projection on her part, yet her answers are not those a loving mother would most like to give. In fact, some of her replies must have been painful to make. "She knew who I was," Kathie said, "but I think the sight of me frightened her. She looked frightened, almost shocked, at the idea that she was part of me."

Tracy asked if she ever touched her, and if not, how close they were to each other. Kathie was not close enough to touch her child, she said, indicating that they were about five feet apart. "I never got any closer . . . but I want to." There were more questions about the little girl's appearance, and Kathie made another observation. "I don't think she had any teeth. I don't know for sure . . . though her lips parted a little when she first saw me, like she was shocked. Her hair was like cotton, and came about to her shoulders, but it was uneven. The ends were kinda snarly. But she was just perfect. When you looked at her it made you tingle . . . she was just so *cute.*" (See illustrations.)

And so there it was, the apparent answer to the problem of Kathie's mysteriously terminated pregnancy of late 1977. If the account in Chapter 6 is correct and Kathie was abducted sometime in December of 1977 and artificially inseminated at the time, then the pieces all fit neatly together. Again assuming that Kathie's recollections are accurate, the fetus was removed during the next abduction in March of 1978. If it was somehow brought to term by the UFO occupants, then the child should have been "born," assuming a nine-month gestation period, in the late summer or early fall of 1978. Her presentation to Kathie occurred in early October, 1983, so at that time she should have been just five years old. Kathie described the child as being a little smaller than Tommy—at the time of the hypnotic recollection, a four-year-old boy. And so we have a further reason to view the child as a hybrid, apart from Kathie's description of her sparse, patchy hair, her very large eyes and her unusually shaped cranium: She was also much smaller than a normal five-year-old child should have been; more in keeping, it would seem, with the reported height of UFO occupants than with the size of typical humans.

The theoretical implications of this kind of genetic experimentation are obviously profound, but like almost every discovery we have made so far about the UFO phenomenon, it raises almost as many questions as it answers. If we know that one of their goals is the interbreeding of humans with their own, why are they producing these hybrids? Are they systematically reducing the differences between "them" and "us" so that they can acclimatize their species to our planet and our atmosphere? Or do they simply want to acquire some of our genetic characteristics to take with them back to their home turf, wherever and whatever it may be, to enrich their stock? Or are both of these assumptions just anthropomorphic guesses, neither of which covers the true, complex situation? I suspect the latter may be the safest assumption, but who knows?

Kathie, for her part, has no interest in such speculation. She only knows that she has a daughter she wants to see again. At one point in her hypnosis, Kathie said this to the tiny, "perfect" child in front of her: "I'm going to miss you. I don't even know you, but I'm going to miss you." And then she asked, as if to the air, "Can you love somebody you don't even know?" Kathie was given another chance to see her daughter, in an even more surprising encounter that took place in March of 1986. Three other women—Andrea, Susan Williams, and Pam, all of whom I dealt with in Chapter 7—have dreamlike memories of being shown tiny infants which they were made to feel were their own. These complex but similar recollections will be described at a later time, but the point that must be made is that, taken together, their accounts form a distinct pattern. We are not dealing with just one or two vaguely related incidents. And the cases I have described in which men have been abducted, immobilized, and subjected to a kind of literal rape are not just one or two isolated events, either. Whether we like it or not the patterns exist—tight, clear patterns which are often buttressed by existing medical evidence. We know, now, a great deal about the content of these long-term, cross-generational UFO abductions. What we *don't* know is, of course, the biggest question: What is the ultimate purpose of it all?

9

More Pieces of the Puzzle

In 1983, before I knew anything of Kathie's or the other women's related accounts, I was given my first glimpse of what has turned out to be the "missing baby syndrome." The clue turned up during a phone conversation with "Lisa," a witness in an unusual UFO incident. After hearing her version of the sighting, I routinely asked a few questions about anything else she might remember that could have a bearing on the case at hand. Because of the nature of her account I wanted to find out if she was really just an accidental observer or if, perhaps, she might be more of a participant than she thought. I phrased my last question this way: "Is there anything else in your past you might want to mention that seems to you even peripherally connected with UFOs—any odd, dangling, unresolved memories that bother you and just don't make much sense?" It's a typical open-ended, fishing question I ask before ending an interview, and I've netted some strange fish this way. The utility of the question lies in the fact that anything answered can be assumed to be associated— perhaps unconsciously—in the witness's mind with the UFO phenomenon. The witness makes the connection, not the interviewer.

Most of the time in situations like these the witness either says that there aren't any such memories, or else takes so long trying to come up with something that I suspect he or she may be only trying to please me.

But in this case when I raised the question Lisa immediately asked me to hold the phone while she went into another room "for a better connection." She then resumed the conversation in what was very nearly a whisper, explaining that she didn't want her husband, who had been nearby, to hear what she had to tell me. "I know this sounds crazy," she said, "but I think I have another child that I've somehow lost." My unspoken thought was, what in the world can this have to do with UFOs? She went on, "I woke up from a dream one night absolutely certain I had a little baby and that I had lost it. I got out of bed and searched the house. I know this sounds crazy, but it seemed absolutely real. I even looked in the closets and under the bed. I know this doesn't make any sense, and it doesn't even make sense to me, but I *knew* I somehow lost a child. I thought I had actually seen it. And I felt this way for weeks after. Sometimes I would just stop what I was doing, put down the vacuum cleaner, and search the house all over again."

Her statement was so bizarre that I really did not know what to make of it. I asked if she had ever had a miscarriage or abortion or a stillborn child, anything of this nature that might provide a reason for her feelings of loss, and she answered that she had not. As a matter of fact she had given birth to a healthy daughter before she had the dream. Yet despite the passing of time and the birth of two more children, her feeling of having a lost child persisted.

My reaction, after we ended our conversation, was that however vivid Lisa's feelings were there was no way they could have anything to do with UFOs. It is highly possible, of course, that they don't, but now, after Kathie and Susan Williams and Pam and Andrea, I'm not so sure. In the context of my question, it was she, not I, who immediately associated these intense and apparently irrational feelings with the UFO phenomenon. I subsequently interviewed some of Lisa's family and friends and they assured me that she is regarded by everyone who knows her as a very sane, very normal person. Under the circumstances, then, both the nature and the unusual tenacity of her recollections constitute a psychological mystery of some sort. But in retrospect, knowing what I know now, Lisa's peculiar "missing baby" dream has to be considered as potentially significant.[1]

To judge its possible importance, her recollection must be seen in context with other, similar accounts. When I first met the psychotherapist Susan Williams in the summer of 1985 and we began hypnosis on her 1953 missing time experience, I asked her to write down any odd memo-

ries or persistent dreams that might help in deciphering her earlier suspected encounters. (See pp. 127–30.) As part of her training Susan has
herself been psychoanalyzed so her dreams and other unconscious memories over the years have been systematically brought to the surface. She
is, by nature, an extremely intelligent, self-aware woman. In response to
my request she wrote a fascinating twelve-page letter detailing this important material. I was particularly struck by one reference which she included under a heading:

Wise Baby Dreams

These have been occurring since about 1978. I love Wise Baby
dreams. The details about the size of the baby may vary from dream
to dream. In a number of them the baby is *very* small—about a foot
long, lying in a little metal container. The marvel is that this baby
speaks at length, eloquently, and the sense I have in the dream is
that I am hearing the truth. I feel good when I wake up—because
the dream was a good-feeling dream, but I feel sad, too, because
when I wake up I'm not with the Wise Baby and I can never
remember the content of what she said. That content is, was, had
been a revelation, but at the same time in the dream I have the
distinct impression that I know it, have known it, anyway. Having
the baby articulate it makes me feel whole while the dream lasts
. . . Wise Baby dreams with the dimunitive baby, *so small,* are
especially precious to me (those Wise Babies have no fat to spare
on their bodies). [Emphasis hers]

Susan was very clear that these were actual dreams, sleep-memories from
which she often awoke; they recurred especially in the late nineteen-
seventies and varied somewhat from time to time. At the outset I was not
inclined to look into these somewhat abstract and philosophical dreams,
but in the context of the other women's recollections I eventually felt that
they must be explored. In June of 1986 we began a hypnotic regression
session for just that purpose.

I set the scene, saying only that we are now going to explore her dreams
about the Wise Babies. In the first surprising detail that emerged Susan
describes the location of her encounter with the Wise Baby as the porch
of her childhood home in Vermont—the place where she had been living
when she experienced the two abductions in 1949. Though her *dreams*

about the Wise Baby dated from nearly thirty years later, their remembered setting now coincides suggestively with her UFO recollections. I ask how, in her dream, she finds the Wise Baby and she says, "It was a discovery . . . or maybe I was drawn to her." She goes on, "I had a feeling of wonder and delight. I'm aware of the size, and some kind of fragility, but that's not the essence of what's wonderful at all—it's the talk, it's the knowledge, it's the eloquence. It's the uncensored truth. That's the beauty and the preciousness."

I ask if the baby is alone, and if so, does it worry Susan that it is away from the mother? She answers forthrightly. She is alone with the baby, but the baby is safe. "The baby [in her little metal container] is in no physical danger. She's fine because she knows she can speak about it." I inquire if Susan feels she has any relationship to the baby, and the question seems to surprise her: "I didn't think that she has a relationship to anyone else."

BH: What about her mother?

SW: . . . I keep going back and forth as to whether she is me, or if I'm her mother, or I'm her mother-to-be. In any event it's a very, very close bond . . . certainly when I find her . . . it's a treasure.

BH: Take a good look at her . . .

SW: *(Pause)* Um . . . She's *too* small. She's not in a fetal position. The skin is very thin . . . very thin, thinner than . . . you know newborn babies' hands, like tissue paper? Thinner than that. The skin is very thin. The odd thing about the physical aspect is that the porportions are not baby proportions. The proportions of a newborn or fetus is . . . the large head. That's the odd thing about this . . . she . . . "it" seems better . . . is that the porportions are those of an adult . . . like a miniature adult. It didn't seem odd to me then, but it seems odd now. And the position . . . she wasn't curled up or anything, like a baby.

BH: *(Uses the black curtain device: The baby is only three feet on the other side of the curtain, you'll get a good, quick look. You'll be able to see her clearly, etc. Counts to three.)* What did you see?

SW: *(Pause)* I saw a pulse . . . above the collarbone, in her neck. I see her face, now. *(Surprised)* Huh. Features are concentrated down in the lower part . . . She looks kinda old, actually. Hm. So the skin is not robust in color . . . it's not baby-pink at all. It's a funny . . . grayish . . . pallor, that I think would be

repulsive, as I look at it now. Features . . . I can't see the eyes
. . . well, I sorta can. They're there. It's all concentrated down,
so the area of the head is . . . the head goes down to a point
. . . the chin. Everything is miniature.

BH: We're going to try an experiment, an experiment in your ability
to visualize and to feel. When I count to three, I want you to
have the experience of reaching down and picking up this little
baby and holding it, the way a mother holds a baby. You've held
lots of babies in your life. Two of them were your own. This is
just imagination. I want you to just imagine holding that baby,
and tell me how it feels to hold it . . . its size and its weight and
everything about it. *(Counts to three)*

SW: *(Pause)* It was very clear. I put my fingers in carefully . . . it was
very fragile. I actually did it in my mind with one hand. Carefully, supporting the head with my fingers. Very, very light. This
baby does not weigh a pound . . . Not sturdy . . . not sick, either.
It's just not . . . I was going to say unformed, but that's not true,
there definitely are arms and legs and little teeny . . . it's not
skin over bones, but everything is so miniaturized that whatever
muscles there are are tiny, and don't have strength yet. It has
the quality of a tiny bird . . . *(Firmly)* She's alive. I felt the living
. . . there was life.

BH: Does she look up at you?

SW: *I* look . . . I could see the features. There's no animation in the
face. I was going to say it was a vacant . . . *(Puzzled)* It doesn't
accord with the richness of the experience.

BH: Is it possible, Susan, that the incredible conversation is not
proceeding from the baby, but is proceeding from elsewhere or
from your own mind as you look at the baby? Or are these wrong
interpretations?

SW: *(Long pause)* I have thought . . . there is that feeling always
that the baby is me, or my voice, or my hidden voice, or something like that. But I was going to say something else. Somehow, what we've done now by *looking* . . . I've separated the
looking we've just done . . . The picking up and examining in
some way teased apart, or divorced the physicalness of the
baby from the content of what I heard. At this point what
seems less real is my original dream that the baby uttered
these wise, profound, beautiful truths. What seems least real is
that that baby, as I see her now, would speak to me that way.
That doesn't seem possible now.

Susan describes her feelings about the baby and the still unremembered things associated with it as being summed up in the phrase "long sought." There was a quality of recognition, she said, as if she'd "known it all along."

We ended our exploration of Susan's Wise Baby dreams at this point and moved on to another topic before closing the session and bringing her out of the trance state. It had been an emotionally rich and highly suggestive hour, as this shortened transcript indicates. Most crucial, I believe, is the metamorphosis of the Wise Baby from an almost mythic, oracular presence to a physically real, fragile infant with a decidedly unnatural size and facial structure. Its skin color was grayish and its expression was almost vacant—very different from the rosy, gurgling, crying infants we're used to. One very important unexplored element in Susan's recollections was the setting of her encounter, aside from her placement of the baby and its tiny metal container near the porch of her childhood home in Vermont. No one else seemed to be present, giving the incident a still somewhat abstract quality, but one wonders what other details might remain buried in Susan's memory. Kathie's recollections, after all, came slowly, in piecemeal fashion. We had begun the session with a series of related dreams of a wonderfully verbal Wise Baby—Susan always capitalized the two words—but the ending was a confrontation with a disturbingly real infant, abnormally tiny, helpless and mute. A pleasant, dreamlike image was now an unsettlingly physical one.

Our second related case (described in Chapter 7) involves Andrea, the New York woman who found herself pregnant at the age of thirteen after a bizarre "dream." When I visited her in June of 1985 I asked if she recalled any other dreams or memories which might be pertinent to her UFO experiences. To my surprise she brought up a troubling recurrent dream in which she was being shown a baby that seemed to be hers, but which was taken away from her. I knew, of course, that her early pregnancy had been terminated by an abortion, so I was alert to any overtone of guilt or sorrow in her account. But after hearing it I felt her story seemed much closer to Susan's than to the remorseful invention of a distraught young woman.

I mentioned earlier that Andrea has not undergone any hypnotic regression; all her memories had surfaced "naturally," without its use. The "lost baby" dream, she explained, occurred a number of times when she was about sixteen or seventeen years old, and again when she was twenty-two or twenty-three. Its setting is genuinely dreamlike, though I found that

Andrea's wording, in the light of many UFO reports, had a certain familiar ring. "It was taking place in a house I've never seen before. The house was sitting in an open field. I parked my car and went in and there was my baby in a crib. There was an odd-looking lady with her. I could see her feet and they were very odd. She had no shoes. Her legs were very skinny. She said, 'You don't belong here and you don't belong with this child.' "

I asked Andrea to describe the baby. "It looked like me, except the eyes were very shiny and they were all black. She had long, thin, black hair. The lady kept telling me, 'This isn't your baby and you don't belong here.' She had the baby. Every time I wanted to hold the baby she wouldn't let me. This baby, Budd, was very tiny. It looked like you'd put this baby in an incubator. This baby was small. And, you know, after this happened to me I constantly dreamed of a baby . . .

"I didn't dream about it too much as a teenager, but when I was about twenty-two or twenty-three years old I would dream about it constantly, and I used to wake up wondering where the baby was. It seemed real. It seemed it was the same lady who held the baby in the earlier dreams."

Andrea reemphasized the baby's strangeness. "Its hair wasn't like normal baby's hair. It was very, very thin. And when the baby would look at me its eyes were very shiny. And I would look at it and reach for it and the lady would say, 'This isn't your baby, you don't belong here.' "

I asked if she had any idea who the father was. "No. Not at all. To this day I wonder where . . . But when I reached out to take the baby, to hold it, to hug it and love it, the woman just said, 'This isn't your baby, you don't belong here.' She walked away, and I couldn't see her very well. I think I concentrated more on the child than I did on her. It's like my eyes focused . . . it's like something hypnotized me with that baby because, when that baby looked at me, something happened to me. I just kept staring at it. Like, how come that baby looks different than a regular human baby? This baby should be in an incubator. It's very tiny. It's *very tiny.* And it scared me. I don't know . . . It seemed like, Oh my God, this is really happening. That's when I was afraid to go to sleep at night."

Andrea's recurring dream of the strange baby ended on a curious note. As she stood in the old house that was "sitting in an open field," she said that "the floor came up and the walls started coming in. I ran out. I couldn't start my car in the dream. I couldn't start it."

Because of Andrea's very great—even crippling—anxiety, no hypnosis has been attempted, and so, unfortunately, her account has not been explored further. I am reluctant even to question her more fully about any of these obviously disturbing recollections. But if, as I suspect, Andrea's childhood abduction memories are accurate, then everything she describes here fits the pattern of an ongoing UFO involvement. Sadly, in this case the subject is an anguished, very vulnerable young woman who seems less able than most to endure the process.

The third female abductee I discussed in Chapter 7 is Pam, the young dancer. In 1979, finding herself "accidently" pregnant, she had decided upon an abortion, only to have the doctor tell her after the operation that there had been no sign of fetal tissue, and that he could not understand what had happened. In the light of the other women's recollections, I asked Pam one day if she had ever had any unusual dreams involving babies. She answered that when she was living with her husband in New Mexico—the same time as her pregnancy and "non-abortion"—she had a series of recurring dreams about a tiny baby. The dreams usually began in an unfamiliar setting, with Pam becoming aware of a very small living thing down near the floor. At first it seems to her to be an animal of some sort, but eventually, realizing it's a baby, she picks it up and holds it. She described it to me as being "tiny and pathetic, so little and thin that it looks like it can hardly survive." She holds it and feels sorry for it because "it seems so pathetic." As she recounted the dream she did not appear to feel any personal remorse or guilt about the sad little creature, emotions one might expect if these memories were triggered by her abortion. Instead, she expressed a kind of detached pity and amazement that the tiny infant was actually alive.

In the fall of 1986 we explored Pam's "dream" through hypnosis, and the results were extraordinarily close to Susan's and Andrea's recollections. Pam's words came slowly and carefully, as if the infant were right in front of her and she was describing it for the first time. She said that at first the baby "looked like a little newborn lamb lying there, a tiny little thing with skinny little legs, and when I picked it up it turned into a baby . . . but it was a pathetic-looking little baby. It was sort of half human, half whatever it was before, with skinny little legs. And the skin is white . . . it's so thin . . . the skin is so thin it's see-through . . . and I feel if I pulled at the skin it would just come right off. It's kind of weird . . . and I feel . . . sort of revolted by it. I feel sorry for it, too." I asked if it was alive. "It's alive, but it's sort of, well it looks almost like a skeleton. It's got a big head and it just lies there . . . and the legs are very skinny, as if there's almost no skeleton at all inside . . . That's why I said it looks

like some kind of animal, 'cause it's got such skinny little legs . . . they're
not human. They're longer than a baby's legs would be at that age, but
it's still a very small thing. It's not proportioned right. It's got a very small
body, like a square body, and then there are long legs, long arms, and it
just doesn't have any weight to it. The only thing that seems to be heavy
is the head. It's got a very big head, and it just lies there . . . It's like a
Raggedy Ann doll, except that its head is heavy, and you'd think the head
would fall right off . . ." I asked Pam to describe its facial features, and
she paused a while before responding. ". . . I don't want to look." I asked
if she was holding the baby. "I'm holding it, yes, but its head is behind
my head, like you hold a baby."

I wanted to know how she came to hold it. "Someone gave it to me."
She sighed and then said again, "I don't want to look at it." In a detail
that was to prove significant, she said that the person who gave her the
infant was watching her carefully. "The person is very small, wearing a
robe, a long robe . . . It's got a round head, just like those other ones
. . . it's that creepy head . . . and shiny skin . . ." Her next observation
was a shock, even in this bizarre context. "It wants me to nurse the baby
. . . It seems to want to watch, to see what I do with it." And then,
speaking softly, as if to herself: "This baby's so odd, I don't really . . . It's
weird. I can see the body but I don't want to look at the face, and I don't
see it. It won't come to my mind what it looks like . . ."

I asked if she actually nursed the baby. "Well, I seem to be trying to,"
she replied, "but there is no milk." Pam chuckled at this odd alien naïveté.
"They don't understand that you can't have milk if you don't let the baby
grow inside of you. They seem to think you'll have endless amounts of
milk. That's sort of stupid." She puts the infant to her breast, but it does
not take the nipple. "I'm sort of laughing inside, 'cause I know it's not
going to work. But I think I'll do whatever . . . I'll show them how it's
supposed to go."

Though the three women's descriptions of the infants they remember
are somewhat different, many of the similarities are striking. Susan's Wise
Baby has very thin skin, "thinner than . . . a newborn baby's hands, like
tissue paper . . . thinner than that," while the child Pam saw had white
skin "so thin it's see-through. It is weird, and I feel sort of revolted by
it." The tiny baby Susan described has a "funny . . . grayish pallor that
I think would be repulsive." Its arms and legs are also "little teeny," and
the proportions of both infants are recalled as not being normal baby's
proportions. Andrea, Susan and Pam all mentioned the extreme lightness

of these children, as if they are far below the weight of normal human babies, and all three commented on the fact that the infants do not appear to be healthy.

Taken together, these three sets of recollections (and as we shall see, Kathie Davis will eventually provide a fourth) echo one another in remarkable ways. When I first became aware of this pattern of "lost" babies and the later "presentation" of tiny, bizarre infants, I decided I should try to find out if this theme is a common one in psychology. I asked two psychiatrists and two psychologists—friends whose advice I had sought in the past on related matters—if they had ever encountered female patients reporting this kind of dream or memory. None of them had. Obviously, special circumstances might lead to this sort of recollection, but all four experienced therapists assured me that in their practice they had never heard of a "missing baby" or "tiny baby" dream such as I described.[2]

In Chapter 4 I described a "dream" Kathie Davis related to me in November of 1983. In outline, what she recalled was waking up on a table with her nightgown pulled up to her breasts. She is very relaxed, and when she opens her eyes she becomes aware of the small, gray-skinned figure standing near her, with his hand on her abdomen. He asks how she is feeling and she answers that she is "real tired and kind of crampy." He pats her gently on her stomach, near her navel, and says, "That's good." In a moment she falls back to sleep. The next day she experienced an unusual vaginal discharge and painful abdominal cramps, and when she checked her calendar she discovered that the incident coincided with her monthly ovulation. There is more to her dream but at the time I put it on a temporary shelf and pursued other matters. It wasn't until May of 1986, two and a half years later, that I explored her recollections of this dream through hypnotic regression. What we learned about the physical aspect of Kathie's experience is extremely important to our understanding of the abduction phenomenon.

I began by setting the scene of that November night, when "you had a particularly interesting dream." I instructed her to "take a few minutes and have that dream again." She moved about restlessly, as if in great discomfort.

BH: It looks like you were feeling pain, Kathie. Is that so?
KD: It's really strange. *(Sighs)* It feels like my stomach is full of air. Not my stomach . . . my hips . . . feel all swollen . . . bloated up. Even my rectum. Everything. My female parts, all across my

lower abdomen . . . just everything feels like I'm being pumped up full of air. It's extremely uncomfortable. It makes my legs feel kinda weird . . . and I had been asleep and I'm feeling really relaxed, and then I start to feel like I'm getting blown up like a balloon . . . all down in my hips and everything . . . real far down . . . *(Sighs)* And I can't . . . *(Pause. Sighs)* It's my abdomen down low feels real cold . . . it's strange . . . crawly.

BH: Crawly? Do you mean being touched or just inside or what?

KD: Just . . . prickly.

BH: Do you open your eyes to look around?

KD: *(Firmly)* No! 'Cause I don't want to. I just . . . want to go to sleep.

BH: Do you have any idea, Kathie, what's going on? Apart from how it feels?

KD: *(Sighs)* I guess . . . I'm just . . . dreaming. *(Pause)* It smells like water. It smells like salt water in here . . . real strong. It's the only thing I can think of. It smells cold in here.

BH: Do you feel that this is taking place in your bedroom?

KD: I don't know. *(Pause. Sighs)* I have the cramps. It feels like my insides are moving around. Like . . . spasms or something. Doesn't really hurt, but it makes my legs feel kinda cold. *(Sighs)* I just feel heavy and half numb.

BH: Have you ever felt anything like this before, Kathie?

KD: No. Not quite like this.

BH: What would be the closest?

KD: When they pulled the tube out of my caesarian scar, but not quite the same. I feel numb, but I feel like I'm puckering at the bottom of my scar. I'm all puckering and it hurts, sort of.

BH: In the middle, or to one side, or where?

KD: More to the right, just a shade . . . little tiny bit. Like a pinch. *(Moves in obvious discomfort, then speaks in a whisper)* Just . . . just want to go to sleep. *(Jumps suddenly)*

BH: *(I guessed that at this point Kathie had opened her eyes and seen the small, gray-skinned figure. She later confirmed that this was true.)* What just happened?

KD: Oh, well, I just don't have to worry, that's all.

BH: How do you know that?

KD: I just don't have to worry. I'm all right. Just go back to sleep.

BH: Do you say this to yourself just to reassure yourself?

KD: *(Avoids my deliberately leading question, but continues to speak as if the reassuring words were coming from an outside source)*

I'm getting used to this. This is nothing. I'm going to be fine.
I'm a good girl. I'm doing good. Very good. Excellent.

BH: Are you saying this to yourself or are you saying it to me?

KD: It's just there.

BH: When you told me about the dream you said there was a part when you opened your eyes.

KD: I already did.

BH: What did you see?

KD: I . . . just . . . I didn't . . .

BH: What did you see, Kathie?

KD: Just a smile.

BH: Just a smile?

KD: I couldn't see very well.

BH: But you said something about a smile.

KD: I think . . . that's what it felt like.

BH: Like you were smiling or someone was smiling at you?

KD: He was smiling at me.

Kathie says that she needs to relax, that she wants to go to sleep, so I tell her she will be asleep in just a moment. But first I try to find out exactly when, in November of 1983, this "dream" took place. Her answer surprised me. "It was more than once . . . Before, I wasn't quite ready, but this time I'm ready." The implication was unmistakable, and when I brought Kathie out of the trance state, she confirmed it: This same operation had been performed on her a number of times. And very soon we were to have a good idea of its apparent purpose.

Susan Williams's 1949 joint abduction with her boyfriend is a complex and fascinating story which unfortunately can only be touched on here.[3] But it is essential to know because of its striking parallels with the "dream" of Kathie's which we have just been discussing. In a June 1986 hypnotic session, Susan described herself inside a round, white room, lying on a table, unable to move. When I asked about any particular physical sensations she mentioned a "pinpoint or something" down near her pelvis, slightly off to one side.

After a few moments she says that her abdomen "feels as though it's beginning to swell and as though there is quite a lot going on . . . in the abdomen, below the belly button. Things are being moved around, like organs. I felt a little bubble of that feeling on the right side, and something that goes up and down, that goes vertically in my body. I don't know what that is . . . colon maybe. But it wasn't unpleasant. It was faint

. . . but of things being displaced, put here, put there." Her descriptions of this abdominal "distension" continued, and I asked what the feeling was like. I mentioned the feelings of distension caused by indigestion, by pregnancy, by constipation, and so forth, but Susan's answer echoed Kathie's absolutely: "It's like being blown up by air. Not the intestines themselves, but the space."

Throughout Susan's ordeal the sensations she describes are both highly specific and nearly identical to Kathie's. I felt almost certain that both women must have undergone the same strange operation, and at the time I had no idea what its purpose may have been. I had never before heard a woman describe the sensations of having her abdominal cavity inflated like a balloon and then having her internal organs "rearranged." Again, as in my recourse to the psychotherapists about the "baby dreams," I sought an informed medical opinion.

At my request, Dr. John Burger, director of gynecology and obstetrics at Perth Amboy Hospital in New Jersey, listened to the tape recording of Kathie's "dream" experience. I asked him what, if anything, he could make of the physical sensations she described. Dr. Burger asked me very coolly what I knew about laparoscopy and the procedures employed to retrieve ova from women for various medical and experimental purposes. One of these purposes, he said, is to harvest ova so that they can be used to produce so-called "test-tube babies"—ova fertilized outside the uterus and then replanted in the uteruses of host mothers for normal develop-ment and eventual birth. I admitted that I really had no specific informa-tion on the subject. The process is a delicate one, he explained. Through a needle inserted in the woman's abdominal cavity a gas—usually carbon dioxide—is introduced to fill the space and lift the vital organs up and away from the probing laparoscope. Then this long, thin, needlelike instrument, which contains magnified fiber optics, pierces the navel and is guided downwards. After it locates the tiny ovum, a second instrument is inserted into the abdomen and is used to harvest the ripe follicle by a suction process. "It sounds to me," he said, "like your friends in the UFOs may be removing ova from women who aren't even aware of it, and they're using a method very much like ours."

A comparison between this known medical practice and Kathie's and Susan's recollections is instructive. At the beginning of her experience, Kathie was apparently taken from her bedroom while she was still asleep or otherwise tranquilized. It is not surprising, then, that she does not at first recall feeling a needle penetrating her abdomen. Susan, on the other hand, was conscious through the entire operation, and she describes feeling a "pinpoint or something" in the pelvic area, slightly off to one side. Kathie says that she feels "full of air . . . swollen . . . bloated up . . . across my lower abdomen . . . like I'm getting blown up like a balloon." Susan describes this same feeling of abdominal distension: "It's like being blown up by air. Not the intestines themselves, but the space."

A laparoscope-type implement probing inside the abdomen may be the cause of the uncomfortable sensations which Kathie describes as "crawly" and "prickly." "It feels like my insides are moving around." Susan puts it this way: "Things are being moved around, like organs . . . displaced, put here, put there." (There is yet another physical reaction which both women mention at the same point in their separate narratives, and which they describe in nearly identical language. I've chosen not to reveal it here in order to provide myself a means to check the veracity of future accounts in similar situations. I've deleted specific details elsewhere in these pages for the same reason, a procedure I recommend to all investigators.[4])

When this abdominal operation is carried out by a physician like Dr. Burger, a general anesthetic is usually employed; the patient would not feel anything "moving around inside." The UFO occupants presumably employ a different method; their subjects remain conscious and relatively pain-free. And there is a second major difference between laparoscopy and these women's recollections: Neither Kathie nor Susan describe seeing or feeling a needlelike instrument penetrating their navels. Kathie's focus seems to be lower down, at her "caesarian scar," where she mentions feeling a "pinch." Susan, during her hypnotic recall, described "a pinpoint or something" in almost exactly the same place. If, in fact, their purposes are the same, these two technologies—ours and theirs—are extremely similar but not identical.

However, Dr. Burger was so struck by the parallels between certain details of the women's descriptions and the basic medical procedure that he wanted to know if either woman had actually had laparoscopy performed upon them for any reason. I checked with them and neither had. As a matter of fact, neither Kathie, Susan nor I knew that the process normally involved "blowing up the abdomen like a balloon" to lift the vital organs away from the probing implement. Susan had had a tonsillectomy as a child, but otherwise had not experienced serious or invasive operations such as the one recalled under hypnosis. Kathie's two children were both born by caesarian section. She had had a tubal ligation after her second child, but the operation was done at the time of the delivery.

There does not appear to be any personal medical precedent for their nearly identical physical recollections.

In May of 1986 Dr. Burger met Kathie and interviewed her for an hour or so, questioning her both about these recollections and her general medical history. He told me afterwards that he was very impressed by her obvious intelligence and integrity. He admitted that as a gynecologist and obstetrician he was fascinated by these cases, and so far has not been able to offer any kind of medical theory to explain their mystery—apart from the unthinkable idea that these events actually occurred.

It would appear that for many decades the UFO phenomenon has been educating its more pragmatic and attentive observers. In this process our delimiting ideas of the phenomenon's nature have been gradually refuted, one by one.[5] From the start, our theories about the UFO phenomenon proceeded from an understandable impulse to narrow and control these truly disturbing reports. For example, when they were first seen, UFOs were thought to be airships of some sort, or some nation's secret weapon. When that explanation proved untenable we slowly allowed ourselves to think that they *may be*—dare we say it—extraterrestrial spacecraft. This, of course, is a radical, "unbelievable" idea to entertain. But even within this disturbing concept we still were able to grant ourselves an edge of detachment and safety by thinking that perhaps UFOs were pilotless, remote-controlled machines of some sort, observing us from a comfortable distance. This idea began to disintegrate with the steady accumulation of "humanoid sightings," reports of strange figures seen in or near UFOs. (It is an interesting fact that for a time the leading civilian UFO investigatory group from the nineteen-sixties, NICAP by acronym, refused to accept *any* humanoid reports as having possible validity.) Eventually we thought—hoped—that even if these reports were true and there were UFO occupants, at least they were keeping their distance and leaving us alone. The Betty and Barney Hill case shattered that complacency: a terrifying abduction and a forced "physical examination," accompanied by an apparently externally imposed period of amnesia.

At each step of the way serious UFO investigators had been operating under as narrow a range of theory as possible, only to find that the UFO phenomenon, through new reports, was itself forcing us to broaden our idea of its scope. In the nineteen-sixties and early seventies it was still widely assumed that the Hills' abduction was almost a one-of-a-kind event —until hundreds of similar abduction reports began to surface. In 1975, when I became actively involved in the investigation of UFO sightings,

I had no theories about the subject beyond the grudging acknowledgments listed above. "They only seem to be examining us—a number of us—in very objective fashion," I allowed myself to think, until invasive physical-implant and sperm and ova sample-taking descriptions became all too common in abduction reports. But as I listened and observed and studied new reports, such as Kathie's and Susan's and all the others I've been recounting here, my ideas of the nature and purposes of the UFO phenomenon have been stretched to truly uncomfortable lengths. A central goal of UFO abductions, I now believe, is the apparent interbreeding of an alien species with our own. And that process, it would seem, is both covert and very widespread.

I stated at the beginning of this book that the reader's credulity would suffer perhaps unsupportable stress. I made that statement just because the limits of my own belief system had been so sorely strained by these unfolding cases. I know all too well what Justice Frankfurter meant when he announced his inability to believe in the historical fact of the Holocaust, despite the eyewitnesses. Our minds can only go so far and then a kind of self-imposed censorship takes over: "I don't care how much evidence you show me—I will not consider it! I will not permit myself to think these thoughts."

The desire *not* to believe, *not* to entertain even for a moment these truly shattering ideas, is a desire shared by researchers and committed skeptics alike. No one—and especially those who have experienced UFO abductions—can comfortably wander the roads of daily life with these frightening images constantly hanging over them as real, perceived possibilities. Most abductees eventually find ways to come to terms with their particular forms of dread and self-doubt. The methods by which they handle their experiences include denial, repression, anger, commitment to helping others through support groups and investigations, and just about anything else that the mind can invent to keep traumatic memories at bay.[6]

Kathie's most efficient self-protective method involves neutralizing disturbing UFO events by first labelling them as dreams and then storing them on a sort of mental back shelf. There, under that designation, she can tolerate them without disrupting her daily routine. No matter how extensive the physical evidence and the external corroboration, Kathie nearly always chooses to refer to her UFO experiences as dreams. It is a useful, agreed-upon fiction that I wholeheartedly support. In these unprecedented situations almost any device that helps to lessen anxiety and stress is preferable to reminders of one's powerlessness and vulnerability.

And so when Kathie called me from Indianapolis in the spring of 1986 to tell me about yet one more remarkable "dream," the underlying meaning of the term was understood by both of us. It had been absolutely real, she said, ignoring the obvious contradiction. When she described this new dream to me I was not yet aware of Kathie's and Susan's "laparoscopy" experiences, the events we have just been discussing. But a natural inference from those experiences is the idea that ova might easily be taken more than once from any particular woman. Andrea, as we have seen, had two sets of "presentation" dreams about tiny babies—once at the ages of sixteen or seventeen and then again at twenty-two or twenty-three. Susan Williams remembered feeling the sensations of "something moving in her lower abdominal cavity" during two different apparent abductions.[7] Kathie recalled under hypnosis that this abdominal operation had happened more than once; it was a procedure she was familiar with, and which she was told could only take place when she was ready. If the production of hybrids is one of the purposes of UFO abductions, and individuals, as we have seen, are usually taken more than once, then a successful breeding experiment with a particular man or woman might well be repeated.

Everything about Kathie Davis's long history of UFO experiences implies an intense interest in her by a specific group of UFO occupants. For whatever reasons these occupants have time and time again involved themselves in her life and in the lives of other members of her family. And so I was not totally surprised when Kathie told me that this new dream involved a second "presentation ceremony," similar to her memory of being shown the little girl during the October 1983 abduction. She remembered it relatively completely when she awoke in her bedroom about four in the morning, feeling marvelously happy and filled with wonder. She told me by telephone the next morning many details which later emerged in somewhat fuller form under hypnosis.

The central event in her dream occurred when she was shown a tiny baby in the presence of the same little girl—now older and taller—that she had seen before. But the most staggering detail of all was this: She was told that these children—presumably her own—were but two of *nine*. The implication was that since 1978, *nine* of her ova had been taken, successfully fertilized and brought to term. And in a strangely personal, human note, she was told that she would be allowed to *name* the children! At this point every reader is permitted the Felix Frankfurter reaction. It is, perhaps, the only appropriate response for those whose sense of things does not accept as a viable possibility the intrusion of extraterrestrial intelligence. Yet once that possibility is entertained, the fertilization of nine ova taken from the same woman is no less plausible than other forms of intervention.

The hypnotic session which dealt with these memories took place in May 1986, in New York. Once or twice I phrased questions that were based on the words Kathie had used during our phone conversation about this experience. I set the scene, holding to our unspoken agreement that these memories, like the others, would be regarded as nothing more than a dream. Throughout the session Kathie's voice was unusually soft and filled with wonder. She seemed completely under the spell of the scene and its undeniable magic.

BH: You told me about a dream you had recently. It was just a dream . . . but you said there was a little baby in it . . . Do you remember that dream?

KD: Yes.

BH: Can you tell me a little bit about it? Where are you when the dream begins?

KD: I'm in a big room. It has to be a dream . . .

BH: I know it's just a dream, but I'm interested in hearing about it.

KD: *(Long pause)* There are nine.

BH: Do you see nine, or are you just told this, or what?

KD: I see two.

BH: Do you want to describe them to me?

KD: The oldest and the youngest. *(Pause)* They want to watch me . . . hold this . . . baby. They want . . . to feel how I love it. *(Whispering, as if to herself)* They want . . . to feel how I love it. I shouldn't worry, 'cause she'll take care of it. *(Pause)* I have something they can't give it.

BH: What is that, Kathie, that you have?

KD: Something . . . to do with touch, and the human part . . . and they don't understand, but they'll learn. And they said I could name them. I would choose. And I picked Andrew . . . and Elizabeth and Sarah and Peter and Caleb and Rebecca and Emily and Paul and Larry.

BH: Are Andrew and Elizabeth the two that are there?

KD: Andrew and Emily.

BH: Andrew and Emily. *(Kathie is suddenly very agitated. I calm her.)* It's just a dream, Kathie, just a dream. Dreams are funny.

... all sorts of things happen in dreams. It's O.K. What just happened, Kathie? It's better to tell me about it. What happened?

KD: They just left. They were here and they just disappeared.

BH: Do you mean Andrew and Emily? *(The odd "disappearance" was discussed later, after the hypnosis ended.)*

KD: Yes.

BH: But you held Andrew?

KD: Yes.

BH: Tell me a little bit about holding him.

KD: I held him close . . . up to my breasts . . . and just . . . cuddled him . . . his tiny head. It was so pitiful. I held his head in my hand. I kissed him on the head. He was all pale . . . he looked dead, but he wasn't.

BH: Does he look like a little newborn baby, or a little older, or what?

KD: He looked like an old man, and he looked so wise. I looked in his eyes . . . he was so . . . smart . . . more wise than anybody in the world. And he understood my touch . . .

BH: It's a wonderful thing to feel that. *(At this point intuition led me to support and reinforce Kathie's obviously deep maternal feelings.)*

KD: And he felt strong again.

BH: That was the way he responded to you . . . you made him strong . . .

KD: *(Softly)* My touch.

BH: *(Pause)* Kathie, is Emily watching this?

KD: Yes.

BH: Can you tell me a little about how it seems she's responding or feeling?

KD: She was just . . . she was learning.

BH: Is she the little girl you've seen before, or is she different?

KD: She's the same. Taller. She's not afraid of me anymore.

BH: That's good.

KD: She's very curious about me.

BH: How can you tell that?

KD: Just the way she looks at me . . .

BH: Does she touch you, or do you touch her, or do you just touch Andrew?

KD: She touched my face. She wanted to feel it. *(Quickly)* She backed away, now . . . It seemed as if when she touched my face and then pulled away it was almost pleasant . . . and she wanted

to touch it again, but she was a little leery. And then she
. . . settled into watching me, inside and out. Just like a sponge.

BH: How does the dream end, Kathie? Sometimes dreams just stop
and sometimes there's a little piece at the end . . .

KD: I was . . . in the dream I was told not to worry about him.
Everything was going to be as planned. Everything was fine.
And I would . . . see them again.

BH: Do you know who it is that tells you this?

KD: That guy *(the same small, gray-skinned figure she'd dealt with
so many times before, as she made clear after the hypnosis
ended).*

BH: Does he have a name?

KD: I can't pronounce it. It's almost a feeling rather than a name.
I have to go soon . . . or I'll get sick. So it's time to go.

BH: So how do you go, in your dream?

KD: I go to sleep. Lie down, go to sleep. I wake up in my bed.
And I start writing all these names down, over and over
again . . .

BH: *(Prepares to wake her up, gives reinforcing suggestions: You'll
have good, strong feelings about this dream. Good, vivid memories of Emily and Andrew, etc.)*

KD: . . . When I kissed his head it was soft. It was real soft. Softer
than Robbie's or Tommy's heads ever were . . .

BH: *(Brings her out of the trance state)*

When she was fully awake, Kathie yawned and stretched and smiled
at me with a very satisfied, happy expression on her face. "What a dream,"
she whispered. "You know his head was real soft, like a marshmallow. It
was no bigger than this," and she indicated something about the size of
an apple. "I went to sleep in the dream and then I woke up and started
writing down all those names. It was about four A.M. and I couldn't go
back to sleep I felt so good." I asked how the little girl looked. "She looked
more . . . a lot better. She looked more like a little girl, more like a normal
person. Her hair was a lot thicker . . . still blond . . . whitish. She's about
forty inches tall . . . about Robbie's height." I asked about her skin color.
"It was pale but pretty normal. Real, real pale. She's more filled out
everywhere, still thin, but not . . ." "How about her mouth?" "Small, but
normal. Little lips. Small. Kind of a heart-shaped mouth."

I was extremely curious about her attentive presence there while Kathie
held the tiny baby. I repeated her remark that the girl was somehow

learning how Kathie felt. "Yes. It's hard for me to describe. It's like I already *knew* what she was doing, so I tried to make it easier for her. And I was so full of emotion for this little baby. You know, it was like she could get inside of me and feel what I was feeling."

I mentioned Kathie's sense that the tiny baby was wise, that its eyes seemed wise. I asked if the baby's eyes were like the little girl's. "No, they were darker. Bigger, darker, kinda purplish-brown, like a newborn's eyes. Kind of a purply color, yet there was something more there. I just fell into them. It's hard to describe. It's like the whole world was in this little baby's eyes. It was like, God, he knew, he *knew* what I felt. He just knew. I can't describe it. It was so intense, so euphoric or something. I was so excited, so up."

One last thing remained to be covered. I mentioned that Kathie had jumped when she said they "disappeared." "My mind just went blank for a minute. I felt disassociated from my body. Under hypnosis I'm aware of this room here, the sounds and so forth, but this time for a minute I felt disassociated from my body and I jumped, sort of to get myself back. I didn't know what was going on. For an instant there I didn't have any arms or legs or anything. Just . . . a being . . ." Her description suggested some kind of mind-body split that I had never encountered before, either as a clear product of hypnosis itself, or as one more new and bizarre element in the abduction scenario. I wondered, of course, if it was connected in any way with the sense she had that the little girl was, as it were, *inside* her, feeling Kathie's emotions as if they were her own.

It is helpful to place Kathie's description of "Andrew" in context with the other women's similar accounts. Pam describes the tiny baby in her recurring dreams as "pathetic, so little and thin that it looks like it can hardly survive." Andrea recalled a baby so tiny that it should have been in an incubator, an infant with dark, shiny, almost hypnotic eyes. ". . . When that baby looked at me, something happened to me. I just kept staring at it." Kathie gazed into her baby's eyes and said that she "just fell into them. I can't describe it. It was like the whole world was in that baby's eyes." She said that the infant was wise, "more wise than anybody in the world." Yet this "wise baby" was still "pitiful. He was all pale . . . he looked dead, but he wasn't." Susan described her Wise Baby as having a "vacant" look, and a "funny . . . grayish pallor . . . that I think would be repulsive, as I look at it now." It was "*very* fragile." She supported the baby with one hand, its head fitting in her palm. Kathie also stated that the baby's head fitted into her palm, and was the size of an apple. Its length, consonant with the others, was about twelve inches.[8]

Every detailed UFO report requires some kind of coherent explanation. One cannot simply dismiss out of hand the accounts of demonstrably honest and sane human beings just because one finds the content of their accounts unpalatable. In summary, the facts we have been considering are these: Two women, Kathie Davis and Susan Williams, describe under hypnosis more or less typical abduction experiences—except that they include a particular kind of abdominal operation. A gynecologist-obstetrician is consulted and finds the details of their recollected operations surprisingly like that of an ovum-retrieval procedure currently in use. The details of this current operation are unknown to the two women (who, incidently, have never met or communicated, and know nothing of each other's case).

Two other women, Pam and Andrea, who also describe UFO abduction experiences, found themselves pregnant under unusual circumstances. *Very* unusual in Andrea's case, since she was only thirteen at the time and "dreamed" that she was, in effect, artificially inseminated by a strange, gray-skinned, large-eyed figure who inserted a thin, tubelike implement into her. The fetus was aborted, but at her first examination the gynecologist found that despite her pregnancy her hymen was still intact. Pam also sought an abortion (*after* a suspected abduction), only to have the doctor who performed the operation announce that despite the earlier positive pregnancy tests no fetal tissue remained, and inexplicably she was no longer pregnant.

Each of the four women—Kathie, Susan, Pam and Andrea—at various times either "dreamed" or remembered under hypnosis that she was shown an abnormally tiny baby, grayish in skin color, oddly proportioned and apparently only partially like a human infant. The women's descriptions of these tiny babies are extraordinarily alike, and again, none of them have ever met or communicated. The psychologists I've consulted on this matter uniformly find their accounts perplexing because they do not fit normal psychological patterns. So we are left with two possible lines of explanation. The first requires the existence of a new and heretofore unknown psychological phenomenon, in which women "hallucinate" nearly identical scenes, involving nearly identical semi-human babies. And this previously unknown psychological phenomenon apparently affects the results of chemical tests for pregnancy, turning negatives into false positives. (Jung would be proud to know of such a powerful new manifestation of the "collective unconscious.") The other remaining explanation is simple but "untenable": These women, Pam and Susan and Kathie and Andrea, are actually remembering what they saw. Their experiences were real. Both of these explanations, it is safe to say, violate conventional wisdom.

It is time now to consider some of the theoretical implications of these truly disturbing, unwelcome reports, and to attempt a further testing of their truth.

10
A Summing Up

When Kathie described being shown the tiny, seemingly hybrid baby, she reported a striking new detail: The UFO occupants apparently wanted her to hold the infant so they could observe something about human touch and human emotion. For the moment Kathie's role was that of an instructor; her abductors—as well as the baby—needed something that only she could provide. "It has something to do with touch, and the human part . . . They don't understand, but they'll learn." It occurred to me afterwards that this need for a demonstration of maternal feeling might be the reason why UFO occupants have apparently shown various female abductees their half-human offspring, if that term is even approximately correct. Something of this sort might explain Susan's encounters with her tiny Wise Baby, or Pam's description of being asked, after she was handed the pathetic little white-skinned creature, to demonstrate how a mother would nurse a newborn baby! In July of 1986, as I was trying to fit this new piece of information into an already bizarre puzzle, I received a phone call from "Lucille Forman," a New Yorker who was spending the summer in Provincetown, Massachusetts. Her own UFO experience, I later discovered, added fascinating details to this new idea.

On the evening of August 20, 1985, Lucille was in her Provincetown apartment watching a film on her VCR. As she learned the next day, she was alone in the building; none of the other tenants were at home that night. The renovated Victorian house in which she lived contains four apartments, and is perched on a hill nearly surrounded by trees. In the woods behind it is a flat area that had been recently cleared for the erection of a new building.

The first odd thing that Lucille noticed that night was the behavior of her cat, which began to yowl as if very frightened. Lucille was deeply absorbed in *Gandhi,* the film she was viewing, and chose to ignore her cat. But after a few minutes she began to feel a "pronounced, enveloping, eerie presence." Her own behavior, as she told me later, was unusual. She did not get up and look around as she would normally have done, but instead she began repeating to herself, "Don't get up, don't look up. Don't do anything but sit in this chair. If you get up something will happen. Don't look up. Keep your eyes on the TV." By profession Lucille is a psychotherapist, so she is naturally observant of her own behavior and clear in describing it. She found herself saying in her mind, as if to someone or something, "Please leave me alone. I'm all by myself. I don't want an experience of this kind right now."

Essentially this is all she remembers about the evening. When she awoke in the morning the cat was still yowling occasionally, and Lucille discovered that the electricity was off in her apartment. There had been a power failure in her part of Provincetown affecting about 2,500 people.[1] She felt a great need to be outside the house, "in the sunshine, where things were familiar." She sat outside for a while, and when she went back indoors she wrote down everything she could recall about the previous night. "I was convinced that something profound had happened, but I wasn't sure what it was."

Provincetown is a short distance away from Wellfleet, where my summer studio is located, so a friend of Lucille's suggested she contact me about her odd experience. There were several reasons why I welcomed this interruption from my work on the Kathie Davis case. Lucille was a very credible woman, and her experience had occurred relatively recently in an area that was immediately accessible to me. But I was also curious to know if the patterns of apparent genetic experimentation that I had discovered might turn up in yet another case.

My first interview with Lucille yielded several significant details. In answer to my question about any odd, unresolved childhood recollections that she thought might bear on the issue of UFOs, Lucille related a disturbing memory of a large-eyed visitor to her bedroom when she was quite small. There were other, similar recollections. But more important in this context was a remark her friend made. "Lucille," she said, "maybe you'd better show Budd that round mark on your abdomen that turned up last summer." It is a small, circular scar located approximately over the region of the right ovary, and hypnotic recall eventually yielded its probable cause.

Again, this is not the place to go into Lucille's abduction account in any depth, beyond a simple outline. Three hypnotic regression sessions and additional normal recall that arose spontaneously between the sessions have disclosed the following: Lucille did look up from her TV screen and saw several large-headed, grayish figures on the deck in front of her. She was told telepathically that if she did not come outside they would come into the apartment and take her. The TV went dead and she saw, instead of the film she had been watching, a face on the screen that was "white with huge shiny black eyes, no ears, small mouth—and it was angry. The message was, 'LOOK AT ME!' I thought back, 'No, I won't look at you.' (I looked at the floor.)"[2] But such is the UFO occupants' apparent ability to overcome our psychological resistance that eventually Lucille stood up and walked out onto her deck. Next she felt that she was floating up the path with two figures flanking her while two more remained in front and back. The UFO was in the clearing behind the house. "I did not feel warmth. They did not touch me but allowed me to enter, myself . . . I see myself walking in with the person whose face appeared on the TV screen. To my mind his behavior was no more or less than our military personnel during a mission . . . there was a sense of urgency conveyed." Placed upon an examining table, Lucille at one point described a "sudden sharp pain in the area I usually feel pain when I menstruate."

As an trained therapist, Lucille is a fine psychological observer. I judged her intuitive sense of the UFO occupants' *purposes* and their general situation to be reliable. It is one thing to accurately recall purely *visual* details, such as height, color and physical appearance. But the more impressionistic territory of "UFO intentions" provides an arena much more conducive to simple old-fashioned projection, wherein all kinds of emotional preconceptions about the phenomenon can come to light. Yet I believe that Lucille's impressions are trustworthy and that some degree of philosophical communication seems to have taken place.

She wrote later that this alien society seemed to be "millions of years old, of outstanding technology and intellect but not much individuality or warmth." She had the sense that "the society was dying, that children were being born and living to a certain age, perhaps preadolescence, and then dying." There was "a desperate need to survive, to continue their race. It is a culture without touching, feeling, nurturing . . . basically intellectual. Something has gone wrong genetically. Whatever their bodies are now, they have evolved from something else. My impression is that they wanted to somehow share their history and achievements and their present difficulties in survival. But I really don't know what they are looking for." Lucille recalled that her captors had shown her a number of realistic (holographic?) images during her abduction experience, as if to illustrate their plight. "I saw a child about four feet tall, gray, totally their race, waving its arms . . . it was in pain and dying. I was told that this is what is happening now.

"We spoke about the lack of touching. I told them that some animals here can die within a day of birth if they are not licked and touched by their mothers or other loving caretakers, since that affects their perceptions of their bodily functions as well as of themselves." And here, in this unearthly context, Lucille, the psychotherapist, the committed helper, made a most unlikely proposal. "Strange as it may seem, I suggested their interpreting Ashley Montague's book *Touching*. I know this sounds utterly ridiculous, but when I arrived back in New York after our hypnosis sessions, I immediately placed the book facing out on the windowsill. This seems a strange thing to do, but I thought 'Who knows?' I don't know what else they need to know, but I feel we should help if we can."

Again I want to underline the fact that Ms. Forman had absolutely no knowledge of Kathie Davis's account of demonstrating, with the tiny gray infant, human touching and holding. The child "understood my touch," Kathie had said, "and he felt strong again." She also reported that while she cuddled him, the older (hybrid) girl was "watching me, inside and out." She sensed that the girl was absorbing everything "like a sponge" —Kathie's emotions, gestures, her thoughts and reactions—just as Pam sensed that the creature who handed her the tiny hybrid baby was carefully observing how she handled the infant to nurse it. It seems to me that Kathie, Pam and Lucille are describing, from different points of view, the same strange extraterrestrial situation. In this unexpected scenario the UFO occupants—despite their obvious technological superiority—are desperate for both human genetic material *and* the ability to feel human emotions—particularly maternal emotions. Unlikely though it may seem, it is possible that the very survival of these extraterrestrials depends upon their success in absorbing chemical and psychological properties received from human abductees.

All of these speculations are unthinkable, though eminently logical in the light of the case material we have been examining. And there is still another dramatic parallel between Lucille's and Kathie's UFO experiences which helps buttress their veracity. During Lucille's first hypnotic session, sometime after she describes being taken off the examining table, she sees a figure who "seems to have a gender . . . and is very pale . . . not gray like the others, but a paler being that seemed to be feminine . . . There also seems to be a warmth emanating from her that seems to be very special. She's maybe even a little taller. I remember being conscious of a pointed chin and the big eyes . . . but more rounded features . . . more roundedness, somehow. Very warm and delicate. And I also had the idea that . . . whoever it was . . . I'll call it a she . . . was a very special being. Very ethereal, very esthetic-looking."

During Lucille's second hypnotic session she amplified her description of this special being: "She is perhaps an adolescent. I don't see ears . . . There is the slight protrusion of a nose. Her eyes are like the other ones with the black eyes, except her eyes are huge and blue. No eyebrows . . . A large cranium . . . and more rounded features. There's a delicacy and also . . . a warmth which, you know . . . since she's maybe a cross . . . partly earthly, partly of them . . . She was not totally 'them' . . . totally alien." In other words, a hybrid very like the little girl Kathie once described, and whom she saw once more as an older child. (See illustrations.) The huge blue eyes, the large cranium, the tiny, pointed chin and the small nose are all described similarly. The basic difference is that the child Kathie saw had thin, white hair, so thin that the scalp showed through here and there, while Lucille described an adolescent who had no hair. Both women, however, said that the children they saw had no eyebrows. Unlike Kathie, Lucille did not experience profound maternal feelings during her encounter, though she remembers at one point sitting cross-legged on the floor and cradling the child in her lap. "I felt what is this . . . what, exactly, is this creature . . . and just wondering 'What do you do here?' I felt helpless because I wanted to help her, and I didn't know what to do."

There is much more to Lucille's account, including an extremely dramatic area or scene that she was apparently allowed to see and that bears directly on the themes we have been examining. Nevertheless I will not go into it here. As I've said before, it's important to withhold certain details to provide a way of checking the veracity of future reports. The scene she described, however, is so unusual and potentially so significant that I eagerly await any corroboration should it someday appear.

Over the decades popular science fiction has presented essentially two versions of contact with extraterrestrial life. In the more common version, such as Orson Welles' radio version of *The War of the Worlds* or the film *Invasion of the Body Snatchers*, aliens arrive like cosmic storm troopers to mindlessly devour and conquer us. The benign alternative scenario, exemplified by such popular films as *The Day the Earth Stood Still*, portrays the aliens as kindly, spiritual beings who have come here to save us from our own self-destructiveness. These two contrasting situations are obviously religious in nature; in each version human beings and aliens have opposing roles as gods and devils. In the film *Close Encounters of the Third Kind* the all-powerful gods thunder down from on high, accompanied by organ music, presumably to save us from our problems and initiate a new cosmic era of good feeling.

But very instructive insights occur when we compare these two basic sci-fi myths with what we have been examining in Kathie's or Susan's or Lucille's vivid accounts—or, for that matter, in the accounts of the men I touched upon in Chapter 7. None of these recollections in any way suggests traditional sci-fi gods and devils. These men and women are neither devoured nor saved. They are borrowed, involuntarily. They are used physically and then returned, frightened but not deliberately harmed. And the aliens are described neither as all-powerful, lordly presences, nor as satanic monsters, but instead as complex, controlling, physically frail beings who apparently need something for their very survival that they are forced to search for among their various abductees.

And behind the abduction phenomenon as it has been described by literally hundreds of witnesses there seems to be a very peculiar and very consistent ethical position. In none of the cases I've investigated have I ever encountered even the suggestion of deliberate harm or malevolence. The abductees are apparently kept as calm as possible and seem to suffer only minimal physical pain—a situation not unlike that of a well-run dental office. People are picked up, examined, samples are taken and so on, and then they are returned more or less intact to the place where the abduction began. There seems to be a definite effort by the UFO occupants to make the operations as swift, efficient and painless as possible. There is reason to believe that the partial amnesia which often accompanies these experiences is intended to help the abductees continue their normal lives as much as it is to conceal UFO activities.[3]

And yet . . . Every UFO investigator who deals with abduction cases, every psychotherapist who has had an abductee as a client, knows the harm these experiences inevitably visit upon innocent people. They almost invariably suffer, in Dr. Robert J. Lifton's term, psychological scarring (as well as *physical* scarring, as we have seen). A woman who had undergone several consciously unremembered childhood abductions around her eighth, ninth and tenth years told me that when she was ten her fear was so profound that she made a nearly successful effort to kill herself. "But it wasn't until I saw my own children reach the age of ten," she said, "that I really understood how strange it was that a child would try to kill herself at that age." She now knows the cause of the unbearable dread she suffered during those childhood years, but her example suggests the possibility that others, not knowing the source of their terror, might actually have succeeded in their own suicide attempts.

And so we come to a central paradox: The UFO occupants, with their apparently hypnotic ability to frame and control at least our short-term behavior, seem, at the same time, to understand almost nothing about basic human psychology. In one case I've investigated, a Minnesota man and his wife were abducted together; the husband was forced to watch helplessly while a long needle was run into the navel of his paralyzed wife. His abductors were completely surprised by his fury and hatred. "But we *want* you to see what we're doing," they explained ingenuously. "We are not harming your mate. Why are you angry?" Kathie's outburst of pain and anguish when her abductors removed the fetus she was carrying apparently also took them by surprise. These incidents, in which UFO occupants seem unable to comprehend even the most obvious and predictable human feelings, are but a few in a long, long list. It is as if they are truly alien to most human psychology, though they may understand enough about human *physiology* to concern themselves with physical pain and its alleviation.

I have made the point again and again in these pages that UFO abduction reports, because of their similarity of content and detail, must be accepted one of two ways: Either they represent some new and heretofore unrecognized and nearly universal psychological phenomenon—a theory which does not take into account the accompanying *physical* evidence—or they represent honest attempts to report real events. Obviously it is absolutely crucial to know if extraterrestrials exist and are, as the reports indicate, experimenting with humankind—or if the reports represent some profoundly radical new mental aberration. When one considers the ethical complexities I have just been discussing, their bearing on the issue of fantasy versus reality is extremely revealing. Because, rather than fitting into a predictably anthropomorphic schema of good and evil, gods and devils (which is, after all, the basic framework of both psychological fantasy and popular fiction), the UFO occupants as described exist in a strangely mixed, nearly incomprehensible ethical world. Their puzzling but consistent morality nowhere intersects with the black-and-white certainties of popular fantasy and imagination. Their psychology, if one can use the term, does not make any more sense to us than human psychology apparently makes to them. The image that remains is one of two different intelligences that lack a common plane of understanding. But there is yet another unlikely factor here—the technologically superior group apparently views itself as more genuinely needy than the more "primitive" culture. One simply cannot reconcile the idea of kindly, helpful, all-powerful "Space Brothers"—a science fiction cliché now dear to spiritualist cults—with the ethically complicated reality of these unsettling UFO accounts. But it is equally impossible to reconcile the familiar image of "Space Invaders," swooping down upon us to conquer and colonize our planet, with the longstanding pattern of subtle and covert UFO interactions with our people. By any standard of comparison, the UFO phenomenon as it has been described seems less like a simplistic product of popular fantasy than it does a highly complex, morally ambiguous and self-contained external reality. A reality, I should add, that none of us understands.

By now it should be apparent that the UFO abduction phenomenon not only profoundly affects the lives of those whom it touches, but has involved far greater numbers of people than any of us had ever imagined. The particular individuals I have been examining in these pages constitute only a tiny sample, and can be misleading to the extent that I have stressed the cases of female abductees at the expense of male. (In actual fact the ratio of male to female abductees is just about fifty-fifty.) An indication of the apparently very large number of people who have been abducted can be obtained by considering, for example, the response from a particular television program on the UFO abduction phenomenon, broadcast locally in a midwestern city in 1986. Two UFO abductees appeared with me to discuss the subject for about an hour, with an intelligent talk-show host respectfully conducting the interviews. The producer of the program told me later that there had been an almost unprecedented number of letters and calls following the broadcast, and a number of the letters were forwarded to me. Of these I answered about ten, and during a later trip to the area contacted the three whose cases had seemed the most promising. One of the three, as I suspected, turned out to have been an abductee —but her case involved other members of her family. I met and interviewed her mother and sister who both described, through normal and hypnotic recall, earlier abduction experiences. In a second case, contacting and interviewing a man who had written to me in care of the TV station led to four other abduction accounts among members of his family. My third contact was with a young woman who had also written, and who also turned out to have been, as I suspected, an abductee. Many hours of investigation and hypnotic regression have been spent on these cases, even though I present them here as mere statistics; each represents an extremely complex, disturbing and emotional series of experiences. But my point is this: The TV program led to a large number of phone calls and letters, yet I was able to follow up in only three cases. After investigation these three cases involved a total of nine individuals who I have every reason to believe are describing genuine abduction experiences. One television program, then, followed up somewhat haphazardly, has so far yielded *nine* highly probable abduction cases. I immediately think of those I *didn't* contact, and what may lie buried in their memories. And what of the others, who only called the station and whose names were lost? And what of those who, for various reasons, lacked the drive or time to write or call, despite what they might have remembered? And most significant of all, how many abductees might there be among the hundreds of thousands of people in that area who did not watch that particular TV program on that particular morning?

Again I want to describe the general pattern of these accounts: An individual, male or female, is first abducted as a child, at a time possibly as early as the third year. During that experience a small incision is often made in the child's body, apparently for sample-taking purposes, and then the child is given some kind of physical examination. There will often follow a series of contacts or abductions extending through the years of puberty. In some cases sperm samples will be taken from young males— I have one case in which this process began during the man's thirteenth year—and ova samples taken from young females. As we have seen in three cases dealt with here, actual artificial insemination can also be attempted very early—with Andrea at age thirteen, with Susan apparently at sixteen, and with Kathie at seventeen. (I have two other cases, not included here, in which the somewhat less clear-cut evidence suggests that artificial insemination occurred to these women at ages sixteen and twenty-one, respectively.)

In the cases in which artificial insemination is attempted, the women are apparently re-abducted after two or three months of pregnancy, and the fetus is removed from the uterus. However, it seems that some of these same women have been taken at later times during ovulation for the removal of ova from the Fallopian tubes. After the ova are retrieved by this process they are then apparently fertilized and brought to term outside the womb, under circumstances one can barely guess at. Why these two very different reproductive procedures have been used on some of the same women is unclear. But in a parallel way some of the male abductees who have had sperm samples taken have also been subjected at later times to a kind of involuntary sexual intercourse. There seems to be no logical reason why two different reproductive methods have been employed with both male and female abductees, but this is what the data suggests. The UFO occupants' genetic curiosity does not seem to extend to all abductees, though the accounts I've received indicate that it may apply to as many as half of them, and conceivably to an even higher percentage if these operations are being underreported for obvious reasons of embarrassment and hesitation.

Perhaps the most unsettling idea of all is the possibility that a child born normally to an abductee may have been, prior to conception, subjected to some form of genetic tampering. I have no evidence to support such a paranoia-inducing suspicion, though I feel that two suggestive coincidences should be described here. During my investigation of the simultaneous abduction of a man and his wife in New England—a case which I have not previously mentioned—the woman told me that she remembers the date and time very clearly. "It happened the night my son was conceived," she reported. She remarked upon this fact very casually, and appeared to regard it as merely an interesting coincidence. In a similar case that occurred in a southern state, the wife told me the same thing, that she believed her UFO experience—the sighting of a UFO hovering behind the trees on her property (and a probable subsequent abduction) —occurred the night her child was conceived. Again, she mentioned it only as a coincidence, and as an aid in identifying the night of the UFO encounter. In both cases the babies were born naturally and are now normal, healthy children; they do not seem to be different in any immediately obvious way from their siblings. For various reasons neither of the two mothers has been hypnotically regressed, so their UFO experiences remain largely unexplored. The coincidences of apparent UFO abduction and conception occurring the same night are probably only that—coincidences—though I feel that this information should at least be mentioned here in an attempt to include all pertinent data.

The long-term effect of these complex abduction experiences is psychological. Though some of the resulting behavior may be similar, UFO abductees are not like people who've had a single traumatic experience, such as the victims of automobile accidents or brutal muggings. They are people who have been, at intervals over the years, involuntarily subjected to a frightening and invasive "secret life," in the phrase of one young abductee. The emotions this secret life engenders can include fear, dread, helplessness, profound maternal confusion and loss, the sense of physical —even sexual—vulnerability, and a thousand other things, ranging all the way up to basic uncertainty as to where one really belongs, where home really is. And all along this road lies a terrible sense of self-doubt, a questioning of one's very sanity. A young Minnesota woman who was abducted as a child and then again as an adult recorded some of her thoughts and emotions both as an attempt to clarify things for herself and, by generalizing her experience, to provide possible support for other abductees:

> For most of us it began with the memories. Though some of us recalled parts or all of our experiences, it was more common for us to have to seek them out where they were—buried in a form of amnesia. Often we did this through hypnosis, which was, for many of us, a new experience. And what mixed feelings we had as we faced those memories! Almost without exception we felt terrified as we relived these traumatic events, a sense of being overwhelmed by their impact. But there was also disbelief. *This can't be real. I must be dreaming. This isn't happening.* Thus began the vacillation and self-doubt, the alternating periods of skepticism and belief as we tried to incorporate our memories into our sense of who we are and what we know. We often felt crazy; we continued our search for the "real" explanation. We tried to figure out what was wrong with us that these images were surfacing. *Why is my mind doing this to me?*
>
> And then there was the problem of talking about our experiences with others. Many of our friends were skeptics, of course, and though it hurt us not to be believed, what could we expect? We were still skeptics ourselves at times, or probably had been in the past. The responses we got from others mirrored our own. The people we

talked to believed us and doubted us, they were confused and looked for other explanations just as we had. Many were rigid in their denial of even the slightest possibility of abductions, and whatever words they used the underlying message was certainly clear. *I know better than you what is real and what isn't. I'm right and you're wrong.* We felt caught in the prison of a vicious circle that seemed to be imposed on us as abductees by a skeptical society:

Why do you believe you were abducted?
You believe it because you're crazy.
How do we know you're crazy?
Because you believe you were abducted!

Our own belief was less an intellectual process than an experiential one, and what finally dawned on us was that others had no proof that the abductions *weren't* real. If the thought of abduction was so threatening to them, that was their problem, not ours. We learned the hard way, through trial and error, whom we could and could not trust. We learned the subtle difference between secrecy and privacy. But many of us experienced a strong sense of isolation. We felt the pain of being different, as though we were only "passing" as normal. Some of us came to the difficult realization that there was no one with whom we could be our complete selves, and that felt like a pretty lonely place to be.

It was common to go through stress reactions after the abductions surfaced. We experienced insomnia, headaches, exhaustion, changes in appetite and a renewed sense of fear and powerlessness. If an abduction happened once it could happen again, at any time, without warning, and there was nothing we could do to prevent it. Those of us with small children felt the weight of our fear for them, and sometimes a vague sense of guilt at our inability to protect them. Nothing in life had prepared us for these experiences, and it all seemed impossible to comprehend.

One of the abductees' most frequently voiced reactions is plain and direct: "Why don't you aliens or UFO occupants or whoever you are simply *ask* me to do what you want? Ask my permission. Respect me as a person. Come in through the front door instead of stalking and kidnapping. If you did, I might go with you willingly, especially if you explained to me what it is you wanted." A reasonable request, but, so far as I know, one that has never been honored . . . perhaps because it has never been understood.

And what is the ultimate purpose of these abductions, these examinations and implants, these genetic attempts to produce hybrids, which have inevitably created emotional havoc among many innocent people? Do the UFO occupants want to lessen the distance between our race and theirs in order to land, eventually, and join us on this planet? And if so, would this be an operation conducted in the open, or in a more sinister, covert manner? Or do these aliens merely wish to enrich their own stock and then depart as mysteriously as they arrived, having achieved their goal and revivified their own endangered species? Or is there yet some other goal we have not even imagined, something unknowable at this point in our intellectual evolution? None of these questions presently have answers, just as no abductee can really, *really* understand and master his bizarre experience. As I said earlier, the situation is the polar opposite of a cult —we have all the mysterious *miracles* one could wish for, but no beliefs. No dogmas. So far as we know we have neither gods nor devils, neither ethics nor evil. The purpose and meaning of it all is as uncertain as ever.

The final words here should be Kathie's. On a spring night in 1986, Kathie and I and about fifteen abductees gathered at my studio to talk about what these events have meant on a personal level to each of us. Each wrestled with internal—and natural—disbelief. Each stated his or her version of Justice Frankfurter's lament, his inability, despite the evidence, to accept the unthinkable. Each dealt with the undeniable emotional cost of these experiences. Kathie chose, in that gathering of fellow survivors, to speak finally of her most intimate secret—her memory of the little girl.[4] But first she dwelt on the reality of all her UFO experiences, talking quietly in a slow, careful reverie. From time to time the sadness she was describing nearly overwhelmed her words.

"It's very difficult for me to accept this. There's a part of me that really does . . . and has known this for maybe nine years. But this is so farfetched and outrageous that I find it extremely difficult to really accept. I wouldn't expect anyone else to, and I believe if I would hear it from any of you I wouldn't accept it either . . . at least not at first. It's just really outrageous . . . for me, anyway. Maybe it's because it comes from me. And I don't know . . . there's only one fact connected with the whole thing and that's the fact that I *was* pregnant. I was medically proven to be pregnant with an exam and a blood test and a urine test.

"And suddenly I was no longer pregnant, and nothing ever appeared

to me to explain what . . . but anyway . . . I was seventeen . . . I wanted
to think that it was one of those things that just happens . . . but inside
I always *knew* . . . that I had a child somewhere . . . a female child. I always
thought that, but I never voiced it to anyone. Then, when I got divorced
and went to therapy . . . the closest I could ever come to mentioning this
was just that I felt . . . we talked about it as a normal miscarriage. But
even my doctor said, 'Why don't we pretend it never happened?' Just a
country doctor . . . he was upset, too . . . But I always knew I had a
daughter . . . and . . . This is really hard . . .

   "I never connected it with any of this, ever. Even when it was brought
to my attention that it could possibly be connected [with UFOs] I still
didn't accept it. But in my last hypnosis session . . . it was the worst I think
I've ever had . . . at first I didn't even want to remember anything
. . . I had always known that something happened to me that night at my
sister's house. I always knew it. And whenever I'd go back to that place
. . . it would pass through my mind, and I would put it away . . . but I
always knew that something happened there. And I just couldn't . . . I
just . . . blocked it out." Kathie continued to describe this most painful
event in her life, the removal from her womb of her developing baby. She
maintained her quiet composure but her tears revealed her emotion.

   "So then we explored it in hypnosis, and it was really hard . . . I don't
know what they took from me . . . I don't know . . . how to say it
. . . I don't know what they took from me . . . but . . . I *knew* what they
took from me, and it . . . upset me . . . a lot . . . I was almost hysterical
. . . and . . . furious. I screamed at them, and I told them it wasn't fair,
and that it belonged to me. I told Budd that I couldn't believe that they
acted surprised at my reaction . . . it astonished them . . .

   "And then in October of 1983 when they came . . . when I had the
dreams . . . and I heard my name being called . . . and that experience
when I ended up in my backyard and my mother let me in . . . then, under
hypnosis I was with . . . whatever these people are . . . and again . . . we
were in the room and I was sitting on a table and my friend or whatever
you want to call him was with me . . . there were a whole lot of them there
and they were acting very pleased . . . They wanted to show me something
. . . and I looked over to one end of the room in front of me and coming
through a doorway came two of them . . . Holding their hand between
them was this little-bitty . . . person . . . about so tall, and I knew it was
a female . . . I don't know why . . . I don't know if they told me or not
. . . I don't understand a lot of it . . . and . . . I don't know if they were

showing me to her or her to me, but she was extremely frightened of me, and all I wanted to do was to hold her. She looked so pathetic . . . and I got . . . kind of upset . . ." Here Kathie paused a minute or so before she was able to go on with her account.

"They told me that I would see her again. That's why I don't want them not to come back . . . on the slim chance that this is not . . . just a dream. That's something I don't want to miss out on . . . and they told me that I couldn't take care of her because I couldn't feed her and she would die if she was with me . . . And she would be well taken care of and I would see her again. And then they took her away. It was . . . really sad . . . very sad. That wasn't the way it was supposed to turn out. I wasn't supposed to react the way I did. And they were surprised at the way I acted . . . I felt that.

"There's nothing in my life . . . I'd never had this kind of experience, or these kinds of feelings . . . so how do I know how to feel if I've never experienced anything like this before? How to feel this intensely? *Now* I know what it feels like to be a parent . . . I have my two little boys, and there's no other feeling in the whole world like when you see your baby . . . even before then. I didn't have any children, yet when they took it away from me . . . I thought I would die. They took a part of me. And how did I know how to feel that? I didn't even have any kids then . . . yet I knew how to feel that. It was so intense, and I understand now that I have kids. It's really . . . the feeling is so strong that I have . . . another. The feeling is so strong and has been so strong for the past nine years that a part of me is gone . . . It's really so strong . . . and a part of me doesn't want to believe any of this, 'cause it's just absolutely the most crazy thing I've ever heard of in my life. And it doesn't make any sense at all . . ." Kathie's sadness and bitterness filled her, and for a while we sat in silence.

A few moments later she added something about her feelings of anger towards the UFO abductors. "When I talk about being angry because of what they're doing, it always has to do with children . . . When they start fooling around with kids . . . like my little kids, Robbie and Tommy. I get mad, really mad. Not for myself, or what they've done with me. But for my kids . . ."

None of us knows what the UFO phenomenon really is or what its ultimate purposes may be, but in the absence of answers, we must at least act upon our feelings. In place of the simple-minded ridicule and dismissal so often encountered, we must offer understanding and heartfelt emotional support to these fellow human beings who have endured such profoundly unsettling, unfathomable, truly alien experiences. They are, in every sense of the word, victims. And yet, unasked, they are also pioneers. For good or for ill, they have seen the future.

Appendix A

Chronology of UFO Incidents in the
Davis Family

KATHIE DAVIS was born in Indianapolis, Indiana on February 2, 1959. She graduated from high school and was married in 1978. In July 1979 she gave birth to her son Robbie, and in September of 1980, Tommy was born. Kathie was divorced in 1981, and the resulting financial situation required that she and her two very young children move back to her parents' house. In 1984 she entered a technical school and learned a vocational skill. In the summer of 1986 she moved with her sons into an apartment, and has since then begun to achieve an independent, financially self-supporting existence. The following list of UFO-related incidents is given in outline form. Some but not all of these incidents are dealt with in previous chapters, and are so designated.

1. Probably the winter of 1966; Detroit, Michigan. Kathie and her sister Laura visit family friends who have moved to the Detroit area. Kathie goes outside to play, and after a flash of light and a loud noise she wanders off. She becomes lost but sees what appears to her as her friends' house. Though it is cold and there is snow on the ground, the door to this house is open. She enters and meets a strange-looking family; a "little boy" takes her into his "playroom," a round, white, windowless place, where she is

asked to sit down on the floor. "I'm going to play a trick on you," he says, and a small machinelike device near her makes a sudden sharp cut on her lower leg. For a moment the little boy metamorphoses into a small, large-headed, gray-skinned figure standing by a table. After an unremembered interim, she is put out of this "house" by the odd family. Still lost, she sees her sister Laura approaching, walking as if asleep. Without a word Laura takes her hand, turns around, and they return to their friends' house. The larger of Kathie's two scars, the upper one, is the result of this experience. She has twice undergone hypnosis on this incident, but Laura, who remembers nothing of it, has so far declined to be hypnotized. (Kathie may have undergone an earlier, as yet unexplored UFO experience when she was two or three years old. She has a recurring dream of her mother's hiding with her in a closet because of "something outside in the sky" threatening them. See Chapter 1.)

2. July 1975; Rough River State Park, Kentucky. Kathie, sixteen years old, visits the park with her seventeen-year-old friend Nan and others. After sighting four spiralling lights, Kathie encounters a normal-looking man—who closely resembles her—and his two tall, silent companions who behave most oddly. Hypnosis has been employed twice on this incident, and it is covered here in Chapter 6.

3. December 1977; Indianapolis, Indiana. In a rural area, eighteen-year-old Kathie and her friends Dorothy and Roberta are driving late at night. An oddly flashing light is sighted which eventually comes down to the ground. Dorothy stops the car to investigate while a frightened Roberta cowers in the backseat. Kathie is taken into a landed UFO and undergoes a gynecological operation. This key event is covered in Chapter 7.

4. March 1978. At her sister Laura's house outside Indianapolis, Kathie is abducted and taken into a UFO where a second gynecological operation occurs. This incident is covered in Chapter 7.

5. Spring or summer of 1979. While pregnant with Robbie, Kathie is taken from her Indianapolis apartment into a UFO. While lying upon a table she experiences, among other things, the sensation of thin probes being pressed up into her nostrils. She is shown a small, black box and is told that she will remember what it is for. This incident is covered in Chapter 3.

6. 1980. Kathie receives a series of enigmatic, indecipherable phone calls at regular intervals during the nine months of her pregnancy with Tommy. No hypnosis has been attempted with respect to these strange calls, and they remain unexplored. See Chapter 1.

7. June 30, 1983. A UFO lands near her parents' house and Kathie is immobilized and irradiated with light. A probe is inserted in her ear, and she suffers what seem to be the effects of mild radiation poisoning. This incident, which triggered her initial letter, is the subject of Chapter 2.

8. October 3, 1983. Kathie undergoes a two-stage abduction. While driving to the store, her car is stopped and a conversation takes place with a small, gray-skinned figure. A little later she is taken from her bedroom and moved into a UFO. After a physical examination of some sort she is shown a small child. Details of the abduction's two stages emerged in two hypnotic sessions, widely separated in time. The earlier details surfaced in October of 1983 shortly after the incident's occurrence. Kathie's recollections of the child only came to light months later, spontaneously, without the use of hypnosis; in fact hypnosis was not employed to flesh out these later recollections until January 1985. The earlier events are covered in Chapter 3 and the recollections of the little girl in Chapter 8.

9. November 26, 1983. The Davis house is entered by a small, large-headed figure who paralyzes Robbie while apparently placing a nasal implant into little Tommy. Kathie, meanwhile, is re-abducted. The incident involving Kathie's sons is covered in Chapter 4. Hypnosis on Kathie's apparently simultaneous abduction was not carried out until May 1986. This account appears in Chapter 9.

10. February 1986. Kathie is awakened by Robbie who describes being frightened by a red light gliding "like a spider" down his wall. Minutes later, Kathie sees a small, gray-skinned figure walk calmly past her door after apparently having emerged from the bedroom where Tommy was sleeping by himself. This incident has not been explored by hypnosis. It is described in detail in Chapter 4.

11. April 1986. Kathie is abducted again from the Davis home and is shown a tiny baby. At this presentation the little girl she had

seen earlier carefully observes the way Kathie handles the tiny
infant. This extraordinary event is covered in Chapter 9.

12. September 1986. Kathie, while driving to her apartment late at
    night with Robbie and Tommy in the car, sights at two different
    times and locations a large, glowing, oval object hovering over
    the treetops. Unaccountably she arrives over one hour late.
    Several hours later Robbie comes into her room suffering from
    a serious nosebleed—his very first. As of this writing the events
    of that evening have not been explored, but the account sug-
    gests that yet one more abduction may have occurred, one that
    was possibly focused upon Robbie instead of his brother, and
    which may have involved a nasal implant.

The twelve experiences outlined above comprise a far from complete list
of Kathie Davis's possible UFO encounters. On at least ten other occasions between 1984 and 1986 Kathie has called or written to tell me about
certain disturbing dreams, suggestive flashbacks, or peculiar physical conditions. A number of times she said that she felt as if she were pregnant,
an "impossible" situation that now, in hindsight, seems not even surprising.

I have deliberately excluded from the above list a number of related
anomalous events in Kathie's life. Some were deleted for a tactical reason
—to provide a means of checking the veracity of any similar future reports
this book may elicit. I have also omitted a number of minor and potentially confusing reports which are not sufficiently clear-cut to warrant
inclusion in what already may be an overly complex history. (Obviously,
this secondary material will be made available to any qualified, serious
researchers who request it.)

LAURA DAVIS, Kathie's older sister, born in 1947. Laura is employed in
a service industry, as is her husband Johnny. The couple has four children
and they live in a rural area outside of Indianapolis.

1. 1949–50. Testimony from both Laura and her mother suggests
   that the two were possibly abducted as they concealed themselves
   in a closet, hiding from "two men" who were threatening them
   outside—though this incident, as explained in Chapter 1, is quite
   ambiguous.

2. 1965. While driving home on a Sunday afternoon in the early fall

Laura finds herself compelled to pull off the main road and park behind a church. It is suddenly dark, and when she looks up she sees a brightly lit UFO rising away from her car. She drives home and becomes aware that she has lost about two hours. In two hypnosis sessions—November 1984 and May 1985—Laura recalled that she was lifted up, apparently car and all, into the UFO. She sees the parking lot below, but her car is not there. Inside the craft she observes a long table and three gray, shadowy figures standing near her, but at this point her memories end. Since she has decided against any further hypnotic regressions, the investigation of this abduction is at a standstill. It is discussed in Chapter 1.

STEVIE, Laura's son, born in 1976. About 3:00 A.M. on a March night in 1985, Stevie awakes when a circular white light about twice as wide as a basketball floats out of the kitchen and into the living room where he was sleeping on the couch (the same couch, incidently, from which Kathie had been abducted while baby-sitting Laura's children in March of 1978). Stevie watches the light travel into the hall where it pauses for a moment outside each bedroom door. After returning to the living room it settles on a table next to his couch. Stevie now finds himself very afraid and unable to move—and in an instant he "goes to sleep." He awakes almost immediately, and sees two small, gray-skinned men, wearing gray one-piece coveralls, standing near him. He is terrified, but still paralyzed. The men act as if they are talking about him, but he hears nothing. They have "funny big black eyes, kind of pointed up in the corners," no hair, no ears, and "their mouths are a line." One of them "says my name." Stevie "goes back to sleep again," and when he awakes the light is still there but the small men have disappeared. The light floats out the way it entered, and there his recollections end. In May 1985, hypnosis was undertaken to explore this incident, but very little new information was forthcoming. Stevie is a very normal, trustworthy and basically unimaginative child. He was genuinely afraid during the session, and I believe there is still more to his experience that he is not remembering. (This incident is not mentioned in any previous chapter.)

Appendix B

Notes on the Use of Hypnosis

My first acquaintance with hypnosis came in 1977 when I was hypnotized by Dr. Robert Naiman, a psychiatrist practicing in New York City. He taught me the technique of self-hypnosis, which over the years has proved quite beneficial. I observed Dr. Naiman's procedures a number of times with various witnesses in UFO encounters, and have since then sat through what must be hundreds of hours of hypnosis sessions conducted by other psychiatrists and psychologists. (These include Dr. Don Klein of New York's Columbia Presbyterian Hospital, Dr. Margaret Brennaman, and psychologists Gerard Franklin and, in particular, Aphrodite Clamar.) In the words of Dr. Ernest Hilgard of Stanford University's Laboratory of Hypnosis Research, "The qualities that make for a successful hypnotist are very, very minimal. Hypnosis is a technique, like using a stethoscope, and what you do with it is more important than the routine skill."[1] I learned this "routine skill" both through years of careful observation and the self-hypnosis I had been taught by Dr. Naiman. Dr. Don Klein has also been helpful to me in refining this technique. Sympathetic insight into one's fellow human beings is the crucial factor, I believe, in the successful use of hypnosis.

For decades this technique has been employed by psychologists, policemen, smokers, insomniacs, overweight people, dentists, doctors, UFO investigators and countless others both as a way to recover "lost" memories and as a quasi-medical procedure—a substitute, sometimes, for more conventional anesthetics. In the past few years testimony elicited through hypnotic regression has been occasionally presented as evidence in court, and it is here, in the legal arena, that controversy has arisen concerning its validity. In December of 1984, in an attempt to address the forensic problem in particular, the Council on Scientific Affairs of the American Medical Association issued a complex report on the subject that has helped to validate its use in missing time cases. After a lengthy study the Council declared that despite its value in many areas, hypnosis does not automatically represent a path to certain truth, as some prosecutors had suggested. The AMA strongly questioned the appropriateness of using hypnosis in courtroom situations. The reasoning behind this reservation should be obvious. Since *all* human observation and memory can be flawed, and hypnosis simply brings to the conscious mind more memories than the subject had previously recalled, these new recollections are almost inevitably bound also to be both accurate *and* inaccurate. For example, let us say that the witness to a robbery originally misperceived the color of the gunman's coat, and trauma and shock later cause him to repress most details of the robbery. Under hypnosis, however, he may now recall a great many of these previously forgotten memories—including his original misperception. Hypnosis cannot guarantee accuracy since it does not improve one's original (possibly flawed) observations—it simply increases their number. And obviously, in a courtroom situation the accuracy of such a small, "insignificant" detail as the color of a gunman's coat is often crucial to the resolution of a case. In a trial of this nature the issue is not whether hypnosis has aided in the witness's general recall of a "traumatically forgotten" bank robbery—that fact may be granted. What is crucial, in my example, is the accuracy of one small detail, and here the AMA urges extreme caution.

In situations involving amnesia and periods of "missing time," however, the AMA report accepts the effectiveness of hypnosis. In contrast to my courtroom example above, the issue of whether a two-hour UFO abduction did or did not take place does not depend upon the accuracy of a specific and trivial detail. Here we are attempting to recover a period of forgotten *hours* in someone's life, involving myriad details and physical sensations which, rather than being mundane and easily forgotten, are memorably bizarre. The form of amnesia we are dealing with in these UFO cases is much more the classic "fugue" type. And of situations like this the AMA report states the following: "In the case of fugues (in which an individual forgets his identity) hypnosis can be an effective clinical procedure to help the person recover his identity. When used in this manner, hypnosis may serve to reinstate the individual's former recollections."[2] The logic of the AMA's position, then, would be to trust hypnosis to reinstate an abductee's general recollections of his experience, though not to recommend that the abductee testify under oath as to his memory of a particular small detail—the exact shade of gray, perhaps, of the alien's skin. My attitude is consonant with that of the AMA. I completely trust the accuracy of these small, highly specific details only when they reoccur in case after case, but I have no doubt as to the usefulness of hypnosis in unlocking the general abduction scenario.

But a final, crucial misconception must be pointed out: It is commonly believed that the validity of the UFO abduction phenomenon itself is somehow inextricably linked with the technique of hypnosis. This false idea began, I believe, with the Betty and Barney Hill case, a situation in which hypnosis *was* necessary to the unlocking of the mystery. But so far I have worked directly with fourteen abductees who have fully recalled their abduction experiences normally, without hypnosis. (In the UFO literature some of the best-known abduction cases—the Hickson-Parker case in Pascagoula, Mississippi, and the Travis Walton case in Snowflake, Arizona, for example—were also remembered naturally, without the use of hypnosis.) Though hypnosis has proved to be useful in the majority of UFO abduction cases to help the subjects overcome what seems to be an externally imposed amnesia, there are many cases in which it has not been required. Hypnosis is simply one more investigative tool UFO researchers use to examine our most disturbing modern mystery.

Appendix C

Hypnosis of Joyce Lloyd on the Events of June 30, 1986

BH: *(Sets the scene, based on what Joyce had earlier described: It's the weekend before the Fourth of July, 1983 . . . you're watching TV . . . it's a hot, muggy evening . . . you're in the dining room, tidying up, etc.)* Can you see yourself in the dining room, wearing light summer clothes?

JL: Uh-huh.

BH: Tell us what you're cleaning up—a messy dining room?

JL: I'm taking everything off the shelves in the dining room.

BH: And does it take a while to do this?

JL: Yeah, I've got a lot of knickknacks to dust. Dusting the table.

BH: What happens while you do this—is the TV set on?

JL: The TV is on in the living room.

BH: Can you see what program you're watching?

JL: I'm really not paying any attention to the TV . . . just listening . . . dusting the furniture . . . and I hear this noise and it's loud and there's lights. It scares the dog . . . I wonder what it is. It shakes the whole house. The lights go off. I looked in the living room . . . the TV . . . the TV turns all red . . . there's no sound. It must be lightning. The lights go on, off. Light . . . there's light in my window. I wonder if I should call the Davises . . . *(Pause, sighs)* Hmm . . .

BH: What's happening, Joyce?

JL: I don't know what to think. Don't know . . . Just loud noise . . . it shakes the house. I'm not scared . . . I'm just curious.

BH: How do you feel when this is happening?

JL: Just hot.

BH: Hot? Do you go to the window and look out? *(This was a deliberately leading question on my part, since I assumed from what Joyce had said earlier that she was probably unable to get up and move to the window. Her later testimony suggests that this was probably the case.)*

JL: I see the light from the dining room table out the window and I hear the noise. It's a loud noise.

BH: What direction do you see the lights from?

JL: From the Davises' house. I'm afraid that maybe somebody got hurt, the noise is so loud. I think I should call . . . *(Note: A rather thick wood occupies the area between the two homes; it is possible to see light shining through the trees, but the houses themselves are largely obscured.)*

BH: Why don't you call?

JL: I don't know . . . something . . . something interrupts me. My body feels real hot.

BH: Where are you right now when this happens?

JL: I'm in the dining room, I think. I just keep looking at the phone. I keep thinking I hope Bernie hurries and comes home. I think maybe it's lightning. I don't feel hot now. The dog's settled down . . . the dog fell asleep. I keep wondering what this is . . . wonder if anyone else heard it . . .

BH: Is it loud enough to move anything in your house?

JL: The light above the table. The house shook like it felt as if the entire yard was shaking.

BH: Sort of like an earthquake?

JL: Yeah . . . I just couldn't imagine what it could be to shake the earth so hard.

BH: Why don't you call the Davises and ask?

JL: I don't know . . . I want to, and I think about it and I don't know why . . . I feel I should call. I don't know.

BH: Do you notice the time this is happening?

JL: I have to look . . . ten-forty-five.

BH: Ten-forty-five. Which clock do you notice it on?

JL: The clock in the dining room, on the wall, in the dining room.

BH: How soon does Bernie come home?

JL: Well, shortly . . . twenty-five minutes.

BH: Do you tell him about this?

JL: As soon as he comes in.

BH: What do you tell him?

JL: He won't believe what happened. Why did it happen? He tells me, "Nothing, don't get excited, it's just a car probably hit a utility pole." I told him no, it couldn't be, it shook too hard, the sound was too loud. So I just gave it up, I didn't think about it anymore. I still don't know why I don't call. I was really afraid someone might have got hurt. I don't know why I don't call . . .

Notes

A NOTE TO THE READER

1. Walter Laqueur, *The Terrible Secret* (New York: Penguin Books, 1982).
2. *Ibid.*, p. 3.

CHAPTER 1: THE SEPTEMBER LETTER

1. A commonly held misconception assumes that those who report UFO experiences must be eager for publicity. The opposite is true. Almost everyone whose accounts are included in this book asked for and have received anonymity. Names have been changed, and in some cases even locations have been narrowly altered. The "Davis" family and the "Copley Woods" are pseudonyms. Throughout these pages each pseudonym, when it first appears, will be enclosed by quotation marks. All other names, dates and locations are literally accurate.
2. Budd Hopkins, *Missing Time: A Documented Study of UFO Abductions* (New York: Marek, 1981).
3. John Fuller, *The Interrupted Journey* (New York: Dial Press, 1966).

4. The most comprehensive and authoritative history of the UFO phenomenon in its postwar American phase can be found in Dr. David Jacobs's book, *The UFO Controversy in America* (Bloomington: Indiana University Press, 1975; New York: New American Library, 1976).

5. Jacobs, pp. 30, 31.

6. A detailed account of my own sighting appears in *Missing Time*, pp. 25, 26.

7. In 1976 I wrote a piece for *The Village Voice* about a UFO landing in New Jersey's North Hudson Park. This article, reprinted later that year in *Cosmopolitan* and in several newspapers, elicited a number of letters and phone calls from readers describing their own sightings. At this time I also acted as consultant for a television documentary dealing with UFOs, and this, too, elicited letters and phone calls from viewers with related experiences. From these and other sighting reports I began to notice segments of unexplained "missing time." And so, with these early cases as a data base, I began my explorations of abduction accounts. (See *Missing Time*, Chapters 2 and 5.)

8. Hopkins, pp. 51–88.

9. Kathie recently confessed to me that she has never been able to read the book completely through; it has always been too disturbing for her to handle in any but small doses.

10. Ted Phillips, "Physical Trace Landing Reports," *MUFON 1985 UFO Symposium Proceedings* (Seguin, Texas: 1985).

11. See Richard Rasmussen's entry "Animal Reactions to UFOs" in *The Encyclopedia of UFOs*, edited by Ronald D. Story (New York: Doubleday, 1980).

12. See, for example, F. Lagarde, "The Aveyron Enquiry," *Flying Saucer Review*, Vol. 16, No. 5 (1970).

13. I learned later that Kathie's recollection on this point is slightly in error. See page 20 and Note 18 below.

14. Subsequent interviews with Laura and her mother place the incident as having occurred in the late summer or early fall of 1965. The Hill case came to public attention through John Fuller's 1966 book-length study, *The Interrupted Journey*, a shortened version of which also appeared in *Look* magazine.

15. Obviously, soil samples presented for chemical study two and a half months late, as it were, could have been affected in the

meantime by a variety of conditions, such as weather, chemical fertilizers, and so forth.

16. "Lucille Forman," a woman whose UFO experiences are dealt with in Chapter 10, reports a similar event, which occurred in 1973. A particularly vivid phone call account appears in Raymond Fowler's *The Andreasson Affair* (New York: Bantam, 1980), pp. 195–99.

17. In the years since 1983 when Kathie related these feelings to her friend, Tommy has made considerable gains in the control of his speech. Special training has been necessary and though the cause of his problem is still not known he is steadily improving.

18. Kathie had said that Laura pulled into the lot, parked, and in the daylight looked up and sighted the UFO. Actually Laura pulled into the lot and stopped—but only later, *after* it had "suddenly" become dark, did she see the UFO above her, apparently moving away. This seems to me to be a minor, easily understandable discrepancy between the two recollections of the incident.

19. An erroneous idea has it that there are many feature films dealing with UFO abductions. In actual fact this film, a TV-movie based on the Hills' abduction, is still the only narrative movie accurately depicting the phenomenon. *The UFO Incident,* which stars James Earl Jones and Estelle Parsons, was made in 1975 and is frequently replayed on late-night television.

20. Hopkins, pp. 51–88.

21. *Ibid.,* p. 70.

22. These papers comprising *The Final Report on the Psychological Testing of UFO "Abductees"* are available through the Fund for UFO Research, P.O. Box 277, Mount Rainier, Md. 20712.

23. Elizabeth Slater, "Conclusions on Nine Psychologicals," p. 14 of the *Final Report.*

24. Suspected implants have been reported by other UFO investigators, such as Raymond Fowler (*The Andreasson Affair,* pp. 51 and 57–58.) So far, none of these tiny objects have been located and removed.

Chapter 2: The Missing Hour

1. Few abduction cases include extensive traces of the UFO's having landed and affected the soil. None that I know of have this sort of physical evidence *and* extensive corroborating testimony from other involved individuals and witnesses.

2. Kathie, in her original letter, remembered only one phone call that night. In fact there were two—one to her mother, in which Mary declined any help, and another *from* her mother moments later. Again I feel this is an understandable and minor discrepancy in their accounts.

3. Being nearly the same size, Kathie and Dee Anne could and often did wear one another's clothes. Because of her straitened financial situation Kathie's wardrobe was less than extensive, so she accepted her friend's spur-of-the-moment offer of a bathing suit. Tammy apparently was not sure she was going to go swimming, so she deferred dressing until she arrived at the Davis home, where she made her decision.

4. Bernie's son was his by an earlier marriage; he was taking the boy back to his mother's after a visit of a few days.

5. Though the vast majority—probably more than 90 percent—of all abductions last not more than two hours, there are a few dramatic exceptions. Travis Walton, for example, was missing for a five-day period. See Coral and Jim Lorenzen, *Abducted!* (New York: Berkley, 1977), pp. 80–113.

6. Hopkins, pp. 107–10.

7. In the December 1980 Cash-Landrum UFO sighting which occurred near Houston, Texas, there were similar physical aftereffects, though far more serious than in the Kathie Davis incident. The three witnesses, Betty Cash, Vickie Landrum and Colby Landrum, all suffered some degree of hair loss, radiation dermatitis, stomach pains, anorexia and vision impairment in the form of photophthalmia—eyes swollen, watery and painful. These physical effects are discussed in an article by John Schuessler, "The Medical Evidence in UFO Cases," *MUFON 1985 UFO Symposium Proceedings* (Seguin, Texas: 1985).

8. Paul Brodeur, an expert on microwave emission, informed me that the heating effect was only one of several indications of the possible presence of microwave radiation.

9. The craft also resembled an object witnessed in broad daylight by police officer Lonnie Zamora in Socorro, New Mexico. This 1964 close encounter, which included a view of two small UFO occupants, is described in J. Allen Hynek's *The UFO Experience* (New York: Ballantine, 1974), pp. 165–67.

10. Kathie's description of the physical effect is similar to Travis Walton's account of being hit in the chest with something like "an electric shock" that traveled through his whole body. See Lorenzen, p. 81.

11. This "scanner" is sometimes described as being like a huge eye, rather than a simple light, but it appears in most abduction accounts. See Hopkins, p. 171.

12. A number of other abductees report nosebleeds or high, nasal pain associated with their experiences, though they do not directly recall having seen or felt needles penetrating their nasal cavities.

13. Again it must be pointed out that ancillary physical effects suffered by "bystanders" in a UFO abduction experience are extremely rare in the UFO literature.

CHAPTER 3: KATHIE IN NEW YORK

1. As a matter of principle I regard interviews which are not conducted in person, face to face, as only marginally reliable. Without all the visual clues of demeanor, body language and so forth, there is a marked lowering of one's ability to decipher what is truth and what is dissembling or, more commonly, what is merely "please-the-interviewer" accommodation. There is simply no substitute for being there oneself, talking directly with the witness.

2. A support group has been set up in New York for just this purpose, with highly qualified psychiatrists and psychologists assisting from time to time. These monthly get-togethers are part social, part group therapy, and since several abductees are themselves therapists these evenings have been quite beneficial.

3. Sue is one of several abductees who have told me that despite years of conventional treatment they never once informed their psychotherapists of their suspected UFO encounters. "I didn't want him/her to think I was crazy" was their sad but understandable explanation.

4. Kathie told me that she and her boyfriend had made love only once before she discovered she was pregnant. She was surprised by this first-time pregnancy, which in retrospect has a different significance than she had imagined.

5. Fowler, p. 48.

6. In this dramatic early abduction the subject, a five-year-old girl at the time, awoke to the sound of gunfire; her mother was at the window of their farmhouse firing a shotgun at a number of small white "men" who had gathered outside, ostensibly threatening her family. The shooting soon stopped (it was the only time she remembered her mother ever having fired a gun), and shortly thereafter the child was floated out of her bedroom between two of the small figures. She vividly described her fear as she passed behind her now apparently "switched off" mother, still kneeling at the window, weapon in hand, her long black braids hanging down her motionless back. The next morning her mother had only vague memories of having fired her gun at some "white-faced children" who she thought were "trying to steal from us"—a most unlikely cause for the pacific woman's violent reaction.

7. Lew Willis's excellent report on the "Elliott" case deserves publication. A drastically shortened version appeared in the *MUFON UFO Journal*, January 1982.

8. This detail emerged in a hypnotic session conducted in New York by Dr. Aphrodite Clamar on October 6, 1979.

9. This observation marked the beginning of an abduction. The subject was surrounded by the five figures who took him out of his car and into a landed UFO where he encountered two more abductees—a man and his wife. His memory of the experience was blocked for a number of years, but gradually, without hypnosis, he began to recall everything that had happened from the moment the military-appearing figures first approached his car till the time two hours later when he "came to," driving on a different road miles away from his original location.

10. Driving through the surrounding area at night, Kathie discovered the place she "mistook" for a Seven-Eleven store. It is a complex of buildings with a large parking lot next to a secluded field—a place where a UFO could plausibly land without being seen. I have been there at night and am satisfied that it is, indeed, the location of her encounter.

11. This type of bedroom encounter—which is far from uncommon —involves the appearance of a strange figure (or two or three) standing near the bed on which the invariably frightened subject lies physically paralyzed. This consciously remembered appearance of the UFO occupants may mark the beginning of an abduction, or, as in Kathie's 1978 attic experience, its end.

CHAPTER 4: ROBBIE, TOMMY AND THE BOGEY MAN

1. The official medical explanation made an unsettling reappearance in the fall of 1986. Kathie had taken Tommy to a doctor for the recommended removal of his tonsils and adenoids. This second physician informed Kathie that the operation had gone well, except that he had discovered a little hole high up in Tommy's nasal cavity, and when he touched it with an instrument it had begun to hemorrhage. Ultimately he had had to cauterize it, and he told Kathie that it had been more difficult to handle than the operations Tommy had come in for. Kathie asked what caused the hole, and he replied that "obviously" Tommy had pushed something sharp, like a pencil, way up into his nose. Kathie said that she couldn't believe he would do such a thing. The physician's answer, which she found disturbing, was this: "It's not so unusual. Several times I've treated children with these little holes way up in their nasal cavities. There must be lots of children who take sharp instruments and poke themselves way up inside their noses."

2. In the fall of 1985, while I was a visiting artist at Denison University, I met Margaret, who lived not far away. Some of the information presented here was included in her letters and phone conversations while the rest surfaced during the one hypnotic session we carried out.

3. Hopkins, pp. 226–28.

4. Fuller, pp. 195–96.

5. Jim and Coral Lorenzen, *Encounters with UFO Occupants* (New York: Berkley, 1976), pp. 61–87.

CHAPTER 5: THE CAMPING TRIP AND OTHER ADVENTURES

1. Fowler, pp. 118, 119.

2. See Jim and Coral Lorenzen, *Abducted!*, pp. 56, 57.

3. Joyce informed me that when she was a teenager her terrified younger brother came rushing home with a story of having come upon a large silver craft in the woods where he had been playing. He described being "pursued," and there is an apparent period of missing time in his account.

4. Lorenzen, pp. 22, 23.

Chapter 6: The Saddest Day

1. Lorenzen, pp. 56, 57.

Chapter 7: Other Women, Other Men

1. During the three long hypnotic sessions I conducted with Al we uncovered a childhood experience in which he recalled being in a strange "hospital" with rather odd medical personnel. Long needles were inserted in his nostrils, and a small incision was made on the back of his calf. Everything about this experience suggests an early UFO abduction.

2. If it is difficult for male abductees to recall and describe other features of their abductions, this particular area is *always* nearly impossible to discuss. It constitutes a kind of rape experience, and the sense of helplessness it engenders deeply undercuts one's conventional masculine self-image.

3. For the history of "foo fighters," see Ronald Story's entry under that title in *The Encyclopedia of UFOs*, pp. 135, 136. *Report on the UFO Wave of 1947* by Ted Bloecher is the authoritative work on this subject. His book is available from The Center for UFO Studies, 1955 John's Drive, Glenview, Illinois 60025–1615.

4. In two of these bizarre cases the subjects' descriptions of their sexual partners suggest that they were possibly hybrids of a sort, with half human, half alien features. The sexual sensations they reported seemed rather normal. However, in the other two cases the subjects' descriptions conformed with the typical small, gray, alien physical type. It should be noted that both of these abductees stated that there was something about the vaginas of their female partners that "didn't seem to feel right." The tactile sensations they described are suggestive of an artificial material rather than normal, human flesh.

5. Steven Kilburn made the interesting observation that the sensations were totally localized. Neither his body as a whole nor his mind were at all sexually aroused. The feelings appeared suddenly and were confined to the genitals.

CHAPTER 9: MORE PIECES TO THE PUZZLE

1. Since my interview with Lisa I have encountered two other women—abductees whose cases had been partially investigated at earlier times—who have described such a "missing baby" dream to me. I hope at some future date to explore these dreams under hypnosis.

2. One psychiatrist reported that upon occasion one of his female patients might dream she was pregnant after he informed her that it was time to terminate the therapeutic relationship. Another psychiatrist—a strict Freudian—said that the missing baby dream "obviously" represented the woman's desire for her lost penis!

3. Under hypnosis Susan described herself as standing nude and apparently paralyzed near a table on which her boyfriend Al reclined. She could see only his bare legs, but when she heard him groan she began to cry at her inability to do anything to help him. The hypnotic session was quite detailed and emotionally intense for both Susan and me.

4. One very important area of evidence which I have deliberately withheld involves signs or symbols that various abductees have recalled seeing inside UFOs. I have compiled samples drawn by six different abductees, and the congruence of these images is remarkable. After a great deal of soul searching and internal debate I decided not to publish this evidence at the present time in the hope that it might provide a means of checking the authenticity of future aduction accounts.

5. David Jacobs's *The UFO Controversy in America* details this evolution in careful detail.

6. An interesting parallel exists between UFO abductees and the survivors of other "unimaginable" traumatic events. Dr. Robert J. Lifton's *Death in Life* (New York: Touchstone, 1967), a study of the survivors of Hiroshima, provides many psychological insights that are equally applicable to those who have undergone repeated UFO abduction experiences.

7. These sensations of internal movement were described during her very first hypnotic session covering her 1953 abduction in Austria, so there is reason to believe that she, too, may have been subjected to more than one ova retrieval operation.

8. One of the tiniest human babies to survive is Trent Petrie, who was born after only twenty-two weeks of gestation. He weighed just twelve ounces at birth and his apple-size head did, indeed, fit into the palm of his nurse's hand. But even without this example it seems possible that a newborn alien-human hybrid —perhaps only about four feet tall or so as an adult—could be that small and weigh so little and yet also survive.

CHAPTER 10: A SUMMING UP

1. There have been many cases reported in which UFOs have been sighted near the areas of power outages, so this conjunction of events may not be coincidental.

2. This and other direct quotes are taken from Lucille's carefully written and thoughtful reconstruction of her August experience.

3. During one hypnotic session I observed a few years ago, the subject, reliving an abduction she'd experienced as a seven-year-old child, said to her captors that she wanted to tell her parents and her friends and teachers all about what she'd seen. The UFO occupants patiently explained that no one would believe her, and that it would be better if she "forgot" the experience. This kind of explanation for the imposed amnesia is frequently reported in UFO abduction accounts.

4. This colloquy occurred before Kathie had had her dream of the other "offspring." She had not yet been told of Andrew, Elizabeth and the others, so her testimony here focused on the little girl as she recalled her from the original 1983 presentation experience.

APPENDIX B: NOTES ON THE USE OF HYPNOSIS

1. *Psychology Today*, January 1986, p. 24.

2. *Journal of the American Medical Association*, April 5, 1985, Vol. 253, No. 13, pp. 1918–23.

How to Report a Suspected UFO Experience

If you believe you have seen a UFO relatively closely and clearly you may send an account of the incident to one of two investigative groups:

MUFON (Mutual UFO Network), 103 Oldtowne Road, Seguin, Texas 78155-4099, or

CUFOS (Center for UFO Studies), 1955 John's Drive, Glenview, Ill. 60025-1615.

If you believe you may have had the kind of experience dealt with in this book you may wish to write your recollections in detail to:

Budd Hopkins, c/o Random House, 201 E. 50th Street, New York, N.Y. 10022.

As time permits an investigator will be in touch with you. All communication will be kept strictly confidential.